INSECTS AND THE LIFE OF MAN

INSECTS AND THE LIFE OF MAN

Collected Essays on Pure Science
and Applied Biology

Sir VINCENT B. WIGGLESWORTH
C. B. E., M. D., F. R. S.

*Emeritus Professor of Biology in the
University of Cambridge. Formerly
Director, Agricultural Research Council
Unit of Insect Physiology.*

LONDON

CHAPMAN AND HALL

A Halsted Press Book
John Wiley & Sons, Inc., New York

First published 1976
by Chapman and Hall Ltd
11 New Fetter Lane, London EC4P 4EE

Printed in Great Britain by
The Lavenham Press Ltd
Lavenham, Suffolk

ISBN 0 412 14700 9 (cased edition)
ISBN 0 412 14730 0 (Science Paperback edition)

Distributed in the U.S.A. by Halsted Press,
a Division of John Wiley & Sons, Inc., New York

Library of Congress Cataloging in Publication Data

Wigglesworth, Vincent Brian, Sir, 1899-
Insects and the life of man.

1. Insects—Addresses, essays, lectures. I. Title
QL463.W69 1976   595.7   76-40479
ISBN 0-470-98962-9 (Wiley)

CONTENTS

06171

ACKNOWLEDGEMENTS

I am most grateful for the Permissions received to reprint these articles. Acknowledgements are made to the British Broadcasting Corporation for Chapter 2; to the *Atlantic Monthly* for Chapter 3; to the Association of Applied Biologists for much of Chapter 4 and for Chapter 17; to the British Association for the Advancement of Science for Chapter 5; to the Editor of *Agricultural Science* for Chapter 6; to the Director of the East Malling Research Station for Chapter 7; to the Royal Society for India, Pakistan and Ceylon for Chapter 8; to Macmillan (Journals) Ltd. for Chapters 9 and 16; to the Royal Society for Chapter 10; to the Royal Entomological Society of London for Chapter 11; to the Permanent Committee, International Congresses of Entomology for Chapter 12; to the Cambridge University Press for Chapter 13; to the Genootschap ter Bevordering van Natuur-, Genees- en Heelkunde for Chapter 14; and to the Company of Biologists Ltd. for Chapter 15.

The original papers have been reprinted unchanged except for the insertion of headings in some chapters; the correction of mistakes; and the updating of certain facts, usually by means of footnotes.

V.B.W.

1

INTRODUCTION

When Patrick A. Buxton was appointed by the London School of Hygiene and Tropical Medicine in 1926 to head their Department of Medical Entomology, he had formed the opinion that the control of the insect-borne diseases of the tropics was being impeded by lack of knowledge about the physiology of insects. He persuaded the Board of Management to agree to the selection of a lecturer who would endeavour to advance the subject of insect physiology; and at the suggestion of Sir Gowland Hopkins, under whom I had worked at Cambridge, and with the support of Sir Walter Morley Fletcher, Secretary of the Medical Research Council and a member of the Board of Management, I was appointed to this post — with opportunity for extensive travel to study medical entomology in the tropics and with abundant time for research.

Some seventeen years later, during the war years, W. W. C. Topley, as Secretary of the Agricultural Research Council, was faced with the urgent need for improved methods of control of insect pests in agriculture and horticulture by insecticidal or other means. As a support for this objective he recommended the establishment of a Unit of Insect Physiology to carry out basic research which would be of potential value to agriculture; and I was invited to act as director. So once again I was able to undertake world-wide travel — to learn the elements of agricultural entomology.

It thus came about that for fifty years I have been occupied with researches in insect physiology — always against a background of economic entomology and in close touch with the applied biologists. Inevitably I have been forced to reflect upon the relation between pure science and its application to the economy of mankind; and it is the purpose of this book to communicate some of the opinions I have formed, and what is perhaps more important, to give some indication of what applied entomology is all about, and at the same time to indicate some of the excitements and rewards of scientific research.

The chapters which follow are all essays or addresses which have been published over a period of nearly forty years. The question at

1

once arises whether, in a rapidly changing world, such words from the past can be of any interest today. In some cases any interest they may have is perhaps historical. In many others it comes as almost a surprise to find that we are now coming back to ways of thinking which were general forty years ago but had been temporarily abandoned; to realize that disillusionment with the over-enthusiasm for potent synthetic insecticides is compelling a return to ecological modes of thought; and to discover that the many-sided attack, universal in the past (fortified, of course, by greatly increased knowledge), is now coming back under the banner of 'integrated control' or 'pest management'.

By way of introduction I propose to run through the chapters in turn, to give some indication of the circumstances under which they came to be written and of the contribution to the argument which each is intended to make. The original papers have been reprinted unchanged, except for the insertion of headings in some chapters; the correction of mistakes; and the updating of certain facts, usually by means of footnotes. In the selection of material I have endeavoured to sustain a varied approach; but the human mind being constituted as it is, the reader must be prepared to tolerate, or to forgive, occasional repetitions.

'Insects and human affairs' (Chapter 2) was a broadcast talk given in 1951. It is in the nature of a brief overture which sets the tone for later chapters that explore the same themes in greater depth. Twenty-five years later there seems little reason for the keynote to be changed.

In the early part of 1945, two years after the establishment of the Unit of Insect Physiology, I made an extensive tour throughout North America, not to teach, but to learn about, agricultural entomology. The visitor from abroad is apt to be valued above his true worth; and soon after my return to England I received a call from the Central Office of Information in London to say that they had had a request that I should write an article about DDT (which was then, and still is, the 'wonder insecticide') for publication in the *Atlantic Monthly*. 'DDT and the balance of nature' (Chapter 3) was published under the editorial caption 'a scientist looks at tomorrow'. DDT had been introduced to us from Switzerland only three years before, and there was unbounded enthusiasm about it; but the article shows that already there were doubts among entomologists about what might be in store.

2

A large part of 'Science, pure and applied' (Chapter 4) was first written for a talk at the Jubilee of the Association of Applied Biologists in 1955 under the title of 'The contribution of pure science to applied biology', but the extended article as here printed was one of three Installation Lectures presented on the occasion of the installation of Claude T. Bissell as eighth President of the University of Toronto in 1958. Besides discussing the relations between pure and applied science it deals with scientific method and the source of discoveries in science.

'The science and practice of entomology' (Chapter 5) was the presidential address to Section D (Zoology) at the meeting of the British Association for the Advancement of Science held in Birmingham in 1948. It deals with the history of entomological studies in Great Britain and with current and future problems in all branches of economic entomology.

'Insects and the farmer' (Chapter 6) was the fourth Middleton Memorial lecture, delivered in 1956. It describes the birth of agricultural entomology in the nineteenth century, the beginnings of Governmental support for science in Britain fathered by Lloyd George in 1909, the contribution of Sir Thomas Middleton in initiating an agricultural research and advisory system in 1911, and the teething troubles which followed in the early days after nationalization of the service in the 1950s — and the hopeful future.

The fruit-growing industry in Great Britain has been well served by its entomologists, but in the course of years the insect problems have become increasingly complex and increasingly unstable. 'The fauna of the orchard' (Chapter 7) formed the Amos Memorial Lecture delivered to an audience of scientists and fruit growers from Kent and Essex at the East Malling Research Station in 1959. It outlines the history of insects and fruit growing and discusses the theories of natural control of insect populations and their bearing upon the management of orchard pests.

The next two chapters deal with malaria, the central problem of medical entomology. Chapter 8 is an anecdotal account of the great malaria epidemic in Ceylon in early 1935, published by invitation in the *Asiatic Review*. This was a classic example of an outbreak in a non-immune population resulting from exceptional weather conditions, which I was lucky enough to witness during a tour through South-east Asia. By reason of its scale and the very high mortality, this epidemic received world-wide publicity. In Britain it was used in

Parliament as a stick by the Opposition to beat the Government. After one of these outbursts the Colonial Secretary referred his questioner to a report in *The Lancet* of a lecture in which I had set out the facts as recorded in Chapter 8 — and that ended the campaign! It may be worth pointing out that after independence, Sri Lanka was one of the countries into which the World Health Organization sent their teams to spray houses with the residual insecticide DDT, to such good effect that even in the highly malarious zones malaria was virtually eliminated — and the population increased at a rate which has raised a new problem. In the malaria-free south-west quadrant the situation remains unchanged; severe drought will give rise to epidemics. But none has compared with that of 1935, and when they do occur 'the killing of adult females in their resting places' as hinted in Chapter 8 has brought the situation under control.

'Malaria in war' (Chapter 9) formed part of a discussion on the 'Relation between Pure and Applied Biology' held by the Association of Applied Biologists and the Society for Experimental Biology in 1941. It gives a review of the dramatic effects of malaria in past wars, particularly in 1914—18, outlines the situation to be expected in the war theatres as envisaged in early 1941, sets out the Government's plans for establishing Mobile Malaria Laboratories and reviews the methods then current for malaria control — methods which are attracting attention once more today. In the event the malaria units did valuable work; but it is probably true to say that the mainstay proved to be the new anti-malarial drugs. From conversations I have had with men who served in the Japanese forces it is evident that these drugs were the real secret weapon in the Pacific Islands' campaign.

'The insect as a medium for the study of physiology' (Chapter 10) was the Croonian lecture of the Royal Society delivered in 1948. In effect it is a brief summary of the researches by the author on a variety of topics. Its explicit purpose was to persuade the physiologists that insects provide unrivalled material for physiological study. Of course, only my entomological friends turned up to hear the lecture. But to-day biochemists, physiologists, molecular biologists and cytologists have discovered how true my claim was. The lecture has been reproduced unchanged, but in the light of more recent work a few errors of fact have been corrected in footnotes.

Sir John Lubbock (Lord Avebury) was the famous banker and

practical sociologist who died in 1913. Like many men who have become legends in their lifetime, much of his work was forgotten at his death. His spare-time work in entomology, which is the subject of Chapter 11, has been neglected by continental authors because he was an 'amateur'. One of his achievements was to adapt the methods used in training animals for the circus to the detection of their sensory impressions; and many of the classic discoveries about the senses of ants and bees were due to him. This article formed the Presidential Address to the Royal Entomological Society of London in 1965. It was intended to put the record straight.

In 1964 the XIIth International Congress of Entomology was held in London half a century after the IInd Congress had been held in Oxford in 1912. 'Fifty years of insect physiology' (Chapter 12) was the Inaugural Address held in the Albert Hall on that occasion. It starts off in an autobiographical vein, and many of the audience must have feared that they would have to listen to a personal saga. In fact the lecture outlines the extent of knowledge of insect physiology as established in 1912, and sketches some of the major developments in varied fields during the ensuing fifty years.

'The epidermal cell' (Chapter 13) formed one of the Tercentenary Lectures of the Royal Society which were a part of the celebrations in 1960. It was published as one of the contributions to a book of essays entitled *The Cell and the Organism* which was dedicated to Sir James Gray on his retirement. It tells the story of the truly amazing diversity of the activities which a single epidermal cell in an insect can perform.

The growth of insects is characterized by remarkable changes in form. Indeed there has always been an air of mystery about insect metamorphosis. It was the famous Dutch naturalist Jan Swammerdam in about 1669 who first gave a physiological description of the phenomenon. Although Swammerdam's conception of 'preformation' was much abused by his successors in the eighteenth century, it forms the basis of all modern studies on metamorphosis. 'Preformation and insect development' (Chapter 14) was a lecture delivered before the Society for the Promotion of Science, Medicine and Surgery in Amsterdam in 1966, on the occasion of the award of the Swammerdam medal. The factual matter in this lecture is much the same as in Chapter 13 but it is treated from a different point of view.

Chapter 15, which was the first George Bidder lecture of the Society for Experimental Biology in 1971, has a title very close to that of Chapter 4; and indeed reverts to the same topic: the nature of the contribution of pure science to applied biology; but it attempts to illustrate this relation by recounting some of the researches that have been carried out during the past forty years on the insect cuticle — a structure of incredible complexity, which holds the key to the survival of the insect in the extremes of climate that it encounters in a world often contaminated with insecticides.

At some time in the middle 'thirties, on a week-end visit to some friends, I made the acquaintance of Sir Richard Gregory, at that time Editor of *Nature,* who entertained us with reminiscences. Until quite recent years the cover of *Nature* was graced by an engraving of the universe as viewed apparently from the moon or from some lesser charted satellite, with a quotation from Wordsworth beneath it. I was amused to learn that after some fifty years a correspondent had called attention to an error in the quotation — which was quietly corrected. And a few years later another correspondent reported a second error. It occurred to me that it would be interesting to check Wordsworth's own opinion of science — which I suspected to be rather low. But it was not until the 75th Anniversary of *Nature* in 1944 that I wrote the brief article (Chapter 16) which shows the strong bias against science that Wordsworth felt. Today Wordsworth's views make a strong popular appeal in many quarters; the preceding chapters make clear why I do not share these views; and the final chapter gives what I believe to be the true answer to Wordsworth and the anti-science faction.

'The religion of science' (Chapter 17) which was the presidential address to the Association of Applied Biologists in 1967, sets out in homely terms the nature of scientific knowledge; and illustrates the implicit faith in the principle of causality on which science is based. This exposition is directed against the anti-science school; it is anti-philosophy only to the extent that it takes the view that science and idealist philosophy (in which I was brought up) have different ground rules and therefore cannot play together.

2

INSECTS AND HUMAN AFFAIRS

It is a commonplace that insects are the chief competitors with man for the domination of this planet. Insects destroy man's growing crops, and defoliate his forests; they are responsible for the spread of nearly all the great epidemic fevers of the tropics and subtropics, and for the infection of his live-stock with some of their most fatal diseases. The structural timbers of his buildings are weakened and destroyed by insect attack; his household goods are ravaged by moths and beetles and a heavy toll is levied on his stored reserves of food, spices and tobacco.

We have learned the greater part of what we know about these insect enemies during the last hundred years. It was only in 1878 that Patrick Manson discovered that filaria worms were carried by mosquitoes. The whole of medical and veterinary entomology dates from that time. When, in the 'sixties of the last century, the American settlers reached the eastern slopes of the Rocky Mountains, a harmless little beetle in Colorado changed its diet from the buffalo burr of the deserts to the succulent potato. Within a year or two it had become a major pest of agriculture. That episode marks the beginning of agricultural entomology as we know it today.

Indeed, it is not merely that we have learned more about the importance of insects, they have become more important. The opening up of the tropics has often encouraged the spread of insect-borne diseases. Improved cattle taken in to tropical lands have rapidly succumbed to insect-borne infections to which the inferior native breeds had become tolerant. Intensive agriculture has created conditions favourable for the insect pests of crops. While increased travel and commerce have led to the introduction of pests into new countries, where, having left their natural enemies behind, they have often flourished exceedingly. The history of agricultural entomology in the United States, or in Australia or New Zealand, during the last sixty years is a catalogue of such accidents.

We are apt to regard any insect that competes with our interests as

7

a pest. But it is of course only a pest if it is numerous. It is necessary to have a sufficient number of mosquitoes of the right kind before they can maintain the transmission of malaria. House-flies are very inefficient carriers of intestinal infections: they must be far more numerous than mosquitoes before they become a danger. Empirical observations in Bombay showed that in that particular locality it was necessary to have an average of 2·5 fleas per rat in order to maintain a noticeable amount of bubonic plague.

The importance of numbers is even more evident where insects are attacking growing crops, stored produce or household goods. On an ordinary apple tree there may be perhaps fifty kinds of insects, any of which may turn out to be a pest if circumstances allow it to become sufficiently numerous. It is only in the last fifteen years that the numbers of the red spider mite of fruit trees have increased to a point when it has become a serious orchard pest in many parts of this country — a change, which, we shall see, is largely the result of chemical treatments. Another mite, *Bryobia,* is common enough in most orchards, although it is usually of no importance; but in the orchards of South Africa *Bryobia* is rapidly becoming a major pest — perhaps for the same reason.

So we are concerned, not in destroying the insect but in limiting its multiplication. The potential rate of multiplication in insects is enormous. Many species will produce a couple of hundred offspring with several generations in the year. The insect population is only kept steady by a prodigious mortality, and even a slight relaxation in the pressure of the mortality factors may quickly result in the numbers of individuals reaching outbreak proportions. Numbers are limited by a great variety of factors: weather and climate, the abundance of the food supply and so on; but mainly by biological factors: competitors, predators, parasites, infectious diseases, the prevalence of which may be influenced in turn by the weather. Under *natural* conditions this intense and many-sided competition tends to damp down the more violent fluctuations in population.

But the growing of plants in the form of a crop is *not* a natural state of affairs. When large areas of land are occupied by a single kind of plant the fauna is immediately simplified and that very simplification creates an increased tendency to fluctuation. The trouble naturally grows with the size of the area under one crop and with the extent to which the crop is grown exclusively on the same land. In these islands we suffer far less from insect pests of growing crops than they do in the United States, for example. And one probable reason for this is that we have small fields with plenty of hedgerows which provide food and shelter for a large complex of insect predators and parasites; and the crop that is grown in one field is regularly changed from year to year.

The reaction of the biologist to this situation is to aim at restoring and maintaining the natural balance among insect populations, as part of normal agricultural practice. There can be little doubt that traditional methods of farming have been influenced and shaped unwittingly in just this way by the need for adopting practices that will diminish insect attack. And in recent years many such methods have been deliberately developed, based upon a scientific study of the ecology of the insect and the crop. Particular times of sowing have been advocated, or particular rotations in the sequence of crops have been devised.

But today there is continuous pressure for more intensive cultivation. Increasing mechanisation encourages the cultivation of larger fields. In agriculture, as in industry, American methods are being advocated. In the presence of these changes can we hope to maintain our traditional comparative immunity from pests without the use of more and more chemical insecticides? As conditions become more and more *artificial* can we still aim at *natural* control?

It is not easy to arrive at a balanced view of this problem. In recent years very potent synthetic insecticides have been produced in vast quantities. These have made possible the control by chemical means of many kinds of agricultural insect pests which were baffling entomologists. They have been a great source of encouragement to the entomologist; for where in the past he could often only diagnose and sympathise, now he could *do* something.

But that first period of uncritical enthusiasm is passing. The indiscriminate use of DDT for instance has produced some very disturbing effects. Following its application in orchards there have been great outbreaks of the woolly aphis or American blight and there have been spectacular increases in the fruit tree red spider mite. As is well known that has come about because the parasites and predators that normally hold these creatures in check have proved more susceptible to DDT than the pests themselves. This is no new problem; it has long been realised that the application of chemicals on a large scale may totally upset the balance of populations. But the effects of DDT and some of the newer insecticides

9

have been so rapid and so spectacular that they have given renewed emphasis to the problem.

Likewise, it has been known for many years that insects tend to become resistant to poisons, presumably by a process of selecting out resistant strains. This, also, has been happening with DDT and other substances.

But there is a strong school which still seeks to bludgeon the insects into submission by chemical means; and which hopes to find chemical means of overcoming resistance to insecticides. The representatives of American firms which supply spray chemicals on a vast scale will tell you that in the United States, with immense areas under single crops, the methods of biological or natural control are unthinkable.

On the other hand, there are experienced entomologists concerned with the crops of the Canadian prairies who will go so far as to say that no insecticide should be released for general use until it has been studied for fifteen years to see just exactly what long term effects it will bring about. For even in large areas of single crops we know far too little to appreciate just what the 'beneficial insects' are doing. In the early days of DDT, when it was used extensively on cotton in Louisiana in place of calcium arsenate, heavy infestations with mites and aphids developed for the first time. That was traced to the elimination by the insecticide of ladybirds, predacious bugs and other insects the importance of which had not been appreciated until then.

In attempting the balanced view we certainly have to reckon with the vested interests of the chemical manufacturer. The Swiss insecticide DDT was the first real triumph in the search for a synthetic insecticide that would kill on contact; and the size of the market that was found for this material was a surprise even to the chemists themselves and has resulted in tremendous efforts to discover new chemicals that would compete with DDT. Many remarkable new substances have been produced, both in this country and in America. The number is being added to every year; and in this hectic race for markets it may be that the true aim of a stable agricultural economy is sometimes forgotten. Even in the United States, where what is commonly called 'spray-gun' entomology often seems to dominate the picture, doubts have recently been voiced as to whether these expensive chemical methods, which are being eagerly taken up during a time of booming prices for agricultural products, will prove economically practicable if prices fall. Already the number of washes that are being recommended in the orchards in some parts of the world is reaching the limit of what it is economic to apply.

We have also to reckon with the make-up of the human mind. That prevention is better than cure is a moral saying which does not really appeal to the heart of man. He prefers cures whether of diseases or of insect outbreaks. It creates a greater impression on the mind to destroy an infestation of insects that can be seen, than by some simple change in practice to prevent any infestation from developing. And that is one reason for the great popular appeal of insecticides.

But insecticides are not the only field in which potent new chemicals are being introduced into agriculture. In the last ten years there have been spectacular advances in the discovery of weedkillers. These are proving a boon to the farmer for very many purposes; but they also raise entomological problems. For besides the insects that attack the growing crops there are many others which play an essential role in pollination. These pollinators must be there in readiness when the crop comes into bloom, and for this purpose they need other flowers to visit while they wait. For some years now the production of clover seed in the United States has suffered from the increasing scarcity of bumble bees.

For it is not only the farmer who is using chemical weedkillers in his crops; they are being used for 'cleaning up' the countryside. The field naturalist delights in the mixed and flowery herbage along the roadsides, or around the hedgerows and dyke sides or on the railway embankments. To clean all this up by the labour saving method of spraying everything with weedkillers and to reduce it all to a suburban trimness where only grass is permitted to remain, will be a tragedy from the standpoint of the naturalist who wants to conserve our native flora and fauna. But it is also a potential menace to agriculture, for pollinating insects cannot be eliminated without endangering the seed crops.

It is possible to answer that, just as we must replace the beneficial insects by more and more insecticides, so we may have to plan and organise pollination. Already bees are deliberately introduced into orchards and clover fields. In the farms of the future perhaps we shall have to go much further.

There seems little chance of reverting to the old ways to escape the

11

troubles of the new. The drive for more intensive agriculture, for higher yields with less labour, becomes inexorable. Must we therefore abandon all hope of using the preventive methods of biology and rely for ever on chemical treatments in an ever more artificial environment?

The biologist has an almost instinctive distrust of chemical control. I do not think this is due wholly to the defence of his vested interests. But he has a deep sense of the complexity of living communities. He is terribly conscious of our present ignorance, but convinced that with more knowledge we should be able to devise methods of cultivation which would favour the crop and discourage the insect pest to the point where a satisfactory balance is established.

To achieve this aim universally without the use of chemical insecticides must be a vain hope. There can be no immediate prospect of abandoning the use of insecticides in orchards for example, where the chemical treatments practised during the last thirty years have completely transformed the quality of the fruit we can produce.

The best hope lies in compromise. There is great scope for discovering just what the insecticides are doing. Just how they are impinging upon the complicated fauna of the apple tree for example. When we have this knowledge perhaps we shall find it wise to relax some of the chemical pressure and replace some of the more potent chemicals by others with a milder action. In this way we may be able cautiously to encourage the beneficial insects to multiply. We may well find that in the long run an insecticide which kills fifty per cent of the pest insect and none of its predators or parasites may be far more valuable than one which kills ninety-five per cent of the pest but at the same time eliminates its natural enemies. Perhaps this is where the future of chemical insecticides lies, not as a substitute for but as a complement to the more subtle and more remunerative methods of biology.

3

DDT AND THE BALANCE OF NATURE

From ancient times diseases conveyed by insects have been the main cause of casualties in military campaigns: the house-fly as a carrier of dysentery and typhoid, the louse as the carrier of famine fever or epidemic typhus, the Anopheles mosquito as the carrier of malaria. There are many ways of combating these insects and breaking the chain of transmission of disease from man to insect and to man again. Among the methods is the use of insecticides.

At the outbreak of the war there was one insecticide which occupied a key position in relation to these insects of medical importance; and that was pyrethrum, the extract from the daisy flower *Pyrethrum cinerariaefolium,* a substance exceedingly poisonous to insects but practically harmless to man. The world's supply of pyrethrum came chiefly from Japan and from Kenya in East Africa. At first there was plenty of pyrethrum available for the British forces. But as the war extended into tropical areas, the supply could not keep pace with the demand. The war with Japan closed one main source of supply; the entry of the United States into the conflict enormously increased the demand, and the situation became acute.

In time of peace the United States was the chief consumer of pyrethrum, and it came as something of a shock to British entomologists to discover that virtually the whole of the available stocks of pyrethrum, grown by British planters in Kenya, had been bought up by America! This situation was met by negotiations which led to restriction in the use of pyrethrum for agricultural or other civil purposes, and to the sharing of the available supplies between the two countries according to their military needs. But these supplies were hopelessly inadequate to meet the rising demands — skyrocketing from month to month — and desperate efforts were made to find a sufficient substitute. It was against this background of anxiety that DDT appeared.

Pyrethrum is a contact insecticide: it kills insects when it comes in contact with the surface of their bodies. So is the other famous

13

vegetable insecticide, derris. For many years chemists had been seeking to produce a synthetic contact insecticide, capable of being made in the laboratory and manufactured on a large scale in the chemical works, which would rival these vegetable products in effectiveness and surpass them in cheapness and availability. But until the war these hopes had been largely disappointed.

ARRIVAL OF DDT

In 1940 the Swiss firm of J. R. Geigy, A.G., of Basle discovered the insecticidal properties of a chemical that is known as 2,2-bis(*para*-chlorophenyl)-1,1,1-trichloroethane or more familiarly as dichloro-diphenyltrichloroethane, later abbreviated to DDT. The firm took out patents to cover the manufacture of this chemical and its use as an insecticide, and early in 1942 the British and American branches of the firm brought these patents to the notice of the entomologists in the two countries, who were seeking a substitute for pyrethrum.

In England we read those patents and were frankly sceptical. It seemed to us that too much was claimed. The new insecticide appeared to be so exactly what we wanted that it looked too good to be true. But clearly the stuff should be tested. A 100-lb sample was obtained from Switzerland. A small laboratory sample was prepared in Manchester. Both had the same properties: they were colorless solids, nearly odorless or with a not unpleasant odor, highly poisonous to insects. The body louse was killed by an amount little greater than the minute dose of pyrethrum needed for this purpose.

Meanwhile the same thing was happening in America. The Swiss claims were fully substantiated. And immediately, on both sides of the Atlantic, entomologists got to work to discover how best to use the new material in the fight against the disease-carrying insects. There was the closest co-operation throughout between the British and American scientists, and development went forward rapidly along parallel lines. New ways of using DDT were discovered, as it seemed, almost daily — until both British and American entomologists almost came to feel that they had discovered the stuff.

The chemists worked with equal speed. Improved methods of manufacture were devised, chemical plants were set up by the manufacturing firms in America and England, and soon after the requirements were defined the supplies were available. As the months went by, more uses were discovered; requirements went up and up; until, with an output of some scores of tons a month, the military demands could still scarcely be fully met.

DDT AGAINST THE LOUSE

Mixed as a dust and rubbed into the clothing, DDT is exceedingly effective in killing lice; and unlike the vegetable insecticides pyrethrum and derris, which soon lose their potency, DDT is extremely stable and will continue to kill lice for three or four weeks after it has been applied.

Early in 1944, an outbreak of typhus occurred in Naples. Judging by what has happened in the past when typhus has broken out among an overcrowded, dirty, and ill-fed population during the winter months, this might have been expected to become a great and spreading epidemic. Dusts, at first containing pyrethrum and later containing DDT, were puffed up the sleeves and trouser legs, down necks and into the waists of skirts and trousers, systematically throughout the affected population. The results were dramatic: the epidemic, instead of rising to a terrifying peak, just faded out.

On the western front in World War I there was an efficient organization for destroying body lice, mainly by heat treatment of clothing, and by soaping and bathing of the men. But the methods employed had one great defect: they left the soldier's clothing ready to become infested again as soon as he could pick up fresh lice from his comrades; thus, in spite of systematic delousing, the men in the trenches were always heavily infested and the louse-borne 'trench fever' was prevalent.

What was needed was some treatment that would leave the clothing proofed against lice for a long period. DDT has proved ideal for this purpose. It dissolves in oils but not in water. By dipping shirts and underclothes in suitable emulsions or solutions of DDT they can be so impregnated that lice which crawl over them are killed. The effect lasts several weeks even in clothing worn continuously. And some effect persists even after washing several times in hot soap and water. This impregnated clothing was highly successful in the prevention of lousiness in the armies that liberated Europe. The percentage of men infested with lice among the American and British forces was exceedingly low — in striking contrast with conditions in the German armies.

MOSQUITOES AND MALARIA

The full story of malaria in the war has yet to be written. But this much can be said. The maintenance and operation of large armies in the highly malarious jungles of Burma or New Guinea could never have been effected without steps being taken for the prevention of malaria. Furthermore, these preventive measures, as well as the medical treatment of malaria, were so much more efficient among the American, Australian, and British Armies (indeed preventive measures were almost non-existent among the Japanese) that, in the war in the Far East, malaria was our most potent ally.

Perhaps the most important single measure in this fight against malaria was the regular use of drugs, quinine or Atabrine (mepacrine), which suppress the symptoms of the disease. But measures directed against the Anopheles mosquitoes which carry the infection from man to man were certainly valuable, sometimes very valuable, and among these measures DDT figured prominently.

Mists containing DDT and a little pyrethrum, dispersed by means of ordinary hand spray guns, proved better for killing the adult winged mosquitoes than the standard pyrethrum sprays. The famous 'aerosol bomb' devised by the U.S. Department of Agriculture, in which pyrethrum was blown out as a fine mist by Freon kept liquefied by pressure, was later filled with DDT instead; and there were many other ingenious methods for producing a suspended cloud of DDT that would kill mosquitoes.

But there is another way of killing the winged mosquito. It was early noted by the Swiss workers that if a thin film of DDT was applied to the surface of a wall, house-flies settling on that surface were subsequently killed. This effect persisted for several weeks. Films of DDT act in the same way against the mosquito; the poison appears to be absorbed through the feet of the insect — and this happens without causing it any discomfort, so that the insect is not repelled from the treated surface but remains there until it has taken in the tiny dose that is needed to kill. Treatment of the surface of huts and tents has been one of the most successful means of controlling Anopheles mosquitoes.

Since the larval stages of the mosquito are spent in water, most of the classic methods of malaria control have been directed against the larvae in their breeding places. DDT proved valuable in this connection too. A mist of DDT in kerosene sprayed over the surface of the water, the addition of DDT to the petroleum oils commonly

16

used to kill mosquito larvae, the spraying of an emulsion of DDT in water — these were some of the methods. It was found that as little as two ounces of DDT would kill all the larvae over an acre of water surface. But there was one disappointing feature. Whereas it had been hoped that the killing action would persist for long periods, it lasted in fact little more than a week.

It has long been the practice to control mosquito breeding in inaccessible places or over wide expanses of water by distributing Paris green from aeroplanes. DDT lent itself particularly well to this procedure. Great advances have been made in the regulated dispersion of oily solutions or emulsions of DDT from the air, and this practice has proved very successful in controlling mosquito larvae.

But it was soon discovered that these aerial sprays yielded a bonus: they also killed the adult mosquitoes. And not only did they kill the day-biting mosquitoes which were on the wing at the time of spraying: they killed the Anopheles mosquitoes which shelter in places beyond the reach of the spray during the day-time and come out to feed only at night. Apparently sufficient poison was deposited upon the surface of the vegetation for the mosquitoes to pick up a fatal dose when they alighted on the leaves during their nocturnal flights. For the rapid improvement of malarial conditions in areas newly occupied by troops, or even *before* the landing of invading armies — that is, until the regular ground organization could get to work — or for maintaining control in difficult or inaccessible country, this method has proved most valuable. It was used with great success in Italy, in India, and in Guadalcanal and many other regions in the Pacific zone.

Bedbugs too, which can be a troublesome pest in barracks, or in native houses, or on board ship, are killed by residual films of DDT — not so easily as house-flies or mosquitoes, but well enough for practical purposes. The result is that virtual extermination of bedbugs has been achieved in jails, barracks, and ships in many parts of the world. DDT was useful in air-raid shelters in London. A suitably prepared film will continue to kill bedbugs for at least three months and often much longer. Promising results have been obtained by the use of paints (water or oil paints) in which DDT has been incorporated.

For other insects, such as roaches or ants, which may trouble the soldier or the sailor, DDT has been good but not much better than materials already in use.

USE OF DDT IN PEACE

The control of malaria by preventing the breeding of mosquitoes has been possible since the end of the last century, when the role of the mosquito in transmitting the disease was first revealed. And it has been put into effect in Panama, in the wealthy Chinese and European settlements in Malaya, in the rich Dutch settlements in Java, and on tea plantations in India and elsewhere — to take a very few examples. This method of control has not been used in the past in the poor rural communities in India or Africa or in the southern part of the United States — because the cost was out of all proportion to the slender resources of people living at a bare level of subsistence.

There are, it is true, certain parts of the world where something has been done for rural malaria by improved water management in the rivers and streams, as in Ceylon and in the Tennessee Valley; or by improved agriculture, as in some of the rice-growing areas in Java; but it is fair to say that where such methods have not been feasible, no *direct* attack on the mosquito has been possible in rural areas.

Has this state of affairs been materially changed by the advent of DDT? It is too early to be sure; but if DDT becomes available at a sufficiently low price, we may have, for the first time, in the 'residual film' deposited on the walls of houses, a really effective method of control that could be applied at a cost within the reach of rural communities.

The control of rural malaria, so long the despair of the malariologist, may at last become a reality. Preliminary trials in West Africa and in India have been highly encouraging. This method figures largely in the 'Extended Program' of the U.S. Public Health Service, in which the energetic campaign for the control of malaria in war areas is being enlarged to cover all the malarious regions in the United States; and in the control of rural malaria by the Health and Safety Division of the TVA. It is acceptable to the people; and it has the advantage that its action is concentrated automatically against those mosquitoes that come into houses — which are precisely the mosquitoes that are carrying the disease.

Nations are becoming increasingly aware of the risk they run of new malarial mosquitoes being introduced by aeroplane from other countries. The terrific epidemic of malaria in Brazil in the early thirties, which followed the introduction of *Anopheles gambiae* from

West Africa, has been an object lesson on what may occur. To meet this risk, international agreements have been made to ensure that aeroplanes are so treated as to kill any dangerous insects that may be on board.

Spraying with insecticidal mists has been the standard method employed; and sometimes this work is efficiently done. But it must be admitted that not infrequently the performance with the spray gun is a mere formality that can cause little inconvenience to any insects present. A residual film of DDT, thoroughly applied at suitable intervals to the whole interior of the aeroplane, would be a very great additional safeguard, and is likely to figure largely in the sanitation of commercial planes.

A residual film applied in houses will be of enormous value in the campaign against the bedbug and in helping to keep houses free from flies. Likewise dusts containing DDT will have their use in dealing with head lice in children and with epidemics of typhus and other louse-borne diseases in the countries in which they are likely to occur. But the real cure for all these troubles is an improved standard of hygiene. DDT is a valuable supplement to hygiene and cleanliness. It will not take their place.

VETERINARY USES FOR DDT

Almost all the vast output of DDT during the war years was earmarked for service users. But enough has been made available for trials to prepare the way for what will soon be its main applications — against insects of veterinary importance, against the pests of growing crops, and perhaps against forest insects.

The swarms of flies in unsanitary cow barns constitute a veterinary problem, and the deposit of a film of DDT on the walls has had a spectacular effect upon their numbers, which at once impresses the observer with the powers of this insecticide. But when we look into the matter a little more closely, the limitations of the method become apparent. DDT as a residual film kills very slowly; it may take two or three hours before the flies resting on the film finally succumb.

However, these flies on the walls do not seriously trouble the herdsman. The flies he is concerned about are those which are brought in by the cows when they come from the pasture to the barn for milking. It is these flies, often quite few in number, which irritate the animals and make them restless during milking; and it is sometimes observed that although the whole population of flies which remains behind in the milking shed is killed by DDT on the walls, the cows are still as restless as ever while they are milked.

Moreover, there are a good many sorts of flies on cattle, and they behave in different ways. The house-flies, which tickle the animals but do not bite, readily leave them and settle on the walls and are poisoned. The stable flies, which are biting, bloodsucking insects, stay on the cattle until they have succeeded in getting a meal of blood. They are a source of much annoyance, and a small number may cause a lot of stamping before they leave the cows and come into contact with the treated walls. The horn flies are little bloodsucking insects which never leave the body of the animal save for a few moments when it drops its dung, in which they lay their eggs. They are quite unaffected by DDT on the walls of the barn.

That suggests the possibility of applying DDT to the back of the animal as a spray or in a dip. The effect of this treatment on the stable fly is only short-lived; after a few days its toxicity is almost gone. But against the horn fly, which remains continuously on the animal, the results have been far more satisfactory. In the northern territories of Australia, in Texas, and in Florida, it has been found that spraying or dipping the cattle in a DDT preparation has kept them free from this troublesome insect for several weeks.

In England very promising results have been obtained against the fleece worm or blowfly in sheep by the same means. Instead of trying to kill the young maggots as they develop in the soiled fleece and skin, the wool is treated with DDT to poison the female fly when she is seeking to lay her eggs. Furthermore, it is possible to treat the wool in addition with materials which make the sheep extra-attractive to the egg-laying female and so to turn the treated sheep into a veritable trap for blowflies.

It may be that something of the same sort will prove of value against the tsetse flies in tropical Africa, which carry a number of fatal diseases of stock as well as human sleeping sickness. These flies collect in large numbers on cloth screens or dummy animals, and there is evidence that they can be killed over longish periods if such screens are treated with DDT.

Lice on goats and cattle, and ticks on sheep, are among the pests of stock against which DDT is proving extremely successful. And it is effective against fleas on cats and dogs.

DDT IN AGRICULTURE AND FORESTRY

In agriculture, DDT has been used with promising results against flea beetles and onion thrips. It has been good against caterpillars, but it has been disappointing against most sorts of aphid or green fly. As a measure for the control of the potato leaf hopper it has been so outstanding that some observers have suggested that its widespread use for this purpose in the United States will create the problem of an excessive production of potatoes unless the acreage devoted to this crop is markedly reduced! DDT is a promising insecticide against the potato beetle. It is without effect on the Mexican bean beetle, however, and it has not proved very successful against grasshoppers.

The codling moth, the Oriental fruit moth, the cotton bollworm, the boll weevil, the corn borer, the Japanese beetle — these are a few of the major pests of agriculture against which DDT is being widely tested. Will DDT make possible control of the corn borer or corn-ear worm on field corn? Will DDT save the United States from invasion by the pink bollworm which is threatening from Mexico and which so far has been kept at bay by quarantine measures? Has an answer at last been found to the problem of the Japanese beetle? These are a few of the questions that agricultural entomologists are asking and seeking to answer.

Most sorts of caterpillars are easily killed by DDT, either from eating vegetation that has been sprayed, or from crawling over a residual film of the chemical. The tent caterpillars which have been so conspicuous in the eastern part of the United States during the past season, although they are not a serious pest, are readily controlled by DDT. The young caterpillars die when they come out from the egg masses in the twigs and creep along the branches if these have been sprayed with DDT — even when the spraying has been done some weeks before.

The gypsy moth too is a ready victim. Although the method has not yet been fully tried out, the spraying of the trunks of trees and debris around the base may prove a useful way of dealing with the gypsy moth in residential areas. Likewise the cankerworm, which so often ruins the shade trees in cities, can be controlled by power sprayers using a variety of insecticides. DDT is proving equal or superior to the best of them.

For use on a really large scale in the forests, the spraying of DDT from the air is a method that has caught the imagination of the scientist and of the general public as holding out some hope of coping with the great outbreaks of the spruce budworm, the various sawflies, or the hemlock looper, which from time to time sweep through vast tracts of forest and defoliate or kill trees over thousands of acres. Highly concentrated solutions of DDT, when discharged from aeroplanes as a fine rain, undoubtedly kill these insects.

WIDER IMPLICATIONS OF DDT

So far I have been giving just a general and somewhat superficial account of what DDT appears capable of doing. What remains to be seen is whether the method is feasible economically and desirable biologically.

The organic thiocyanates, which were coming to the fore in the pre-war years, were a big advance in the search for synthetic chemicals which would rival as contact insecticides the natural vegetable products. DDT is another big step forward in that search. But it is quite certain that it is not the last word. DDT has unquestionably provided a tremendous stimulus to experimentation; even the insecticide manufacturers have been amazed at the size of the potential market for a really good insecticide. There are doubtless other chemicals on the way. One has already appeared — the British material Gammexane, or 666, which rivals DDT and for certain purposes seems even to surpass it.

What the chemists have been seeking so far is a universal insecticide: a material that will kill every insect with which it comes in contact, and at the same time a material that does not injure the plants upon which it is spread or poison human beings when they eat those plants or when they come into contact with it in the course of manufacture or use. Has this aim been achieved in the discovery of the properties of DDT and is it an objective that is wholly desirable? Those are the questions which biologists are asking themselves today.

DDT seems to have the effect of poisoning some part of the nervous system. Insects which have walked on films of DDT soon begin to stagger in a drunken manner. Their legs twitch and they cannot co-ordinate their movements. Sometimes they remain for several days in this 'drunken' state before dying. The poison appears to enter in minute traces through the feet and elsewhere on the surface of the insect.

In mammals such as rabbits, rats, mice, or guinea pigs, DDT has a somewhat similar effect. There are muscular tremors and spasms, incoordination, and finally paralysis and death. But for reasons that are not understood, a much larger dose of the chemical in proportion to their weight is required by mammals than by insects. Poisoning in the animals can be produced most easily if the DDT is dissolved in oil and then either eaten or rubbed into the skin. It seems harmless when eaten in the dry form and is certainly harmless when applied as powder to the skin.

Large amounts of DDT have been handled and experimented with during the past three years; yet only one case of DDT poisoning in man has been described; and this was in a laboratory worker who had deliberately rubbed into his skin very strong solutions of DDT in a way that could never happen in practice. The symptoms produced were like those in other animals, but when contact with DDT was stopped he gradually recovered completely.

It is therefore generally felt that, used with ordinary care, DDT is a safe insecticide so far as man and domestic or farm animals are concerned.

Tadpoles and fish are more susceptible to DDT. They are not affected by the very small quantities that are applied to the surface of the water to kill mosquito larvae. But when strong solutions, such as are used for spraying the forests from the air, fall on water, not only are all the aquatic insects — may-flies, dragonflies and others — killed, but trout and other fish are destroyed and the streams rendered practically devoid of animal life.

Plants, on the other hand, are not much affected by DDT if it is suitably applied. Where they have been injured, the harm has generally been traced to the action of other chemicals with which the DDT has been mixed.

HARMFUL AND BENEFICIAL INSECTS

Man is the measure of all things. We judge the world by its impact upon ourselves. Insects which convey diseases to domestic animals or to man, or insects which feed upon the crops we wish to eat, are described as harmful. And these insects attract so much attention to themselves that we come to regard all insects as enemies of man. But among the teeming millions of insects there is incessant strife. Under favourable conditions insects can multiply with incredible rapidity, and in the course of several months may increase their numbers a millionfold or more. Their numbers are held in check by fluctuations in the climate, sudden cold or heat, drought or flooding; by the limitation of the available food supply; and by the biological pressure of competitors or of insects and other animals which prey upon them.

Insects, I have said, can multiply at a prodigious rate. But as a rule their numbers do not change very much. Although a female may lay perhaps three hundred eggs, the one generation may be only a little larger or a little smaller than the next. Of the three hundred offspring, two hundred and ninety-eight must have perished. In this colossal mortality other insects play a large part. There are 'predaceous' insects which attack and devour their fellows; and there are 'parasitic' insects which lay their eggs within the bodies of their victims so that their young may slowly devour them.

This process is commonly known as 'biological control', and many instances could be quoted in which insect parasites have been introduced to deal with an insect pest and have done so to such good purpose that failing industries have been restored to prosperity. It is not surprising that the method has caught the imagination of the world. But aside from these spectacular achievements, our insect friends the insect predators and parasites are everywhere quietly working all the time, and any decrease of their activities is followed by an outbreak of some insect pest.

Insect pests in farm crops are on the whole much less severe in Britain than in America; and the chief reason for this lies in the better opportunity afforded to the insect friends and the birds in preying upon the pests. In Britain the fields are small, the crops are changed in rotation each year, there are hedgerows around the fields providing shelter for the birds and insects which serve in the defence. But in America the large areas under the same crops, grown perhaps for several years on the same land, provide ideal opportunities for the pests to build up vast populations which decimate the crops.

DDT AND THE BALANCE OF NATURE

Now let us look again at the action of DDT, bearing in mind that alongside the pests at which we are aiming is a complex assemblage of interacting organisms and that perhaps DDT is like a blunderbuss discharging shot in a manner so haphazard that friend and foe alike are killed.

It may be said at once that the various insects in the house are not limited in numbers by parasites and predators sharing their domestic haunts. Even though spiders kill a certain number of insects indoors, few housewives regard spiders as friendly inmates of the house. John Keats, with the sympathy of the poet, may write in kindly terms of the crickets as 'little inmates' of the house, 'full of mirth', and call them to witness that the 'poetry of earth is never dead'; and the English naturalist of the eighteenth century, Gilbert White, writing in 1790, may refer to the detestable roach, which had then only just arrived in Britain, with something more than tolerance, and may express the hope that this interesting insect which had appeared in his friend's house might soon visit his own. But today all insects in the house are regarded as unwanted aliens. If we can eradicate them all, so much the better. In so doing there is no risk of upsetting the balance of nature.

DDT is popular, when used in houses, precisely for the reason that it destroys insects of all kinds. In America I was told of the coloured housewife who complained bitterly, after her house had been treated with DDT to kill malarial mosquitoes, that she was forever having to sweep up 'dem damn dead flies'! But some people are never satisfied.

The point is that conditions in the house are such that there is no risk of killing friends along with the enemies. DDT used in this way seems to confer nothing but benefits.

The same is true when we consider the insects which live on the bodies of man and animals. There are no friendly insects which haunt our persons. When we can kill such insects without risk of poisoning their hosts (and we can with DDT) the result is wholly good.

When we turn to the control of mosquitoes in the open we are on less safe ground. The very small quantities of insecticide which need to be applied on water to kill mosquito larvae do not normally kill fish; but they kill a variable proportion of the other aquatic insects. This result may not matter very much. But it may have far-reaching effects which it is impossible at present to predict. The broadcasting of sprays from aeroplanes in order to kill the flying mosquito is still more prone to upset the balance of nature. These sprays settle on the vegetation and kill vast numbers of insects of all sorts. Without careful study it is impossible to guess what the ultimate results of this process may be.

Still more drastic are the effects of the highly concentrated sprays of DDT that are being used against the forest pests. These sprays kill other kinds of insects, in addition to the pests against which they are directed. They settle into the streams and kill the aquatic insects. Some fish, such as the speckled trout, are reported to have been killed when they fed on poisoned insects. Crayfish and tadpoles are killed either by contact with the poison or by eating contaminated food. These again are important sources of food for fish, which must suffer when they are destroyed.

There seems little doubt that the general insect population in the forests is greatly reduced and that the natural waters may be nearly sterilized and lifeless. It has even been suggested that nesting birds may suffer from the shortage of insects and be unable properly to feed their young. Only careful experiments can prove whether birds will suffer or not.

When DDT is applied to a small area of woodland it will not matter very much if almost complete destruction of insect life results: the area will soon be colonized again from the surrounding woods. But where really large areas of forest, extending over hundreds of acres, are treated, the effects may be more serious. That problem also must be resolved by experiment, and the results of the trials carried out this year in the United States and in Canada will be awaited with interest.

We already know a little more about the results of applying DDT to farm crops and orchards. We know that DDT sprayed on peach trees with the object of killing the caterpillars of the Oriental fruit moth is even more effective in killing the parasite that is being liberated to control this pest than it is in killing the pest itself. We know that DDT is not much good for killing the woolly aphis. But it is a wonderful insecticide against the Aphelinus parasite that normally keeps the numbers of woolly aphis down. Already it has been observed that orchards containing woolly aphis, when they have been sprayed with DDT, have developed outbreaks of this pest such as had never been seen before.

The same thing has happened with the fruit tree red spider. In orchards where this mite has normally been kept within reasonable bounds by the enemies that prey upon it, trees have been literally scarlet with the red spiders after being sprayed with DDT.

26

DDT AND HONEY BEES

There is one insect that is generally regarded as the friend of man; and that is the honey bee. Honey is itself a useful article of commerce, but the making of honey is not the only service we receive from the bee. Unless flowers are pollinated they will not set seed. Bees are among the most valuable pollinators of flowers, and at the present time most beemen consider that the chief value of the bee to man lies in its activities in transferring pollen from one flower to another. In orchards or in the clover fields, the crop may depend upon the bee. In certain areas the yield of clover seed drops from year to year, and one reason is thought to be a growing shortage of bees.

Now there are pests of apple flowers, such as the apple-blossom weevil of Europe, and pests of clover or alfalfa, such as the lygus bugs, which are well controlled by DDT. But DDT kills honey bees. If bees are confined in cages with plants that have been sprayed with DDT they are soon killed. On the other hand, there is some evidence that the effect on bees visiting sprayed blossoms in the field may not be so serious as was feared. Entomologists are cautious as to what they say about the matter at the moment. But beekeepers are a vociferous race. Like the bees they care for, their more lovable qualities may become obscured when they are roused — and they do not take kindly to DDT.

This is no new problem. Beekeepers have suffered in past years from the use of arsenic in orchards during blossom time or from derris. Only careful and unbiased work can determine how and when DDT can be used so as not to impede the invaluable activities of the honey bee.

CHEMISTS AND INSECT PESTS

It is obvious enough that DDT is a two-edged sword. We can see how seriously it may upset the balance locally between insect enemies and friends.

Now this too is no new thing. The manufacture of chemical insecticides and fungicides for the use of the farmer has increased enormously during the past thirty years; yet more and more of these chemicals are called for. Time was when a couple of arsenical washes were adequate to control the codling moth on apples. Now, five, six, or even seven washes are needed in some orchards. As time goes on, the codling grub, for reasons that are not wholly understood, becomes more resistant to arsenic. Early in this century the California red scale on citrus was readily controlled by fumigation of the tree with hydrogen cyanide. But in recent years a 'resistant race' has developed and it becomes increasingly difficult to keep this scale down with cyanide gas. Three or four years ago it was discovered that tartar emetic was the perfect control for the citrus thrips in California. But within two years a race of thrips resistant to tartar emetic had replaced the normal race and tartar emetic ceased to work.

It is the same story with the fungicides used in the orchards. One of the best chemicals for the control of apple scab is sulphur. Sulphur is good for killing the red spider. But it also kills other mites; and in some localities there are many sorts of mites which prey on the red spider, and in order to replace the activities of these mites, more and more chemicals have to be sprayed upon the trees.

All this is grand from the chemist's point of view. The more chemicals are applied, the more they are needed, and the demand for chemical insecticides goes up and up. It is not so good from the grower's point of view, and it is certainly bad from the standpoint of the biologist, who likes to feel that he is controlling nature in an intelligent manner, and not merely throwing grit into the works.

FUTURE OF CHEMICAL INSECTICIDES

Chemicals which upset the balance of nature have been known before. DDT is merely the latest and one of the most violent. It can bring about within a single year a disturbance that it would take other chemicals a good many years to produce. It has thus focused attention on the problem and has provided a great stimulus to entomologists to reflect upon what is happening.

One conclusion they have come to is that we know far too little about the interaction of pests with their physical environment and with the other insects around them. We need to know far more about their ecology — that is, about their natural history studied scientifically. When the ecology of an insect pest is fully known, it is often possible to modify the conditions in such a way that its world no longer suits it. The crop may be planted too early for it; the order of crops in the rotation may be changed; varieties of the plant that are unfavourable for the insect may be grown, and so forth.

28

But when all these so-called cultural or naturalistic methods of control have been developed, there remains a large residue of pests for which insecticides must be used. Here again more ecology is needed. We want to learn how to apply the insecticide at such a time or in such a way as to touch the pest and not its enemies. We want to choose insecticides which discriminate between friend and foe.

This is probably where the future of insecticides lies — in the development of materials with a selective action. It may well be that in the long run an insecticide which kills 50 per cent of the pest insect and none of its predators or parasites may be far more valuable than one which kills 95 per cent but at the same time eliminates its natural enemies. It has been found in England that in fumigating truck crops with nicotine it is possible to adjust the dose of fumigant to such a level that the aphids or green flies are killed but the insect enemies are spared. That is an example of the type of selective insecticide we need. The development of such materials will provide unlimited scope for the ingenuity of biologists and chemists.

POSTSCRIPT

The subsequent history of DDT is well known. Residual films inside houses have provided the central method employed by the World Health Organization in the attempted 'eradication' of malaria. Eradication did not prove feasible; but spectacular reductions in the incidence of malaria were achieved. The weakness of the original plan (now corrected) was that local public health organizations, to develop and maintain *all* methods of malaria control, were not always set up; and reversion to malarious conditions has sometimes occurred when the WHO teams have left.

Most of the other developments, as foreshadowed in the foregoing article, have come about. Local strains resistant to DDT have developed in many insects; effects on beneficial insects have been so severe that use of DDT in orchards and in the cotton fields was soon abandoned; there have been almost no detectable effects of DDT on the health of man, whether among manufacturers, users or the general public. Indeed DDT has remained one of the safest of insecticides. But widespread and often excessive use, particularly the continuous use for fly control on stock animals, has led to transmission to man in his food and its accumulation in substantial amounts in the stored body fat of the general population. This appeared alarming; and in many countries the use of DDT has been banned. By that time it was no longer a necessary insecticide in agriculture; it remained useful for some forest pests — though destructive of wild life; it is still extremely valuable as a safe residual insecticide for malaria control.

4

SCIENCE, PURE AND APPLIED

It is a great honour, and a great responsibility, to be invited to give one of the Installation Lectures on this auspicious occasion. I am ill qualified for this task; but at least I may justly claim that the subject on which I have chosen to speak is one that is of the greatest importance to every university in every part of the world. In England, at least, we sometimes forget that our universities owe their origin and their development in great part to the demands of practical affairs. They arose in the Middle Ages, mainly to provide better education for the hosts of 'clerks' or subordinate clergy who undertook all the tasks in mediaeval society for which some degree of learning was necessary.

With the great expansion of trade and affairs in England in Tudor times there was a corresponding expansion of the Universities of Oxford and Cambridge with an increased emphasis on medicine and law. At that time and later the universities were tolerably active and effective; but after the violent disturbances of the Civil War and Restoration there followed a long period of stagnation and privilege extending throughout most of the eighteenth century. Then came the Industrial Revolution. This was based on the achievements of practical men, drawing upon the experience of craftsmen; and England quickly climbed to a position of ascendancy which for a time seemed unassailable. But there were far-seeing people who soon perceived that such a position could not be sustained unless techniques and procedures were continually improved, and that the source of such improvement was to be found in the natural sciences.

The turning point was the Great Exhibition of 1851. Although British products were still outstanding, the progress that had been made by our competitors, basing their techniques on scientific study and research, was alarming. This was the immediate stimulus which led, during the second half of the century, to the establishment of technological institutes of many kinds and to the foundation and expansion of a series of new universities. The depressed state of

31

farming in this same period led to a corresponding improvement in agricultural education and in the development of the sciences basic to agriculture.

In our own time two World Wars have underlined the dependence of our present society upon science. And the demand for new sources of energy has led to a renewed expansion in teaching and research in science and technology, which is now in full swing. But those of us who work in universities soon forget these origins. We forget, for example, that the standard course of zoology, as taught in most universities for the best part of a century, was the creation of Thomas Henry Huxley who was appointed to teach zoology in the Royal School of Mines in South Kensington; and that Huxley owed his appointment to the very practical need for mining prospectors, who could find their way among the strata of the earth by means of the fossils which these contain.

In this lecture I propose to consider the relation between pure and applied science. But first I must say a few words on the methods of science.

SCIENTIFIC METHOD

New knowledge in science comes in many different ways, but in the deliberate search for knowledge it is customary to recognize two quite distinct procedures. There is first that formulated by Francis Bacon and called by him the 'Novum Organum'. It consists in the accumulation of facts. These, it is anticipated, will eventually all fall into place; and without the exercise of any more thought than that required by a committee, a complete understanding of nature will be achieved. This method still has its advocates and its practitioners but it has always proved singularly unproductive.

The second method is the experimental method. This has often been described, perhaps nowhere better than by Claude Bernard a century ago in his *Experimental Medicine*. It consists in the formulation of an hypothesis which the investigator then attempts to prove, that is, to demolish, by a series of experiments. If all attempts fail, the hypothesis is provisionally accepted as a theory or base for further hypotheses; and thus the provisional edifice of scientific knowledge is gradually built up.

The essential ingredient is the hypothesis. Where does this come from? It comes, of course, from the imagination which formulates ideas. Claude Bernard describes graphically how the investigator outside the laboratory should allow his imagination full rein; but when he enters the laboratory he should shed his imagination like his overcoat. We all recognize that the progress of science is constantly dependent on improved techniques. But technique alone is not enough. (One has only to contemplate the wasted effort that can be expended on new techniques just because they are new.) When we say that we lack a knowledge of techniques, as often as not we mean that we lack ideas.

Where then do the ideas come from that form the basis of these precious hypotheses? They come by thought. But thought is a difficult and painful process: most people would rather die than think; and that is why they are so ready to escape the necessity by adopting empiricism, or Baconianism, which sometimes appears in modern dress as the substitution of statistics for thought. But in scientific research there is no substitute for thought. That is not a truth which we readily admit. We are glad enough to extol the merits of teamwork, to demand heavier endowments for research, and to admire fine equipment, but we are reluctant to speak of the necessity for thought and the generation of ideas.

THE IMPACT OF PRACTICE ON SCIENCE

But where do thoughts come from? To conceive good thoughts you need a good brain, and a brain prepared by education and experience to associate ideas and derive new conclusions from diverse observations. Even the best brains, however, do not operate in a vacuum. They are subject, among other things, to the influence of fashion. In science they may be led by fashion to pursue particular lines of study until these have become more and more specialized and less and less productive of important results.

Take the examples of muscular contraction or nerve conduction, both fields of research which have engaged the attention of highly specialized schools of physiologists for many years. From time to time these schools have looked like becoming so specialized as to produce results which none but their own members could under-stand. But always the subject has been revivified by ideas from outside. At the present time, with techniques and ideas coming from physical chemistry, biochemistry, nuclear physics, X-ray crystallography, electron optics, these subjects are once more in a most exciting phase of eruption.

Now one of the most efficient correctives to the dangers of over-specialization is provided by the stimulus of contact with practice. The research worker in pure science who has reached the point where his ideas are going round and round in circles like a bee in a bell-jar, may have a new direction and stimulus given to his work by contact with some practical problem. One is tempted to borrow the jargon of the dialectical materialists and claim that the interaction of the opposites of theory and practice, of pure and applied science, is one of the most potent dialectics in the advancement of knowledge.

The zoologist studying the natural history or autecology of an animal is generally satisfied with a comparatively superficial knowledge of it. After all, there are so many animals in the world to know about. But when the applied biologist is confronted with some animal in competition with man, a mosquito carrying yellow fever or malaria, a migratory locust, an aphid bringing virus diseases to the potato crop, a sawfly destroying the wheat crops of Alberta, he requires a depth of knowledge of quite a different order. It is in these fields that the principles of ecology are being hammered out. It is a question of personal preference whether we regard this as an example of the pure science of ecology coming to the rescue of the applied biologist or as an example of the applied biologist showing how ecology should be studied.

We see the same state of affairs in taxonomy. Taxonomy provides the essential basis of any work to do with living creatures; and that, of course, is the real justification for the existence of our museum staffs. But museum workers were slow to appreciate the full implications of Darwinism. Although the principle of evolution was soon accepted, the museum worker, almost of necessity and by the very nature of his work, has clung to the idea of the fixity of species. During the last fifty years the development of genetics and ecology has been changing that, and today we hear much of the 'new systematics'. But what is not always appreciated is the contribution of the applied biologist to this change in outlook. The museum worker has long recognized geographical races; but it has been the applied biologist, looking at his animals in nature, at all stages in their development, far more intimately than the museum worker could possibly do, who has realized that a single species may present a variety of 'biological races' differentiated by their ways of life. Although it is requiring the painstaking work of the geneticist to analyse the nature of biological races and their relation to species formation, I do not think it would be an exaggeration to say that the discovery of these races was due to the applied biologist.

I have spoken of the need for thought. But one of the dangers by which science is beset is too much thought: an undue faith in the capacity of reason. For hundreds of years the great physicians of Europe based their medical practice upon systems of medicine which had been arrived at by a process of pure thought. And scarcely a vestige of those systems has remained: the purely rational process has indeed proved extraordinarily unproductive.

On the other hand, the scientific method has proved so amazingly successful during the past century or two that in these days reliance on pure reason is at a discount. Yet the risk of science, or parts of science, becoming enmeshed in some fabric of logic is by no means negligible. If one were to search the annals of current science I do not doubt that one would find small islands of scholasticism where existing theories are considered self-sufficient and the mind is satisfied with formal explanations in terms of these accepted theories. But the cold rude breath of experimental science blows everywhere and these sheltered corners do not remain undisturbed for long.

In the universities today there is a revival of interest in the philosophy of science, the study of logic and so-called 'scientific method'. There can be no doubt that these matters provide an admirable exercise for the mind — they will be harmful only if students come to believe that scientific knowledge is in fact built up and advanced by any such logical procedure.

TRADITIONAL KNOWLEDGE AND EMPIRICISM

In the past, in the absence of that organized body of fact and theory that we call science, no discovery had permanence unless it was incorporated into the traditional procedures of some practical art. And since it is very difficult to be sure whether a given change in the practice of an art represents progress or decay, the practitioners of such arts have always been extremely conservative. Indeed such a system of knowledge could remain stable only so long as it was intensely conservative.

Science has changed all that. A body of classified knowledge is being built up, held together and summarized by laws and theories which make possible an almost infinite number of predictions from a minimum of brief generalizations. We professional scientists know that all these generalizations are only provisional. They represent 'summaries of current opinion', some of which may endure for a thousand years or more, like the Ptolemaic conception of the universe; others may last a century or two like the system of Copernicus, Galileo and Newton; while yet others, which we ordinary folk formulate, are destined to be current for no more than a few years at the most.

But the general public does not appreciate the provisional nature of scientific knowledge. It is no wonder that the practitioners of crafts of every kind have come to rely more and more on science and have developed a flattering faith in the opinions of the scientist. On the whole I believe that faith is well founded; but there have been many examples, even in the recent history of science, of scientists discrediting most valuable discoveries and beliefs because the knowledge and methods available to the science of the day have been inadequate.

There had long been a belief that fleas were connected with human plague; but when plague first appeared in India in 1896 and a strong scientific commission was appointed to investigate the matter they wrote in their report that 'the theory that the plague is carried to man by some biting insect is scarcely worthy of statement.' The transmission of plague by the rat flea was conclusively demonstrated a few years later. When my father was a medical student he was taught that one Steinhaeuser had claimed that rickets could be cured by the administration of cod-liver oil, but that, in fact, chemists had shown that cod-liver oil contained only the same sorts of fatty acids as olive oil, and since olive oil was much pleasanter to take it was just was well to prescribe that!

In medical practice the fungus-infected rye grains known as ergot have long been used to induce prolonged contraction of the uterus and so control post-partum haemorrhage. At one time this action was attributed to certain alkaloids present in the drug. But when I was a medical student I was taught that none of the characteristic alkaloids of ergot had this effect, and that any prolonged action of this kind upon smooth muscle which might be claimed by the doctors was simply due to the putrefactive bases, notably tyramine, which developed in the decomposing fungus. However, practising doctors, influenced I am afraid by an obstinate empiricism, continued to use extract of ergot for the treatment of post-partum haemorrhage, and this preparation continued to appear in the British Pharmacopoeia. Indeed, it was not until 1935 that Chassor Moir and Dudley reported that the watery extract of ergot did in fact contain an alkaloid 'ergometrine', which had been overlooked by earlier workers, and that this alkaloid had just the properties for which the obstetricians had been using the drug for a century or more.

All this is not intended to depreciate the contribution of science to the practical arts but to illustrate the nature of that contribution. So very often it is not to *discover* some phenomenon of practical use, but ultimately (and sometimes long after that use has been adopted on purely empirical grounds) to provide a rational explanation for it. I submit that such rationalization is of the highest importance, for the two reasons I have already stated. First, because it gives stability and permanence to knowledge. Secondly, because there is a limit to the amount of empirical information which the mind can retain; when that knowledge has been given a rational basis it will appear as the necessary consequence of natural laws, and a few general laws may be sufficient to predict an infinite number of special properties. One has only to think of the predictions that are possible in organic chemistry with the aid of a comparatively limited number of general principles.

EMPIRICISM OR DIRECT EXPERIMENT

When the scientific method is brought to bear upon the practical arts it is *not* usually by the procedure of the hypothesis, the experiment, and the theory, but by the empirical method of direct experimentation. It must warm the heart of the applied scientist to quote John Hunter's famous advice to Jenner: 'Don't think; try the experiment!' For to try experiments without too much thought is often the quickest way of arriving at a practical objective. When the limits attainable by such experimentation have been reached, scientific study of the problem may lead to a new outlook and provide the starting-point for a new empirical attack.

For man is an empirical animal. Each new advance in scientific discovery provides him with new weapons for his irrational procedure. His empiricism often leads to surprising observations which could never have been made if every step in the procedure had been rational. That, of course, is why bad experimenters can sometimes get results where good experimenters fail. Claude Bernard missed the presence of trypsin in the pancreatic juice because he was so skilful as a surgeon that he obtained juice uncontaminated by the contents of the duodenum and so the trypsinogen remained inactive. And how many new discoveries in organic chemistry have been made because the operator broke the thermometer and obtained syntheses catalyzed by mercury.

The production of a new material or a new process is soon followed by its trial for all kinds of purposes, a series of 'experiments' the results of which may provide the basis for subsequent systematic investigation and rationalization by scientific research. We are impatient, and such random experiments are often the quickest way of getting results. A large part of scientific research consists in proving what we have already learned by such methods; scientific research is a slow way of gathering information, but information so obtained is more likely to survive.

In 1939 Paul Müller and his colleagues in Switzerland discovered the insecticidal properties of the chemical now known as DDT. In 1944, Läuger, Martin and Müller wrote up a fascinating account of the steps which led to the discovery. I do not pretend to know whether these were the logical steps which were actually followed or whether (as in the writings of most of us) the logic was inserted afterwards to give coherence to the story. What is quite certain is that few would now accept the toxicological basis of their argument, which turns on the hypothetical association of particular chemical groupings with particular types of toxicity. In the parallel case of the discovery of the gamma isomer of benzene hexachloride in England and France, there has never been any suggestion that this was a product of the human reason; it was discovered by the wholly empirical procedure of testing as potential insecticides any chemical that chanced to come to hand.

What immediately caught the eye was that both these chemicals were heavily chlorinated aromatic compounds. The significance of this has not yet been adequately explained, but it led chemists all over the world to set about chlorinating every ring compound they could think of; with the result that we now have upon the market a further series of potent synthetic insecticides. Some day scientific research will have to provide an understanding of these triumphs of empiricism.

We have had an instructive example of the relation between scientific research and applied biology in the problem of the fruit tree red spider mite, which has been engaging the attention of orchardists increasingly in recent years. Ten years ago it was agreed as between the Agricultural Research Council, a group of insecticide manufacturers and the growers to undertake a joint attack upon this problem. The investigation was planned upon a broad front. Direct trials of insecticides were made against the mite and its eggs; the life cycle and habits of the mite were studied in the field; its relation in competition with the rest of the fauna of the orchards was studied. In the laboratory, the behaviour of the mite, and the nature and determination of the arrested development or diapause in the overwintering egg were studied in great detail; and finally the complex nature of the egg shell and its relation to the entry of insecticides were partially unravelled.

As the result of ten years' study we have now for the first time a real understanding of the life of this mite. No one working on this problem in the future can fail to benefit from all this knowledge (incomplete though it is) which enables one to think intelligently about this pest in a way which was quite impossible in the past, and to utilize to some extent the natural fauna of the orchard as a contributory factor in control. From the practical standpoint the investigation was wholly successful, for new methods of control have been introduced into the orchards which appear to have solved the problem. But the interesting point is this: control is being effected primarily by the use of summer ovicides. The production of these ovicides was based, of course, upon a century of organic chemistry; but from the standpoint of biology their discovery was wholly empirical; it owed nothing to the scientific investigations of the remainder of the team, and their mode of action is unknown!*

---

*These ovicides were highly effective at the outset; but after a few years the red spider mite developed resistance to them. At the present time the fight goes on — to devise effective chemical treatments (insecticides and fungicides) which will spare the predators that commonly prevent the build-up of large populations of spider mites in untreated orchards.

SCIENCE AS THE BACKGROUND FOR THOUGHT

That is not an experience which should in any way discourage the student of the ecology or physiology of insects. Some years ago I had the privilege of attending a luncheon in Winnipeg at which I was asked to speak about the 'contribution of insect physiology to medical entomology'. The burden of my address was that it made no contribution; that is, no *direct* contribution, and it is not its function that it should.

I think that is a matter about which we should be clear. We often hear the young man sigh deeply and say: 'It must have been wonderful when you were starting research and all the field was wide open. Nowadays it is different — everything easy has been done'. And yet we all know that you have only to take up the most familiar matter in pure or applied science and almost at once you find that almost nothing is known about it. Indeed, most of us thank God for our ignorance, and happily contrast our lot with that of the classical scholar who has long since worked out his mine and is now reduced to picking over the slag heaps in the hope that he may have missed a little of the ore.

The prime contribution of pure science is to make good this deficiency in knowledge. Very rarely can the applied biologist or the applied scientist in general put his finger on some discovery in pure science and say that it was this which solved his problem — but in thinking about any practical problem he is continually making use of the whole range of scientific knowledge that exists about all its component parts.

When one reads the discourteous remarks that are made in certain quarters about 'reactionary mendelismus — morganismus' one might imagine that the professional breeders of plants and animals in Western Europe and the Americas were all geneticists. Nothing, of course, could be farther from the truth. Most of the complex systems with which the breeder is concerned are still beyond the grasp of the geneticist — or he is only just beginning to extend his science to include them. In very many instances, breeding is still an empirical art which relies on gifts of intuition and experience. Even the production of hybrid corn, which is often claimed as one of the practical triumphs of genetics, although based upon a most penetrating genetical analysis, could be fairly described as the result of an informed empiricism operating on a grand scale.

The production of the mule, that other classic example of hybrid vigour, certainly owed nothing to Mendel.

No! The role of the geneticist has consisted largely in explaining what the animal or plant breeder has already done. By so doing he gives stability to knowledge, provides starting-points for further empirical steps, and, what is perhaps of equal importance, he provides the background or climate of thought.*

I made my approach to the physiology of reproduction and inheritance by the historical method. My early researches were conducted in an ancient volume of Buffon's *Natural History* which I discovered in the lumber room; and I waded through the controversy on whether the female contributes anything to the embryo at conception. Then a year or two later I came across a translation of Haeckel and learned all about the amazing story of the ovum and the spermatozoon. Finally, this must have been about 1915, I noticed a slim little volume in the school library entitled *'Mendelism';* and being curious to know what on earth mendelism might be I took it down and read all about the particulate inheritance of characters. I am afraid that my knowledge of the subject has not greatly advanced since those days. But what an astonishing range of ideas one is left with: the independent inheritance of characters; recessive characters uninfluenced in heredity by the dominant characters in the zygote; the equal contribution of the sexes; the reappearance of characters in later generations by recombination, and so on and so forth. My point is that even genetics at its simplest provides an indispensable background for thought for the breeder of plants and animals, which he will inevitably have in mind even when he uses such more or less empirical procedures as progeny selection or hybridization.

SCIENCE AND THE PRACTICAL ARTS

This background of scientific knowledge may find its application in quite remote fields of practice. Think, for example, of the preparation of food. During the present century there have been remarkable

---

*It is more than twenty years since these words were written; the predictive use of genetics has grown immensely in the interval; and the assertions made above, though true enough at the time, are now an 'over-statement'!

advances in physical chemistry and colloid science; and it has come to be realized that many of the finer products of cooking owe their special qualities to the physico-chemical properties of the traditional ingredients. The ingredients in question are often the expensive ones like egg albumen and cream. But armed with this knowledge it has not proved an insuperable task for the colloid chemist to produce cheap substitutes from gelatin, seaweed, soya beans and the like which have approximately the same properties for the specific purposes required. This has been a most profitable achievement. As a result, millions of our people have never tasted those exquisite delicacies: meringues, ice creams, sponge cakes, cream buns or lemon curd as they used to be. We hear much about the moral responsibility of the atomic physicist. Some might feel that the colloid chemist must have a heavy conscience when he views this field of applied biology. (Although, of course, he can tell himself that these young people have never known what real food was and therefore cannot feel its loss.)

In reading a recent report from the Pest Infestation Laboratory I was struck by that section which describes how the kaffirs in South Africa complained that since the introduction of hammer mills for grinding maize (in place of the ancient pestle and mortar or grinding between stones) the flour did not taste the same and it upset the stomach. Examination in the laboratory revealed the presence of numerous rodent hairs and some 22 000 insect fragments per 25 g of the meal. One is inevitably reminded of the homogenizer, another contribution of technology to the preparation of food which is equally liable to abuse. I recently enjoyed some soup in a well-known London hotel which (having kept hens during the war) I had no difficulty in recognizing as homogenized vegetable peelings.

This brief sketch of the recent history of cooking almost inevitably leads to a consideration of the allied science of immunology. The familiar history of immunization as a practical craft can be traced from the practice of inoculation against smallpox in Constantinople and elsewhere in the East and its introduction into England by Lady Mary Wortley Montague. This was followed by the equally empirical procedure of vaccination developed by Jenner from the traditional observations of peasants. The efficiency of vaccination was proved by Jenner by careful experiment. It was followed in the succeeding century, during the golden age of bacteriology, in the hands of Pasteur and his successors, by a whole series of immunizing procedures against various pathogenic organisms. These practices, an elaborate form of cookery, are still extremely valuable in medicine, but we are still almost completely ignorant of the nature of the immunizing process — and indeed of the whole mechanism of protection by the body against infective organisms. The systematic study of these matters is the science of immunology, the key to which is likewise held by biochemistry and colloid science. The utilization of artificial immunization in practice is scientific only in the sense that what are essentially empirical procedures have been reduced to some degree of order by careful experiment.

There is, indeed, no hard and fast line between what I am calling empiricism or direct experiment and what I am calling scientific research. Both are supported by the same implicit faith in the constancy of natural laws — a faith so absolute that few other religious faiths can equal it. The spread of this faith among people of every kind is perhaps the greatest of all the contributions of pure science to every day life. It is certainly one of the major contributions of science to medicine or to farming.

I am far from supposing that such convictions are universal; there is still a widespread belief in magic — which often masquerades as a belief in science. If we were to take a free vote among the English people I think there is little doubt that we should find a majority in favour of the spontaneous generation of complex organisms, a phenomenon which most biologists would class with the miraculous. Nor am I suggesting for a moment that the doctor should always be made to 'think scientifically'; this is, 'to adopt the mental process necessary for the satisfactory pursuit of experimental science: to demand severe standards of evidence and proof, to draw no conclusion that is not strictly justified by the evidence, to leave in suspense any decision for which the materials are not quite complete'. The last thing the doctor can afford to do is to exercise scientific suspense of judgement. To advise him to think scientifically would risk paralyzing his judgement rather than activating it. No! the practice of medicine, like the practice of government, is a practical art which demands not the limited instrument of the scientific method but a soundly cultivated judgement. And one element in the cultivation of that judgement I hold to be a sympathetic familiarity with the outlook and achievements of science, pure and applied. That is all the more necessary today, when, as part of his improved technique, the charlatan adopts the language of science (that itself is indeed a highly lucrative form of applied science) and it is no easy matter to distinguish the genuine from the spurious.

PURE SCIENCE AND APPLIED BIOLOGY IN THE FUTURE

Thus far we have been thinking mostly of the past. What of the present and the future? How are we to ensure that the pure sciences, the roots of the tree which provides such valuable fruit for all men, are helped and encouraged to grow unimpeded?

It is the universities which cherish the tradition of free enquiry in science — uninfluenced by any considerations of possible usefulness. We must have a wide margin of enthusiasts in the universities whose enquiries are *totally* unrestricted. Not only is that desirable in the interests of learning, it is absolutely necessary in order to safeguard the applied science of tomorrow.

For it is notoriously difficult to foresee just which discoveries in pure science will prove to be of practical value. When writing the first edition of his *Grammar of Science* in 1892, Karl Pearson chose as an example of a discovery which had no apparent practical value, the recently described Hertzian waves, the waves of radio. And who could possibly have foreseen where the infant organic chemistry of 150 years ago was going to lead? For at that time it had no conceivable connection with industry. Who can foresee today where theoretical chemistry is going to lead? It is possible that this may provide the real key to the biology, medicine and industry of the future!

But the fact remains that as all the costs of running a university increase, a relatively greater proportion of the total funds available is deflected away from the costs of research. As a result, the head of a university science department who wishes to develop the research work of his team must seek outside aid. This almost always involves seeking extra financial support from one or other of the Research Councils. In Great Britain we have three such Councils concerned respectively with Medicine, Agriculture and Industry.* Thus they all have practical objectives.

---

*In recent years a fourth Council, the Natural Environment Research Council, has been added and the D.S.I.R. has been replaced by the Science Research Council.

The Research Councils have always interpreted the needs of applied science in a most liberal and enlightened way. The Department of Scientific and Industrial Research, for example, makes grants for any research projects which are judged to be of exceptional 'timeliness and promise'. The difficulty is that the most original ideas are at the outset both unpromising and untimely. Only research which is totally unfettered can advance into the most unpromising fields. And, in any case, a research project with some obvious practical importance very rightly makes the strongest appeal.

The threat to fundamental science is therefore real, and in the future it could become serious. The problem is universal. Writing of conditions in the United States, Professor Paul Weiss has pointed out that the system of allocating grants for a specific purpose is admirably suited for development work or for organizing trials of some existing theory; it is not suited for encouraging the most original research. He suggests that all organizations which contribute financially to the development of medicine, for example, should assign a fixed fraction of their budgets, perhaps no more than 10 per cent, to a common pool for the promotion of the biological sciences as such — this pool to be used as a mobile reserve, without restrictions, for the support and encouragement of men with ideas.

In Sweden the problem has been met by the establishment of a fourth council — a council for pure science. In Norway a steeply rising tax is levied on the profits of the 'Football Pools' (the betting on English football!). In Denmark a·great part of the profits of the Carlsberg brewery is earmarked by the Carlsberg Foundation for general scientific research.

We sometimes hear complaints that the universities are not interested in the needs of the applied sciences. I hope I have said enough to make clear my conviction that some contact with the requirements of industry (including, of course, agriculture and medicine in that term) can be extremely stimulating for the research worker in pure science. But it would be most dangerous to go further than that. Knowledge is a delicate plant — and to keep pulling plants up to see how the roots are getting on is not the best way to encourage growth.

Pure science provides the tools that can be applied for man's benefit. When and where these new tools are going to be produced is utterly unpredictable and is not amenable to planning. Perhaps we are too inclined to think of these tools as things like wireless waves, or antibiotics, or vitamins, or new insecticides, or hormone weed-killers. But these are only valuable side products of pure science. The primary objective of science is to provide the theories which are the tools of thought. To equip the mind with *these* tools is, I submit, the real contribution of pure science to practical affairs.

5

THE SCIENCE AND PRACTICE OF
ENTOMOLOGY

Entomology in Great Britain remained for long enough the care of amateurs. A long line of distinguished naturalists whose chief interest lay with the insects runs through the nineteenth century. There was A. H. Haworth (1767—1833), a lawyer by profession, the founder of the first entomological societies in this country; there was William Kirby (1759—1850), Fellow of Gonville and Caius College and rector of Barham in the county of Suffolk for fifty-eight years, who, with William Spence (1783—1860), produced the standard work on insects that was to hold the field for half a century. There was George Newport (1803—54), physician and surgeon, who published a remarkable series of papers on the anatomy and physiology of insects. There was the lawyer's clerk and engraver John Curtis (1791—1862) and Miss Ormerod (1828—1901) who, in the second half of the century laid the foundations of agricultural entomology in Britain. There was Sir John Lubbock (Lord Avebury) (1834—1913), worthy of remembrance indeed, for it was he who sponsored the Early Closing Act and gave us our bank holidays. As a relaxation from a most active public life, Lubbock laid the ground-work of our knowledge of the sensory physiology of the Hymenoptera; it was Lubbock who proved that bees distinguish colours and can be trained to associate particular colours with the presence of food; that the vision of ants extends into the ultra-violet; and who suggested, far ahead of his time, that ants find their way home by remembering the direction of the sun.

Professional entomologists there were, in the museums: W. E. Leach, J. F. Stephens and others at the British Museum from early in the century, Westwood at Oxford from 1861; David Sharp at Cambridge from 1885. But the tradition of the subject remained that of the naturalist and the collector. It was the private collector who built up systematic entomology in this country — and he still plays a valuable part. Implicit in all I shall say in this address is the need for sound taxonomy. We are unlikely ever to have enough taxonomic specialists in our museums to deal with all the multifarious groups of insects. We still need, and I think we shall always need, the competent amateur to fill the gap.

It was probably this tradition which led to the neglect of insects when the scientific teaching of zoology in our Universities was being established during the second half of the last century. It is true that in formulating his 'type' system T. H. Huxley adopted the cockroach as one of his 'types' — but there the study of insects stopped, and there it has tended to remain.

INSECTS AS A MEDIUM FOR THE STUDY OF BIOLOGY

This was singularly unfortunate, because the insects compose perhaps three-quarters of the known species of animals. They are exceedingly diverse in form and habit, readily available for study, and well suited to illustrate, often in the most vivid and accessible form, most of the problems with which the student of living things is concerned.

One by one the natural sciences have found among the insects ideal material for study. The laws of heredity in insects provide one of the main pillars which support the science of genetics; the role of the genes in the determination of sex was first deduced from a study of sex-linked inheritance in the Lepidoptera; the insect has provided and is providing wonderful raw material for the organic chemist and for the student of fine structure on the frontiers between chemistry and physics; insects have proved excellent material for the assay of vitamins and they can be expected to provide opportunities for the recognition and physiological study of new vitamins; the phenomena of growth, metamorphosis, wound healing and regeneration can be seen in the clearest light in the comparatively simple epidermis of the insect. The study of neuromuscular physiology in insects and other arthropods is contributing greatly to our knowledge of that subject. The aerodynamics of insect flight is not only interesting in itself but can illuminate the problems of animal flight in general. And for the mechanistic analysis of simple types of behaviour, insects have provided more varied material than any other group. One would, of course, be guilty of a grave solecism in the hierarchy of learning if one were to stigmatize students of such matters as 'entomologists' — but the fact remains that zoologists, physiologists, physicists and chemists have turned to the insect with increasing frequency in recent years.

Last, but not least, the insects provide some of the best material for the ecologist. In his Presidential Address last year Professor Hardy was covering so vast a canvas that he could scarcely find place to mention that much of the most illuminating work on the balance of populations in nature is being carried out among the insects. Within this group the interactions of climate and food supply, predators, parasites and infectious diseases of all kinds provide one of the most fertile fields in which to cultivate zoology outside the laboratory. Indeed, this is where most of our current ideas on the subject have come from.

THE GROWTH OF APPLIED ENTOMOLOGY

There is another side to the picture. The period during which zoology became established in the Universities in this country was also the period of development of intensive and large scale agriculture and of great improvements in communications, with the consequent emergence and dissemination of insect pests. The change was heralded in the 1860s by the transformation of the harmless little Colorado beetle into a major pest of agriculture, sweeping across the American continent and, to-day, across Europe. The production of Paris green and lead arsenate as agricultural insecticides was the result. And since that day the pests have become ever more prominent and the insecticides and other methods of control more powerful.

During this same period, starting with the work of Patrick Manson on filariasis in 1878, came the discovery that insects or related arthropods are responsible for the transmission to man of nearly all the great epidemic fevers of the tropics: yellow fever and dengue, malaria, the relapsing fevers, typhus and all its varieties, bubonic plague, five-day fever, sleeping sickness, kala-azar and the rest. The same proved true of many diseases of livestock: trypanosomiasis in Africa, the tick-borne fevers of cattle in South Africa and the United States, and many more.

The increasing adoption of plantation methods for growing crops in the tropics, and now the first beginnings of large scale food production for export in Africa, are fast creating conditions for more and more insect problems. The current instability of human society is leading to more attention being given to the possibilities of storing large reserves of food. Storage brings in its train the problem of controlling insect pests in stored produce. It was a great step forward when the millers in this country, ten years ago, became interested in controlling infestations of insects in grain. If, as seems likely, food is to be stored in the hot climates of Africa this problem is destined to thrust itself more and more upon the attention of Governments. The locust has been with us since the dawn of history; but it can still bring famine to a whole community. Only improvement in communications and the development of food storage enables the importation of food to soften the blow. The importation into this country of infested hardwoods, and the widespread use of timber of poor quality in which sapwood is abundant, have led to a great increase in those insects which destroy structural timbers; and their importance is likely to enlarge as new pests become distributed and as the world shortage of timber continues to make itself felt.

All these developments have led to an ever increasing recognition of the significance of insects in human economy. The insects have surely come into their own — in pure science and in applied.

TRAINING AND OUTLOOK OF THE ENTOMOLOGIST

It is upon this present state of affairs that I want to reflect for a little while in this address. The use of insects for the study of the fundamental problems of physiology is a subject on which I have spoken elsewhere (Wigglesworth, 1948).* Insects not only furnish ideal material for the detailed investigation of many of these problems, but by reason of their relatively small size they encourage the observer to think about the body as a whole and to reflect upon the unity of the organism — an important matter, of which the classical physiologist seems at times to be scarcely even aware.

I do not propose to say much about the insect as a medium for the study of biology in general — beyond this: I think there are still unbounded opportunities for exploitation. But these opportunities will only be developed to the full if we turn out *entomologists,* men who know the world of insects in the round; who are at once

---

*See Chapter 10.

morphologists, taxonomists, physiologists and field naturalists. As the painters' dictum has it: if we take care of the shadows, the highlights will take care of themselves.

The majority of entomologists, professional entomologists that is, must be applied entomologists; and it is of applied entomology that I wish chiefly to speak.

In some branches of science man seems to be confronted with a fixed set of relations which successive generations of students are patiently uncovering. But the world of insects is like human society; it is in a constant state of flux. Of course, the student of insects is inspired by that same religious faith in the fixity of natural laws which is the sheet anchor of all scientists. But he is acutely conscious of the inconstancy of his material. Changes in nomenclature seem to be rendered interminable by the laws of priority, operating like the old Court of Chancery. But it is not only in this artificial science of synonymy that the insect world is inconstant. The fixity of species which disappeared in theory with the acceptance of the doctrine of evolution, is found to have disappeared in practice when the entomologist looks as closely into his insects as the applied entomologist is often obliged to do. The *Anopheles maculipennis of* the museum dipterist has been splintered to a dozen entities more or less sharply defined by differences in physiology or behaviour or in the morphology of their eggs or other stages. The student of the aphids is trying to find some way of dealing with groupings which would surely be regarded as good species were it not impossible to find morphological differences between them. Indeed, the applied entomologist is often embarrassed by the discovery of what must be so if evolution is in progress — that the species tails off into the geographical race, or into the biological race, where clear cut differences in physiology or mere statistical differences in behaviour exist in the absence of detectable morphological characteristics. And, apart from such major changes, species are continually changing in abundance and in distribution, in their choice of foodplants and in the amount of damage to human interests they bring about.

Some of these changes we see going on around us are no doubt the product of natural evolution outside the control of man; but very many of those with which the applied entomologist has to deal are the result of human activities — changes in agricultural practice which disturb the balance of populations, an unfortunate choice of crop rotations, or the abandonment of any rotation at all; or, may be, the introduction for other reasons of varieties of crops that prove highly susceptible to insect attack.

APPLIED ENTOMOLOGY AND RESEARCH

If I am correct that the world of insects is in a state of flux, it follows that the entomologist must be constantly investigating. Indeed, it is my contention that *applied entomology is research*. Once a problem in applied entomology is solved the preventive procedure can be incorporated into the practice of the industry in question and the entomologist is no longer required. That, of course, is an overstatement; despite the advances in preventive medicine we still need the general practitioner. Some procedures demand the special knowledge of the entomologist for their proper application; or their correct timing may depend on accurate identifications possible only for the trained entomologist. It has been found by Dr. Massee and his colleagues in Essex that in the presence of certain insect predators it may do more harm than good to carry out summer spraying in orchards (after June) against the fruit tree red spider mite. Only an entomologist can recognise the predatory species among all the other insects present. The classic example is the infestation of field crops by aphids. It takes more than the intelligent farmer to decide whether it is wise to apply insecticides or whether the infestation is about to collapse before parasites or infectious disease.

But I think the assertion is broadly true. The entomologist, in fact, is continually working himself out of his job. It is, however, a provision of nature that, as a result of man's activities, sometimes, it must be confessed, as a result of the activities of the entomologist himself, no sooner is one problem solved than another, often more difficult, arises for solution.

The entomologist, I repeat, must be an investigator. He must acquire and retain the research outlook, the inquiring mind, the determination to find out for himself by experiment. I have spoken already of the value of the insect as a medium for the study of physiology. Here I should like to enter a plea for the study of insect physiology for a different reason: for the reason that it forces the applied entomologist to look far more closely into his problem than he would otherwise do. Last year you listened to an admirable defence of ecology by Professor Hardy. I wish to detract no word from that. But again and again it has been my experience that the physiologist has been able to point out the key problems in the life of the insect in its natural environment and so to give a valuable lead to the ecologist who is concerned with the balance of natural populations. The physiologist who comes to take an interest in populations, who combines the aspirations of the zoologist within and without the laboratory, will in my view make the best ecologist. And, by the same token, some experience in physiological research will provide one of the best introductions to a career in applied entomology.

INTERACTION OF RESEARCH AND PRACTICE

If those are the implications of my thesis so far as scientific education and outlook are concerned, what are the implications in the field of practice and administration? It is a truism that the applied entomologist, if he is to be effective, must come to regard himself, primarily, as a member of the industry which he serves. He must acquire the outlook and sympathies of the sanitarian, the farmer, the wharfinger or whatever it may be. But when that is done, the basic problem as I see it is how to keep the entomological investigator in close touch with the day to day problems of his industry without stultifying him as a research worker.

We are all familiar with the plea, made as a rule by those of limited acquaintance with both research and practice, that we should call a halt to all this research and concentrate on using existing knowledge. I have no wish to disparage the very great importance of the dissemination of knowledge (the British Association exists for that very purpose), but anyone with the smallest acquaintance with practical problems knows that at every point practice is held up by lack of knowledge. The sense of frustration often comes from the fact that the applied entomologist who sees what we need to discover is so occupied with petty tasks that he has not the chance to fill the gap.

I have spoken of the value of physiological studies on insects in opening the eyes of the ecologist and applied entomologist. Of no less importance is the stimulus which the study of practical problems gives to the physiologist. The interest in insecticides, which became so widespread during the war, has been a potent factor in bringing about the revolution in our knowledge of the insect cuticle which has taken place during the past ten years. The intensive study of the moisture and temperature relations of insects which has yielded results of great physiological interest was very largely stimulated by the applied entomologist. And he it was who started the study of population ecology in insects. But if these mutually beneficient influences are to be felt there must be an unbroken chain of research workers at all levels in sufficiently close touch with one another to appreciate each other's problems.

ADMINISTRATION

The administrative requirements will vary in the different branches of the service; but the keynote throughout should be the same: the safeguarding and encouragement of research. Anyone who has tried both, knows that administration is so immeasurably easier than research that it becomes the line of least resistance and that is why research needs encouragement.

Let us consider a few examples of what I mean, selected from the field of entomology in this country and empire, and reviewed in a spirit not of criticism but of detachment. Take a small example first. In my opinion an institution like the British Museum (Natural History), apart from its most important function of exposition, is primarily a centre of research in the classification of animals; and in the interests of this research the staff should be protected from trivial incursions by the existence of a screen of public relations officers who would provide the connecting link between the general public and the specialist — to the advantage of both.

The problem is a larger one in the applied field and it is encouraging that some of the latest recruits to the entomological service of this country seem to have shown the clearest grasp of the requirements. The Pest Infestation Laboratory built up by the Department of Scientific and Industrial Research during the past ten years, upon the foundations laid by Professor J. W. Munro, is a research laboratory. It covers the whole range of problems from such technical matters as the disinfestation of bulk grain in huge silos, or the devising of insect-proof wrappings for packages of foodstuffs, down to the physical and physiological factors concerned in the passage of toxic substances through the cuticle of the insect. Close touch with the practical world is maintained through the Infestation Branch of the Ministry of Agriculture, which deals with all the day to day matters concerning insects in produce and which in this way provides the research laboratory with the practical problems that are in most urgent need of investigation and with the industrial contacts that are necessary for their solution, but at the same time protects the investigators from unprofitable distraction.

The same desirable gradation is to be seen in the Anti-Locust Research Organisation — although this still rests on a temporary footing, with all the resultant uncertainties. The Anti-Locust Research Centre* under the Colonial Office† in London provides a clearing house for all information about the current activities of locusts and locust control organizations in all parts of the world. The various colonial governments have their own schemes of locust control. But the bulk of the research on all locust problems in the colonial empire ranging from the techniques for killing locust swarms, or studies in ecology which aim at preventing the emergence of swarms, down to research on the detailed physiology of the locust in all its varying phases, is administered and co-ordinated by the centre. The virtue of this scheme, which has yet to come to fruition, lies in the opportunities which it affords for many-sided contacts and for mutual stimulation by research workers at all levels.

These are fields in which advances in both science and practice have been rapid during recent years. The same cannot be said for our knowledge of infestations by insects in timber; and I think the reason is not far to seek. The entomology section of the Forest Products Research Laboratory, which is our chief centre for work on this subject, has no screen between it and the building industry. As a result we find the research workers so occupied in answering letters and giving advice, using knowledge that is admittedly inadequate, that although very creditable advances have been made, the extension of knowledge by research has been severely handicapped. We are caught in a vicious circle which will be broken only when it becomes possible to insert a screen of advisers or inspectors, stationed in immediate contact with the research laboratory (responsible perhaps to the Ministry of Health) who would provide the research workers with the essential link with practical problems but would shield them from trivial interference and enable them to get on with their proper work of investigation.

---

*Now the Centre for Overseas Pest Research.
†Now the Overseas Development Administration.

By far the largest employer of entomologists in this country is the National Agricultural Advisory Service.* Built up under the guidance of the late Sir John Fryer, the specialist advisory service for the farmer was taken over by the nation three years ago. The entomologists in the service, who in the past were associated with the various centres of teaching and research in agriculture throughout the country, were then reorganized as an entirely independent service. It is not difficult to appreciate the attractions of such a scheme from the point of view of administrative tidiness and convenience. But it will be no easy task after such an uprooting to build up a new tradition of first class research — research, not into those general principles with which the student in the Universities is commonly occupied, but research into the fluctuating insect problems that confront the grower in the locality in question; research which differs in kind but should not differ in quality from that carried out in the institutions from which the service is now detached.

There is within the service a provision of County Officers who should become increasingly competent to deal with most of the day to day matters of entomological advice and so leave the provincial specialists with a substantial part of their time free for the investigation of those problems needing close study. Perhaps the first step will be to convince ourselves that the specialist branch of the advisory service, at any rate in entomology, must be concerned primarily with investigation; that the entomologist cannot cope with the changing problems that arise in agriculture without research and experiment as a broad basis; and that the final link in this chain of research must be forged by the specialist adviser. One thing is certain; without this the service will not attract or retain (as it did in the past) entomologists who will be known by name and who can really contribute to the improvement of agricultural practice in this country.

Behind the advisory service will stand in due time the series of oddly named 'husbandry farms' more specifically concerned with trials and experiments; presumably the entomologist will sometimes play a part here. Then there is the series of crop research stations,

---

*Now the Agricultural Development and Advisory Service (ADAS).

some long established and others coming into being. And behind these again the Agricultural Research Council with its co-ordinating committees and conferences, its research units devoted to special subjects (I myself am associated with one of these dealing with insect physiology), and its special research grants to University Departments. The machinery is there; it is highly flexible and is in the hands of independent scientists in the University Departments and elsewhere. If we do not make use of it in advancing the science and practice of entomology we have only ourselves to blame.

ENTOMOLOGY IN THE COLONIES

The same problems arise when we consider entomology in the colonial empire; although here are several new elements that demand consideration. There is so much that remains unknown in applied entomology in the tropics that the duty of the entomologist to pursue research is patent to all. But if we are going to get the best value for money spent on research we must aim at providing the right conditions. The entomologist in the tropics often has adequate equipment; laboratories are often more spacious than at home and assistants more plentiful. What he is apt to lack is the stimulus of emulation (the most potent factor in breeding research) the intellectual stimulus of scientific contacts, and access to libraries and centres of research.

The scientific services in the colonies differ from the administrative services fundamentally in these respects. It should therefore be recognized that the entomologist ought to put in a very substantial part of his time in this country (or in some suitable centre in Europe or in the Dominions) not on leave, but at work. The presence of a changing population of such men in our institutions at home to which they would be temporarily attached, could not fail to have a mutually stimulating effect.

The practice of a liaison of this kind would facilitate the exchange of staffs. The young, or not so young man taking up entomological research in the tropics should be able to feel that he will not lose touch with work at home, and that if he makes good there will be no insuperable obstacle to his transfer later to a post at home (and vice versa). From this point of view the service would be much more attractive if the terms of appointment and of pension were of a kind that would make possible transfers of this sort. That is one of the attractive features about the Colonial Research Service that is gradually coming into being. This is not a matter on which it is useful to express dogmatic opinions in a few words, but there is something to be said for treating other entomological appointments in the colonies in the same way.

INSECTICIDES

But there must be many here who are asking themselves: Is all this harping upon entomological research really necessary? Is not the entomologist in fact outmoded by the discoveries of the organic chemist in the realm of insecticides? There is indeed a belief current today, a belief that is very naturally fostered by those whose material interests lie in that direction, that the future of insect control lies not with the entomologist but with the chemist.

Now, here let me add my meed of praise to those chemists in Switzerland, Great Britain and Germany who discovered respectively the insecticidal properties of DDT, Gammexane and the organo-phosphorus compounds, materials which have transformed the control of insect pests during the past ten years. This has been a remarkable achievement; and its impact is by no means expended, for more and more synthetic insecticides are produced as one manufacturer vies with another. Not only is this a remarkable achievement in itself, but it appeals to the human mind. The public loves the hospital, the doctor and the bottle of physic; while the advances in preventive medicine which have transformed our lives are scarcely noticed. So too it creates a greater impression on the mind to destroy an infestation of insects that can be seen, than by some simple change in practice to prevent any infestation from developing. Effective methods are known for preventing the breeding of house-flies, methods based on simple biological principles. But I know of at least one institution which could not be interested in such methods but adopted instead the practice of spraying the walls with DDT. The house-flies in that institution are now among the most DDT-resistant in the world.

It is indeed becoming increasingly evident that the use of more and more insecticides is creating insect problems as fast as it solves them. This is no new discovery. It has been realized for many years that in the orchards, for example, an ever increasing number and variety of washes were becoming necessary to secure clean fruit.

A. D. Pickett (1949) points out that in the orchards of Nova Scotia during the early part of this century two or three applications of spray applied with hand-operated pumps were sufficient to give fruit of good quality. To-day, with greatly improved equipment and far more potent chemicals six or even ten applications are required to produce crops reasonably free of insect damage. The familiar mussel scale *Lepidosaphes* has been known in these orchards for more than fifty years; but only in the past fifteen years has it become a pest — and then only in those orchards which have been most thoroughly treated with lime sulphur for the control of apple scab. That is because the chalcid *Aphelinus mytilaspidis* and the predaceous mite *Hemisarcoptes malus* which normally hold the scale in check are killed by the sulphur. The same has happened with DDT which has produced great outbreaks of the woolly aphis, the red spider mite and other pests. We can, as Pickett points out, probably control any specific pest with which we have to deal — but the problem of pests in general gets worse. New machinery and new chemicals are developed, and we are carried from crisis to crisis, always hoping that the newest chemical or the newest technique will provide the final answer.

Where is this process going to end? Already the number of washes recommended in some parts of the world is reaching the limit of what it is economic to apply. We do not know what the end is going to be. Not even the most enthusiastic entomologist believes that chemical control in orchards can be dispensed with. What we need is more control of the chemists. We need more biological research to see just exactly what effect the chemical applications are having upon the insect populations as a whole.

THE FUTURE OF APPLIED ENTOMOLOGY

We need not less but more entomological research. By all means let us use insecticides when we can do no better. But we should regard them, as C. B. Williams has emphasized more than once, as an admission of failure, to be replaced by the more subtle and more remunerative methods of biology as soon as these can be worked out.

Can this be done? Even in the twentieth century necessity is still the mother of invention, and when economy requires it will be done. It was the economic depression of the early 'thirties which provided the stimulus for the working out by G. C. Ramsay (Ramsay and

Macdonald, 1936) in Assam of the cheap and highly effective means of malaria prevention by the shading of the breeding places of *Anopheles minimus*.

Not long ago we were told by politicians that the problem of veterinary trypanosomiasis in tropical Africa had been solved by the discovery of the drug 'Antrycide'. No one would wish to depreciate that brilliant achievement in chemotherapy; but can anyone who is familiar with the tsetse problem in Africa believe that it can have been solved by the use of this new tool alone? And yet, in the Northern Territories of West Africa (admittedly a special case — but *all* problems in applied entomology are special cases; that is why we need research) in the Gold Coast it has been proved by Morris (1949) that sleeping sickness can be reduced by 98 per cent simply by removing from the riverine habitat of *Glossina palpalis* and *G. tachinoides* a few species of evergreen trees and shrubs, and so changing the environment in the dry season retreats of these flies just enough to render then untenable. In South Africa the pine thrips *Heliothrips haemorrhoidalis* has been controlled simply by thinning out the trees to give them more light and air.

The virus diseases of potatoes in this country are carried mainly by aphids, particularly by *Myzus persicae*. Seed potatoes largely free from virus can be raised if conditions are unfavourable for the migration of winged aphids to the potato crop. These aphids overwinter in numbers in localities where crucifers are grown on a large scale. High atmospheric humidity and exposure to the prevailing westerly winds inhibit migration. Bearing these factors in mind it has been possible to select good sites for growing virus-free seed potatoes in North Wales, South Devon, and other places. That is a crude example of applied ecology. But there can be little doubt that with more understanding of the behaviour of aphids we shall be able to manipulate the cultivation of many of our crops in such a way that we can come to terms with the aphids that affect them.

One would find no difficulty in adding endlessly to these examples. All I wish to do, without discouraging for one moment the study of insecticides and the search for new toxic materials, is to emphasize the increasing scope and need for entomological research — to guide intelligently, to supplement, and sometimes even to supplant the application of chemical methods. Far from being exhausted, I believe there are still unbounded opportunities within the science and practice of entomology.

REFERENCES

Morris, K. R. S. (1949) The Science of tsetse control. *Nature,* **164,** 1114—1115.

Pickett, A. D. (1949) A critique on insect control methods. *Canad. Ent.,* **81,** 1—10.

Ramsay, G. C. and Macdonald, G. (1936) The species control of Anophelines in India. *Indian Med. Gaz.,* **71,** 699—710.

Wigglesworth, V. B. (1948) The insect as a medium for the study of physiology. *Proc. Roy. Soc.* B., **135,** 430—446.

6

INSECTS AND THE FARMER

Insects have been in competition with man for the products of his labour ever since the cultivation of the soil began. But in course of time some kind of balance of power was established. Agricultural methods were gradually improved and if the whole historical process could have been followed by an ecologist he would probably have found that many of the cultural practices that farmers came to adopt by methods of observation, trial and error owed some part of their success to their swaying this balance of power against the more destructive insects.

The same applies to the work of the agricultural improvers of the eighteenth century: the success of the modern rotations of crops, and of the mixed husbandry of crops and stock, rests upon very many factors of different kinds, but one of the factors and an important one is the discouragement of harmful insects. In the first half of the nineteenth century technical improvements in agriculture were coming from all directions and one gets the impression that in the heyday of 'High Farming' in the 'fifties and 'sixties of the last century, the farmers got along very happily without being unduly concerned with the ravages of insects.

But it was during these years, when the American settlers reached the eastern slopes of the Rocky Mountains, that a harmless small beetle in Colorado changed its diet from the buffalo burr of the deserts to the succulent potato. Within a year or two, sweeping across the United States to the eastern seaboard, it had become a major pest of agriculture. That episode marks the beginning of agricultural entomology as we know it to-day. Agricultural insecticides first came into use for the control of the potato beetle. In 1877 the beetle made its appearance in the potato fields of Mülheim on the Rhine. The German government intervened with characteristic vigour. A cordon of Prussian troops was thrown round the area and five litres of benzene per square meter were sprayed on the soil and set alight. This country became alarmed; and in this same year parliament passed 'an Act for Preventing the Introduction and Spreading of Insects Destructive to Crops'.

I do not propose to discuss the legislative side of entomology in this lecture, important though that matter is from the standpoint of the farmer; I merely want to recall that what was probably the first governmental measure directed against insects in Britain was a measure of international quarantine that has formed the basis of the brilliant campaign which has kept this county free from one very important pest after Western Europe had become completely infested.

At that time, 1877, the Colorado beetle did not arrive. But agricultural depression from other causes set in rapidly. Only improved techniques could save the industry from complete decay and, as is well known, it is from this time that modern agricultural education dates.

Already in 1860 the lawyer's clerk and engraver John Curtis had produced his famous book on *Farm Insects* in which he says, 'I wish to impress in the strongest manner the absolute necessity of the agricultural observer, however talented he may be, calling in the aid of the scientific entomologist in his investigations.' Miss Ormerod's *Manual of Injurious Insects* appeared in first edition in 1881 and for twenty-four years (from 1877 to 1900) she produced her remarkable series of annual reports on insect pests and their control.

The Board of Agriculture was established in 1889; and the way in which, in the following year, education in agriculture, supported by the Government, came to its strange birth, endowed with the 'Whiskey Money', is a well-known story. Entomologists make their appearance in the names of Cecil Warburton at Cambridge, F. V. Theobald at Wye College, supported on a part-time basis to provide teaching and advice, and a little later Stewart MacDougal employed on the same footing.

That was the position of agricultural entomology in 1909. In that year I made the headlines in our local paper in the Fylde. For I had attended a fancy dress ball in the guise of what the paper called a 'diminutive policeman'. In the middle of the proceedings a large figure was observed in the centre of the ballroom dressed as 'The Budget'; and acting on instructions I drew my truncheon and amid much approving laughter I am reported to have 'thrown out The Budget'. Fortunately this symbolic act had no permanent effect upon the course of history; after the general election Lloyd George's budget was passed by the Lords, the Development Commission was set up under the provisions of the Development and Road Improvement Funds Act, and governmental support for science had really begun.

It is curious to reflect that Lloyd George, who certainly did more for science in this country than any other of our prime ministers, is the only one of modern times who was never elected a Fellow of the Royal Society.

In September 1911 the Development Commission recommended the payment of annual grants from the Development Fund to selected universities and agricultural colleges to enable them to supply technical advice to farmers, and to provide for the investigation of local agricultural problems. The intention was that this framework of scientific specialists should be linked with the county staff who would deal with inquiries of a straightforward character — all according to the pattern that we are familiar with to-day. 'There has thus been created,' wrote Sir Thomas Middleton at this time, 'a system for bringing within the reach of English agriculture the knowledge resulting from the vast amount of work now undertaken in the research laboratories of all civilized countries. But all this knowledge will be valueless to any particular locality until it has been applied by farmers to the cultivation of their land. How is this application of scientific discoveries to the commercial questions of the ordinary farm to be accomplished?' That is the question, so far as it concerns the insects, that I want to consider in this lecture.

In 1913 the Board of Agriculture appointed their own whole time entomologist in the person of J. C. F. Fryer. Many will recall Fryer's racy descriptions of entomological work in those early days when the duties of the new post and the most elementary needs of an entomologist were almost equally unknown to the Board. He set out the story in its outline in his Presidential Address to the Royal Entomological Society of London in 1940.

The full implementation of the plans, as formulated by Middleton in his report, had to wait until after the First World War. Then entomologists were appointed to all the thirteen provincial centres in England and Wales. The research institute in entomology, which had been established at Manchester under A. D. Imms, was moved to Rothamsted. Active entomological departments were set up in the fruit research stations at Long Ashton and East Malling, and in the glass-house research station at Cheshunt. Fryer himself at the head of an expanded Plant Pathology Laboratory was now established at Harpenden.

This was the pattern of the research and advisory service in agricultural entomology as it developed between the wars. I first came into close touch with the enterprise in the middle of the Second World War. I had the privilege of attending the meetings of the advisers in London and of visiting nearly all the research institutions and advisory centres in the country and of accompanying the advisers on their visits to farms. And I was then able to follow this up with a similar tour of the United States and Canada, criss-crossing these vast countries from north to south and east to west and visiting some sixty centres of entomological extension and research work.

All this constituted an intensive elementary course in agricultural entomology of a kind that few people have been privileged to enjoy. But the chief impression that I wish to recall at this time is that of the spirit which animated the advisory entomologists in this country during those years.

It had been clearly foreseen in advance by Fryer and others that if war broke out there would be widespread ploughing of old grassland and consequently a recurrence of the wireworm problem of the earlier war. The 'Wireworm Survey' had been promptly organized and staffed. The advisers, strengthened in numbers by the staff of the wireworm teams, found themselves in a key position in agriculture. The 'Wireworm Survey', with all its inevitable shortcomings, was a valuable contribution in itself; but perhaps even more important in the long run was the way in which it brought the advisory entomologists into touch with very many farmers who in the past had not known of their existence. All this helped to build up a most refreshing atmosphere of keenness and enthusiasm.

All these specialist advisers were, of course, employees of the Universities or Farm Institutes where they were stationed. These bodies were subsidized to provide staff and research facilities; they were not subsidized to provide accommodation, and this was sometimes of the most inadequate kind. I recall one centre, for example, where the plant pathologist and entomologist were obliged to occupy opposite sides of the same table in the attic which was their accommodation. Both were able and energetic workers who handled so much incoming material that this was constantly infiltrating across the neutral zone of their table and provoking recurrent states of acute tension.

65

It was at this time that the Luxmore Committee made their investigations and issued their report. They observed the same inadequate accommodation and, as everyone knows, they decided in favour of a complete severance of the advisory system from the universities and other teaching institutions and the unification of the provincial specialist and county advisory services directly under the Minister of Agriculture. Their recommendations were implemented immediately after the war.

It is not my intention to criticize these recommendations — I am in no way qualified to do so. I am concerned only to record their impact on the advisory services in entomology.

That impact was severe in the extreme. Francis Bacon had laid down long ago that 'there will hardly be any main proficience in the disclosing of nature, except there be some allowance for expenses about experiments'. And the Luxmore Committee had written with equal wisdom: 'the specialist advisory officer must . . . take a lively interest in agriculture and have adequate practical experience of it, but although he must keep in constant touch with the industry, he must first and foremost remain a scientist, for it is through science that advances in the practice of farming are made. He must therefore be allowed the freedom on which original thought and successful investigation must depend'. But almost overnight the advisory entomologists found themselves cut off from their familiar surroundings and caught up in the atmosphere of the Civil Service, with fixed hours for clocking in and out — when they had been accustomed often to not getting back from farm visits until ten o'clock at night. A number of the best men, whom the service could ill afford to lose, resigned; and the general atmosphere was one of numbed depression and frustration.

There was one bright spot. In the early 'twenties Fryer had established a Conference of Advisory Entomologists which met from time to time in London, and every summer at one or other of the Provincial Centres. I started attending the meetings in the later war years. No one could fail to appreciate the friendly and co-operative atmosphere of these family gatherings; and when Fryer became wholly occupied with the Agricultural Improvement Council and later, the Agricultural Research Council, the same spirit was perpetuated under C. T. Gimingham.

I do not know whether this conference may not have been originally an unofficial body; at any rate it receives no mention in the

Luxmore Report. But under nationalization it continued as an official conference of the Ministry and the same people (or some of them) met round the same table. Here was an atmosphere where it was possible to think once more about the science of agricultural entomology; where it was possible to see the less serious side of even the most exasperating frustrations.

Gradually the growing pains have been overcome. The human spirit can triumph over the most adverse circumstances. If there are elements of tragedy in the story, it is a tragedy without a villain. Perhaps entomology suffered for the good of the others. Perhaps entomology was a victim of that same enthusiasm for paper planning whose memorials lie rusting by the roadsides of Tanganyika. A sympathetic and widely experienced visitor from the Dominions once told me that his chief criticism of the new advisory service was that it was so un-English — by which he meant that it had all been thought out on paper instead of growing empirically in the usual English style.

But two things are clear: the advisory service in entomology is working; it is making effective contact with many more farmers than it did under the old regime; and in any case it is not possible to put back the clock. What I want to consider is how it is working in relation to the needs of the farmer.

What is the object of the service anyhow? The first and obvious purpose is the education of the farmer in good farming methods — that is why the Luxmore Report is primarily a report on agricultural education. To provide such general education, guidance and moral support is the function of the County Adviser or District Officer. The District Officer should become increasingly able to deal with the day to day insect troubles of the farmer; and when he is sufficiently knowledgeable and sufficiently self-confident to appreciate his own limitations, he will not be too proud to seek the assistance of the provincial specialists. But if that were all, the service ought soon to render itself redundant and every entomologist would soon work himself out of his job.

It was clearly envisaged in the memorandum sent out by the Board of Agriculture to the Universities and Agricultural Colleges in 1911, and which came, one would surmise, from the pen of Sir Thomas Middleton, that 'to gain the confidence of farmers . . . it is necessary to convince them that the college staff is able to advise not merely in regard to the general principles of cultivations and management which are within the knowledge of skilled farmers, but as to difficulties which lie outside ordinary experience, and which may demand exhaustive investigation and patient research.' 'There is reason to believe,' the memorandum adds, 'that the existing demand for special assistance for the investigation of difficult local problems will very greatly increase in future'.

That was a fine prophetic statement of forty-five years ago, and it brings us to what I consider to be the real purpose of the advisory service. When I hear reference to the 'American way of life' it always raises in my mind a picture of carefree expenditure of the resources of nature. Perhaps that conception is a little out of date. But the fact remains that most of America has only been farmed for a hundred years; the reckless pioneering stage is hardly passed; the welfare of posterity is only beginning to be thought of. (After all, as the farmer protested to Abraham Lincoln: 'What has posterity done for me?')

In this country things are very different. The land has been farmed for thousands of years, at least since the terraces of megalithic times. And now we are in the throes of another agricultural revolution. This takes the form of the application of more and more science to agriculture, and pressure for more and more intensive cropping.

When the synthesis of indigo in 1870 led to the ruin of thousands of unfortunate cultivators in Bihar and Orissa, they eventually went over to the production of sugar. This was grown year after year on the alluvial soil which was scratched with primitive ploughs to give small but steady yields. A few years before I was in Bihar in the middle 'thirties some agricultural enthusiast had introduced deep ploughing — with the result that they obtained bumper crops for two or three years, and then failure.

That is the position with which we are faced. Every improvement or intensification in farming creates new problems. Insecticides which eliminate the codling moth in the orchards create conditions which favour the woolly aphid or the fruit tree red spider mite. The mixed farming and crop rotations, with unploughed stubbles and strip cultivation, which saved the soil of the prairies in Alberta, have provided ideal conditions for the increase of the wheat-stem sawfly.

Our aims must be to restore the balance of nature — by which I mean, of course, the balance between the effort put into his land by the farmer and the yield of crop that he gets in return.

All kinds of agricultural scientists are bringing their influence to bear upon the farmer and his insects. Every change in rotation, in variety of crop, in fertilizer treatment or type of cultivation will have entomological repercussions. All these have to be watched. The insecticide manufacturer is sometimes depicted as a villain in this piece; and since the long term effects of an insecticide regularly applied may take years before they become apparent, it can be claimed with some justification that most insecticides are rushed upon the market too soon. One of the triumphs of agricultural entomology since the war has been the effective control of soil pests such as wireworms and cabbage root flies by means of insecticides. It is only now that D. W. Wright at the Vegetable Research Station is pointing out how important a part in the destruction of these pests is played by Carabid beetles and other predators. Thirty species of beetles and two species of mites have been found preying on the young stages of the cabbage root fly, and when low rates of insecticides have been broadcast a week or two before transplanting cabbages, the plants have suffered actually more damage from cabbage root fly than in the untreated control plots.

My argument is that the prime objective of the specialist advisory service in entomology is to safeguard the long-term stability of an intensive agriculture — and this objective requires ceaseless research.

One of the weaknesses in the position of the agricultural entomologist, and this applies all the world over, has always been his ignorance of how much damage insects are doing. Some eighteen months ago the Agricultural Board of the National Research Council of America set up a Committee on Agricultural Pests which will try to obtain reliable data on losses attributable to pests. But the leaders in this field are the entomologists of our own advisory service.

Ten years ago the N.A.A.S. conference of entomologists started routine assessments of the annual peak population densities of about a dozen insect pests throughout England and Wales. And in 1950 the Ministry of Agriculture appointed A. H. Strickland to their Plant Pathology Laboratory to co-ordinate this work and to widen its scope to include measurements of population density in relation to economic damage. The results to date show, for example, that damage by cabbage aphid to brussels sprouts alone is equivalent to something like 5—10 thousand acres a year, the average financial loss over the past ten years being £868 000 per annum.

A comparable extensive survey on the frit fly shows that this may be estimated to cost farmers in England and Wales some £16 million annually. Complete frit control could raise the average national oat yield from 18·6 to about 24 cwt/acre.

Such conclusions are not reached easily. They are based on an immense amount of data carefully collected and collated along agreed lines. Though still only a beginning, this co-operative effort represents one of the outstanding achievements of the new service.

There are many other types of co-operative experiment at which the Conference of Advisory Entomologists is cautiously trying its hand — keeping always to rather simple procedures and measurements which can be standardized and subsequently analyzed to give informative results. The limitations of such kinds of experiments are obvious: they are necessarily superficial; they deal only with results and not with causes — but they are the sort of work which no other organization could carry through, and they are well worth doing; their value will increase with the years. And there is always the hope that when we know enough about these insects it will be possible to realize the aim formulated by C. B. Williams: to forecast and prevent outbreaks rather than to diagnose and attempt to cure them after they have occurred.

The specialist advisers are also concerned in carrying out experiments to test the recommendations of the various research institutes. I have in mind the kind of work being done by L. Broadbent on the production of virus-free potato seed by means of insecticidal treatments. Getting such things done depends, of course, in the last analysis upon the interest and enthusiasm of individuals. As always in government service all the world over, the key man is apt to be transferred to a new position at the critical moment and other impediments arise — but such is the human spirit that somehow the system works.

The question is whether the research structure is really sound. The farmer's needs are wholly practical: he wants improvements in applied entomology; and the agricultural entomologist, like every other scientist who serves some economic purpose, is always being urged to keep his feet firmly on the ground and to stick to down-to-earth problems. But the fact is that there is often very little useful research to do that is of immediate practical importance. At the present time such a variety of new insecticidal chemicals have come upon the market that there is a good deal to be done in the way of testing their use under field conditions. But work of this kind is soon accomplished: it took only a very few years before the usefulness of DDT had been gauged for most agricultural purposes. Whereas the chemical and toxicological work which lies behind such practical tests is almost unlimited.

The structure of research with a practical objective is that of a pyramid — with the 'down-to-earth' investigations at the apex. It is this fact which renders so meaningless the discussion of the relative merits and virtues of 'fundamental' and 'applied' research. From the practical point of view the proper classification of research is into 'useful research' and 'futile research'. Useful research is research at any level in the pyramid which contributes to the solidarity of the structure of knowledge. Futile research is research which is being continued in a direction or to a point where it is no longer likely to give valuable returns. Only the director of research who year after year has to formulate problems for hungry Ph.D. students can know how difficult is the selection of useful projects for research. It is easy enough to drift into doing futile research in any field of study, but contrary to popular belief, it is particularly easy at the apex of the pyramid where the 'down to earth research' is done.

In the minds of those who employ the expression I think it usually means that the practical man, the farmer, shall decide what investigations shall be carried out. Now the farmer may or may not have a clear idea as to what his insect troubles are, but he cannot know what investigations are required to put them right. The specialist adviser in entomology has a much clearer idea of the problem — he may be able to specify an insect pest about which he feels his knowledge to be inadequate. But unless he has had time to look into it pretty closely he will be quite unable to formulate a really worthwhile programme of research upon it.

During the past twelve years the Unit of Insect Physiology of the Agricultural Research Council has been concerned with the study of three pests in Northumberland and Cumberland: the sheep tick, the garden chafer, and the leatherjacket. In each case the story has been the same. The farmer has been conscious of the existence of these troublesome creatures. The advisers have had a limited acquaintance with their life histories. But only when my colleague A. Milne has got down to the close study of their ecology, and other members of the group have begun to try and interpret their ecology and population fluctuations in terms of their physiology, have we come to realize how limited was our knowledge, and what were the problems requiring study.

Other creatures with which the Unit had been concerned, the fruit tree red spider mite, the bean aphid, tell the same story: close study and close thinking are needed if useful research is to be done. This, of course, is in no sense to deny that there have been some fine pieces of applied research carried out within the advisory service. One might mention the co-operative work on seed treatments; or, within the field of insect ecology, the work of H. C. Gough on the wheat bulb fly. But I do not think that it is an exaggeration to say that about every insect on which the agricultural entomologists are giving advice, our present knowledge is inadequate.

It is clear that we need very much more ecological research, and ecological research informed and stimulated by the simultaneous study of physiology. Why are we not doing more in this direction? It is clearly impossible for specialist advisers with all their multifarious distractions to carry out work of this nature; but I feel that the unrivalled knowledge of the country, of its farmers, and of its agricultural pests, of which the specialist advisers are the repository, is far too little used — and that goes back in part to the divorce of the service from the centres of thought, teaching and research.

It is claimed by some that ecology is the Cinderella of the biological sciences; that the Agricultural Research Council and other grant-giving bodies are reluctant to support work on insect ecology. But that is not the weak spot. The truth is that it is easy to talk lightheartedly about insect ecology, and in the long warm days of summer it can be very enjoyable to do it. But when the ground is muddy and there is a piercing wind from the east, it is very much nicer to get quick results in a warm and cosy laboratory. The fact is that it requires patient and hardy enthusiasts, and intelligent and patient statisticians to study the ecology of agricultural insects as it should be studied; and their numbers are strictly limited.

What is perfectly obvious is that the entomologists in the advisory service cannot combine the exacting and time consuming discipline of research of this kind with their advisory duties. But the thinking which permeates the system should be all one. The advisers should know what the entomologists in the research institutes and universities are thinking; and, what is at least equally important, the entomologists engaged wholly on research should know the problems which are developing on the farm.

All this is obvious; and this cross-fertilization does occur. But, in my opinion, although the National Agricultural Advisory Service in entomology has now been in existence for ten years, it has still not fully recovered from the intellectual evisceration that it suffered at its birth. There is still room for much closer liaison.

As I wrote on a previous occasion,* 'the world of insects is in a state of flux; it follows that the entomologist must be constantly investigating. Indeed, it is my contention that *applied entomology is research.*' And the results of all this research have to be translated into a form which can be utilized by the farmer; and communicated to him in imaginative and sympathetic terms. The specialist adviser in entomology has a supremely difficult job to do; as Sir Thomas Middleton wrote in 1912: 'For the purpose of translating the results of research into successful practice, a highly trained scientific man is required having a special knowledge of his particular branch of science and a sufficient acquaintance with agriculture to command the respect of skilful and enlightened practical farmers.' There could be no better summary to the argument I have been trying to present.

---

*See Chapter 4.

7

THE FAUNA OF THE ORCHARD

You must all have already a copy of Dr. Massee's book on *The Pests of Fruit and Hops*. There is, therefore, no need for me to emphasize the vast array of insects, mites, and spiders that are to be found on the trees and bushes of the orchard. In addition, there is a rich and complex fauna underground, ranging from the helpful earthworm, continually and unobtrusively cultivating the soil, to the troublesome nematodes that invade the roots of the fruit trees; and a moving population of birds which are searching the twigs and trunks for insects or pursuing other less worthy aims.

But there is no doubt, I think, that we should all agree upon which is the most important central figure in the fauna of the orchard. That is certainly the fruit grower himself. In his endeavours to produce more and better fruit the grower is continually interfering with the rest of the fauna. And the purpose of this lecture is to reflect a little upon the significance of that interference.

Insects and mites were always a source of trouble for the grower of fruit. And the larger the orchards, the more pronounced this trouble became. The remedies employed — whitewashing, scraping, washing with simple chemicals, grease-banding — amounted to little more than tinkering with the orchard fauna; and in some years the insect populations were appalling. Dr. Tom Wallace, speaking of conditions forty years ago in the Vale of Evesham (if I may be permitted to mention such a locality to the men of Kent and Essex), gave some indication of what conditions were like in an aphid year in those days. 'In many of the orchards, not only were the trees crawling with aphids but the soil under the trees was also green with the insects; it looked as if moss was covering the soil. If you drove a car through the area on a fine day your vision was completely blacked out by dead aphids which had committed suicide on your windscreen, and you had to get out and wipe off the bodies. . . . In those days to visit plum growers during the period when aphids were hatching in the spring was almost a dangerous occupation.'

Then, in the early 'twenties, came the tar-oil washes — and the situation was transformed.

I am sometimes reminded, in this connexion, of the patient afflicted with trigeminal neuralgia, one of the most excruciating diseases to which the human flesh is heir. The sufferer is prepared to submit to anything to get rid of his pain. He will readily allow the surgeon to cut out the trigeminal ganglion — a formidable operation, for this ganglion lies in the skull right underneath the brain. And when he comes round from the operation — the pain has gone. He is prepared to lay half of all he has at the feet of the surgeon. Of course, the surgeon has warned him that the operation will necessarily lead to permanent paralysis of the cheek muscle on the one side; but that is a little price to pay for such relief. However, as time goes on it becomes a little troublesome that food should collect between the gums and the cheek. Indeed, this becomes increasingly irritating — until, in the end, the excruciating pains of neuralgia are forgotten and no words are too bad to describe the surgeon who has caused him so much inconvenience!

Perhaps our attitude is a little like this when we complain of the evil effects of insecticides. The tar-oil washes did not clear up every trouble. The fruit tree red spider mite and the apple capsid raised their ugly heads; and petroleum and DNC were in due course introduced into the spray programme. And so it has gone on; as one insecticidal treatment has been introduced to cope with one problem, another problem has arisen. But, when all is said and done, the state of the patient is very different indeed from what it was at the time of the First World War.

According to Dr. Massee there are something like a hundred sorts of insects and mites inhabiting the apple tree. Most of these are actually feeding upon the tree and therefore, from the standpoint of the grower, 'doing damage'. But the great majority are so few in number that the harm they do is insignificant. It is only a handful of species which are regularly present in sufficient numbers to be called 'pests'. All, however, are potential pests.

From time to time a new pest may be introduced or find its own way from abroad. (A few years ago, for example, we saw the arrival of the summer fruit tortrix moth, *Adoxophyes orana*.) But most new pests have been there all the time, living their own lives in their own quiet unobtrusive way. Then something happens, and what was merely an interesting insect becomes an offensive pest. I think the best way to appreciate the explosive nature of the situation in the orchard is to read Dr. Massee's 'Notes on Some Interesting Insects' over the years. Every year you will find that some forgotten insect has broken through the cordon and for a brief period has flourished as a pest in somebody's orchard. (Dr. Massee does not reveal his inmost thoughts, but I sometimes feel that he gets a wicked satisfaction when some obscure insect momentarily gets the upper hand.)

It is not my intention to speak at length about the physiology of insects. But I would remind you that most insects lay several hundred eggs. Suppose the female of a given species lays 200 eggs on the average. Then it is obvious that if the population is to remain steady only two insects, one male and one female, must survive to the stage of sexual maturity, and 198 must perish. There is clearly an appalling rate of mortality.

It is impossible, with any given insect species, to know exactly how this total mortality (99% in the ideal example I have given) is made up. That must vary from year to year and from tree to tree. It is instructive just to observe with a hand lens a few twigs from the neglected apple tree in the back garden. They are teeming with life. Mites and mite eggs are on the leaves and small twigs. Typhlodromid mites are moving up and down in search of smaller mites to prey on. Here an anthocorid bug may be actually caught in the act of sucking up the contents of a mite egg. Everywhere small parasitic wasps (chalcids, ichneumonids, braconids) are running feverishly to and fro, searching for the caterpillars of the winter moth or the rare clusters of woolly aphid. In neighbouring trees, tits and other birds are diligently searching the branches for some purpose or other. Everywhere there are forces of destruction. If the pressure of these destructive forces is reduced, more insects will survive and the insect populations will increase, perhaps to the level of becoming a pest.

This situation is so complex and many-sided that it hardly seems possible to describe it in a few simple terms. But the scientist likes to have laws and classifications. Indeed, that is what he is paid to do — to describe everything in nature by means of the simplest possible laws and theories. One of the most helpful classifications of the factors regulating insect populations was drawn up twenty-five years ago by Harry Smith, of the Citrus Research Station in California. Smith divided the mortality factors into two main classes: (i) 'density-dependent factors' — those which destroy a steadily increasing or a steadily diminishing proportion of the whole as the population increases in density; (ii) 'density-independent factors' which destroy more or less the same proportion of the population whatever the density may be.

To take a few examples: insectivorous birds will be among the density-dependent factors. In any one season the number of birds is fixed. Their appetites are limited; moreover, they soon get tired of an insect that is too plentiful. So that the proportion of the insect population they destroy soon falls off as the density of the population increases.

Many insect parasites and predators and certainly insect diseases are density dependent in the opposite sense. The parasites and predators may themselves multiply rapidly and since the densely crowded insects are very easily found they tend to destroy a steadily increasing proportion as the population density rises. The same happens with infectious diseases of insects.

None of these factors is, of course, 'perfectly density dependent'. As Milne has pointed out, the only factor that is perfectly density dependent, in the sense that it acts more and more severely as the population rises, is intra-specific competition. For example, the competition for food among the members of a single species.

Examples of factors that are independent of density are adverse weather conditions, applications of insecticides and the like, which may be expected to kill more or less the same percentage of the population whatever the total numbers.

An immense amount of doctrinal argument has developed about this theory. In the controlled conditions of the laboratory, experiments can be so devised that the population is limited by intra-specific competition, and so illustrate beautifully the control of the population by density-dependent factors. Particular cases can be selected from nature where the unpredictable effects of weather are evidently more important in deciding the numbers of a particular species — and these weather effects may be acting either directly on the insect under study or indirectly by their effect on food supply or on enemies and diseases of one sort or another.

In fact, to the simple-minded observer the influences controlling survival (as well as those controlling rate of growth, rate of reproduction, etc.) are often so numerous and varied that the situation in nature may appear unpredictable.

In the ultimate limit it is the competition between the members of the species (for food and shelter) which limits their numbers; but there is a broad range over which the numbers can fluctuate widely and often as the result of purely chance alterations in weather conditions, or the malign activities of the fruit grower.

The fact remains, of course, that density-dependent mortality factors *do* act like the governor on an engine (or what we should call nowadays a feed-back mechanism), and they do tend to keep the population within bounds and to bring the numbers down again if these bounds are greatly exceeded. And this balance is far more steady in those environments that are least disturbed by man. The numbers of the different kinds of insects remain tolerably steady in derelict orchards. But the fauna of the well-cared-for commercial orchard is very much disturbed by man. The grower generally uses density-independent factors, such as insecticides, for killing off those insects which he does not want. Here there is no feed-back mechanism, and such methods naturally cause violent fluctuations in the numbers of insects present.

That is how the biologist sees the orchard or any other community of animals and plants. Just a little persistent increase in the pressure upon a species and its numbers will fall; a weakening or removal of some mortality factor and the numbers will rise. He feels that there is safety in numbers and variety. He likes to have a fair number of pest insects about in order to sustain a population of the parasites and predators which feed upon them. He feels that the presence of these is a valuable insurance against some unforeseen change that would otherwise lead to a great increase in the pest.

But there are many who find the biologist's way of looking at things rather woolly. They don't like the idea of having to be gentle with nature. They want to bludgeon her into subjection, rather than humour her and try to win her co-operation. The instinctive aim of the grower is, quite naturally, to make a clean sweep of the orchard; to exterminate the pest species from commercial orchards and hold them permanently in that state. Is this aim an impossible and unreasonable one?

We must admit straight away that there is nothing wrong in principle with this idea. We do not tolerate in our beds a 'reasonable number' of fleas, or a strictly moderate population of lice upon our persons. We expect to eliminate these insects completely from our homes and bodies. In many parts of the world the medical entomologist is aiming at the complete eradication of malaria-carrying mosquitoes. In the last few years American entomologists have eradicated from the whole of Florida both the Mediterranean fruit fly and the notorious screw worm fly. Why should the orchardist be satisfied with less? Why should he be expected to harbour permanently a large number of pests and potential pests on his fruit trees?

No one would venture to give a dogmatic answer. It may be that the time will come when man really will have tamed the earth. When wild nature as we know it will no longer exist and only a few species of plants and animals, chosen to suit the needs of man, will be permitted to exist within the few restricted areas of earth which break the universal desert of reinforced concrete.

But that glorious future has not yet arrived. We still have to compete with nature on something rather less than equal terms.

Now the key qualities of nature as seen by the biologist are variety and change. That was pointed out by Charles Darwin a hundred years ago. Darwin's doctrine of natural selection and the survival of the fittest was soon accepted. He had produced such massive and carefully accumulated evidence to support his theory. But Darwin himself was never satisfied. He was unable to get a clear conception of the laws of variation and heredity; and he was never able to see evolution actually in progress. He got round this difficulty by supposing that the changes take place slowly over immensely long periods of time.

The irony of the situation was that within six years of the publication of the *Origin of Species,* Mendel published his *Laws of Heredity,* which provided exactly what Darwin had been looking for. That was in 1865. Mendel was familiar with Darwin's work, and was fully aware of the impact which his own discoveries made upon the idea of evolution. But so far as is known, he did not communicate with Darwin or send him a copy of his paper. Of course, Mendel did send out reprints. When I was working in Berlin in 1939, the botanist von Wettstein told me that when he was going through his father's library (his father had been professor of botany, I believe, in Vienna) he found a reprint of Mendel's famous paper, duly filed away. But it had failed to make any great impression.

It is ironical also that one of the most spectacular examples of evolution by natural selection was going forward under Darwin's eyes during the second half of the nineteenth century. I refer, of course, to the appearance of black moths in the industrial regions of western Europe. We now realize that these black moths were there all along. That is, an occasional one appeared from time to time, as an occasional albino may appear in man, but their proportion failed to increase. These black forms, however, are generally more hardy and robust than the paler forms, and whereas the pale forms are wonderfully concealed when they rest on the pale bark of trees covered with moss and lichens, they are at a serious disadvantage when the trees and fences are blackened, and the lichens killed off by the pollution of the atmosphere. In recent years it has been proved experimentally by Kettlewell and others that the black forms do in fact survive the attacks of birds more successfully than the pale forms in the polluted regions; whereas the pale forms are at an advantage on the uncontaminated lichen-covered trees. This process of selection has been going on at least since the middle of the last century. It continues with increasing intensity; more and more sorts of moths are becoming predominantly black, and in some the caterpillars are becoming black also.

In the case of the black moths the pressure of selection is pretty intense, and the changes in the population take place with corresponding rapidity. But one of the most important developments in the past thirty years has been the demonstration, chiefly from the mathematical studies of Haldane and of Fisher, that a very small selective preference for one form will lead, surprisingly rapidly, to its becoming the predominant one.

The extraordinary efficiency of natural selection, and the existence of persistent inheritable changes within the species, the so-called 'mutations', provide the background for our picture of nature at the present time. The great question is the origin of the mutations. Many of these are present all the time, but are concealed by being 'recessive'. They only become evident when the animals or plants are inbred for a number of generations. Other mutations occur anew. Whether there is a mechanism which provides that they appear when there is a need for them is highly dubious — although it often looks as though that were so.

Whether man, and in our present context that means the fruit grower, is evolving, is a matter for opinion and debate. But he certainly changes his habits, and such changes must affect the fauna of the orchard. The tar-oil winter washes of the early 'twenties were a great triumph. They virtually disposed of the insects that were most troublesome at that time, the mussel scale, the rose apple aphid, the green apple aphid, the apple sucker, and gave partial control of the winter moths and their allies and the woolly aphid. But there were some insects and mites which they hardly affected. The eggs of the fruit tree red spider mite, the eggs of the apple capsid, and so on. At the same time they did kill off a number of predatory insects, anthocorid bugs, the black-kneed capsid and many more; and they effectively cleaned up the bark of the apple trees, eliminating the lichens and mosses which provided a natural cover for many of the beneficial predatory forms.

Thus the fruit tree red spider mite, the apple capsid, the apple sawfly, the apple blossom weevil, became the important figures in the commercial orchards — and year by year new insecticidal formulations and new spray programmes were devised to cope with each new problem as it arose. I will not recapitulate the story as it developed in the late 'twenties, in the 'thirties and in the early 'forties. But what an opportunity for a Darwin: evolution going forward under more or less controlled conditions before our eyes.

Two main changes have come about. When I was first introduced to the commercial orchards — and that was by Sir Ronald Hatton and Dr. Massee in the early days of the war — I was disappointed by the poverty of insect life which they displayed. The number and variety of sorts of insects had been drastically reduced — but, as a corollary, the situation was in some ways potentially more explosive than ever.

The insects had not stood still under this treatment. We spoke of the moths of England becoming black under the impact of the industrial revolution. That really means that there were black moths in small numbers all along, but that under industrial conditions they have been selected out (and modified genetically in the process) so that they have become the dominant forms. As Kettlewell has pointed out, that did not invariably happen. Some species did not produce black mutants in time and were therefore exterminated from the industrial regions.

Similarly, we speak now of insects 'becoming resistant' to insecticides. But all the evidence suggests that the varieties resistant to the insecticide in question were there all along. They have been preferentially selected out. In North America and elsewhere in the world where the codling moth is a serious pest of commercial orchards, it was controlled for many years by arsenical washes. But the number of these washes had to be progressively increased as the years went by, until it was necessary to apply seven or more in the course of a single season. They had been selecting out a strain which was perhaps able to avoid the arsenical particles when entering the fruit or was resistant to the poisonous action of arsenic.

When DDT appeared towards the end of the war, it seemed to provide the solution to this problem. It controlled the codling moth completely, after a single application. But in these same orchards the fruit tree red spider mite and the woolly aphid appeared in such quantities as had never been seen before. That, of course, was due to the elimination of their natural enemies under the action of the DDT. That result is still liable to occur; but it is less dramatic nowadays, and the suspicion grows that DDT-resistant parasites and predators are making their appearance.

In this country we have not experienced quite such violent effects. Perhaps we are not so efficient or drastic as the Americans in the application of insecticides; perhaps we are not quite so enthusiastic for what is new. Whatever the reason, good or bad, we have tended to be a little more conservative and to do things a little more gently. But in all walks of life we are getting more and more Americanized. A few years ago we produced some magnificent bumper populations of the fruit tree red spider mite in Essex by the application of parathion in the late summer, when the population of predators ought to have been building up. And we have produced mites resistant to the summer ovicides chlorbenzide and others, with very creditable speed.

Meanwhile the insects change in other ways. The classic example is the apple capsid, which early in the century was found only on willow. Even when the branches of the willow tree mingled with those of the apple tree these bugs kept themselves to the willow and left the apple alone. Then, within a comparatively few years it became a serious pest of apple.

We are all familiar with the apple fruit rhynchites, *Caenorhinus aequatus* and the punctures which it makes in the apple fruitlets. The early stages of this weevil are normally passed within the fruits of hawthorn; but in recent years it has been showing an increasing tendency to lay its eggs within the apple fruitlets. If we decided, for some reason, to eradicate all the hawthorn trees in the neighbourhood of orchards, perhaps we should be able to produce a form of *Rhynchites* which always bred in the orchard itself and thus provide the grower with a new major pest.

Indeed, it is impossible to read the 'Notes on Interesting Insects' without being struck continually by the odd things that insects will sometimes do. How they will suddenly, for no apparent reason, change their habits, appear locally to breed in the orchards, where they have no business to be, and sometimes even to become pests for the moment. It may well be that we have here a 'biological race', that is, a mutant form in which the change concerns not some attribute of structure or colour, but an alteration in behaviour. I notice that Dr. Dicker or Dr. Massee usually stamp out these interesting insects — but they serve to illustrate the point that the fauna of the orchard is in a continuous state of flux.

What of the present and the future? In spite of everything that has been done during the forty-six years since Jesse Amos joined the Research Station at East Malling, the fauna of the orchard still presents us with a question mark. We are in a phase of intensive activity and uncertainty. The initiative in the production of chemicals for the control of fungi and pests in the orchard has passed from the research stations to the large chemical firms in this country and abroad. These powerful new chemical materials are necessarily put upon the market, and come into the hands of growers, long before their long-term effects on the fauna of the orchards can be known. To elucidate these effects is a slow and difficult business; and before it can be done the entomologist is overwhelmed by the arrival of more new products which demand assessment.

One thing is clear. The Research Station still occupies a key position in the scheme of things. Only the workers in the research stations are in a position to sort these problems out in an unbiased fashion. But they cannot do it in a day. The serious investigator cannot just hop like a flea-beetle from a problem here to a problem there, making no more than a minute puncture in each. He must make the difficult decision of what we really need to know, and then pursue that enquiry to its logical conclusion undisturbed by back-seat drivers.

I hope I have said enough to make clear my opinion that the fauna of the orchard is still an immensely complicated problem. The grower has digged a pit for himself. He has educated the public to expect fruit of a quality which they never demanded in the past; and yet the pests and diseases are not fully under control.

We have a fair knowledge of the general principles by which the fluctuations in the fauna are brought about. But the grower is like a boxer who is faced with an actual opponent. The general principles of pugilism will help him up to a point; but no opponent is ever quite the same as the last; the pugilist is dependent on quick thinking and past experience — guided by the general principles of his trade. The day when the orchard is really under control, and the fauna and flora will do the bidding of the grower, will come in time — but it has not come yet.

8

MALARIA IN CEYLON

Malaria has been prevalent in Ceylon for many centuries. As long ago as 1638 a map of the island, published by the Dutch, showed great areas, particularly the North-Central Province, depopulated by 'fever sickness'. These depopulated regions were the site of the ancient civilization of Ceylon; and there can be little doubt that malaria played a part in the ruin of that civilization. But today we can only speculate whether, as some believe, the importation of malaria from India was the primary factor in that decay, or whether the repeated Tamil invasions so disorganized the elaborate system of irrigation and agriculture developed by the Sinhalese as to create everywhere breeding places for Anopheles mosquitoes, and cause such general poverty and distress, that malaria which existed previously in manageable proportions became an insupportable disease.

Modern knowledge of malaria in Ceylon was put upon a sound basis by a monumental report presented to the Government by their Medical Entomologist, H. F. Carter, in 1927. To make clear the situation revealed by that report it is necessary to give some account of the physiography of the island. Ceylon lies in the tropics between 5° and 10° north latitude. It is 270 miles in length and 140 miles across, with an area of about 25 000 square miles. The greater part of the country consists of low-lying, undulating plains; but there is a central system of mountains in the southern half of the island, rising to 8000 ft. The rainfall varies greatly in the different regions. Briefly, the south-western quadrant receives the full benefit of both the south-west and north-east monsoons, and constitutes a wet zone with an annual rainfall of more than 100 in, which occurs chiefly from May to July and November to January. The northern and eastern parts get rain principally from the north-east monsoon, mostly from November to January, and constitute a dry zone with a long period of comparative drought from March to October. The total population is about 5·5 millions; and of these 3·5 millions reside in the wet zone, where the rubber, tea, coconut, and cacao of Ceylon are grown.

Eighteen species of Anopheline mosquitoes occur in Ceylon; those with an evil reputation as carriers of malaria elsewhere in the world being three: *Anopheles culicifacies, A. maculatus,* and *A. varuna.* Omitting a great amount of detail elaborated by Mr. Carter, we can divide the country from the malaria point of view into three zones: the dry zone, the wet zone and the foot-hill zone. *A. maculatus* and, to a less extent, *A. varuna* are foot-hill species, breeding abundantly in the streams; and by analogy with the Himalayan terai, with Malaya and Java, we should expect the foot-hill zone to suffer from the most intense malaria. But, fortunately for those sections of the planting community concerned, this zone is only moderately malarious: the 'spleen rate', the percentage of children with the enlarged spleens of malaria, is about 20. Why that should be so is uncertain; perhaps the *A. maculatus* and its associates in those parts feed on cattle more readily than they do on man. That is the case with the *A. maculatus* of Assam; whereas this same species in Malaya prefers human blood.

The most malarious part of the island is the dry zone: an area of more or less broken jungle country where the scanty and uncertain rain that falls in the wet season is stored in tanks — that is, embanked lakes — and used to irrigate the crops throughout the remainder of the year. The rivers and streams regularly dry up during the dry season, leaving only a series of pools of clear water. *A. culicifacies* breeds prolifically in these pools, in seepages from the water storage tanks, and in the irrigation channels. When the rain comes, innumerable temporary pools are created in all the natural and artificial depressions in the countryside. These provide more breeding places for *A. culicifacies*; and every year throughout the dry zone there is a peak of malaria incidence about a month after the onset of the rain.

The spleen rate over the greater part of the dry zone is around 60—70 per cent. The amount of malaria varies somewhat from year to year, but the people are so saturated with the disease that true 'epidemics' of malaria are impossible. Some indication of the incidence of malaria in Ceylon is given by the fact that in 1932, an average sort of year in respect to malaria, there were 1·5 millions of cases treated in hospitals and dispensaries: that is, about one-quarter of the total population. Twelve thousand pounds of quinine and over two million tablets of quinine costing £23 000 were distributed free by the Government. That was in a normal year.

In the south-western quadrant, as we have seen, the climate is far wetter. The rivers and tributaries contain running water throughout the year, and irrigation is comparatively little used. *A. culicifacies* is present everywhere, but in small numbers only. The relatively harmless swamp-loving species, *A. hyrcanus, A. barbirostris, A. annularis,* are the dominant Anophelines. Malaria in this zone is usually unimportant; the spleen rate is only about 5 per cent; and this area naturally received little attention in the earlier reports. But in recent years it has been realized that malaria can be of considerable local importance even in this wet zone. The natural history of this malaria was clearly described in a paper published by Colonel W. W. Clemesha (rather aptly in point of time) on the eve of the recent epidemic. This account showed quite convincingly two things: (i) that malaria in this part of Ceylon is *river malaria* — that is, it occurs mainly along the banks of the chief rivers and their tributaries; and (ii) that it is *drought malaria* — that is, epidemics occur only when there is an exceptionally low rainfall, and the volume of water in the rivers is so reduced that they become broken up into a series of relict pools. In other words, malaria spreads into the wet zone only when the climatic conditions there approximate to those in the dry zone. Indeed, I was told of one planter who claimed that malaria always broke out on his estate when a particular rock became visible in the river.

From a consideration of data accumulated over a number of years, Colonel Clemesha showed that the healthy years in the Kurunegala area are those in which the July, August, and September rainfall is plentiful, or above 20 in. Unhealthy years are those in which the rainfall in these months is scanty, or under 20 in. The relation between death rate (usually a good index of malaria incidence) and drought over a period of twenty years is clearly seen in charts from Kurunegala, in the heart of the area affected by the recent epidemic. This malaria is again carried almost solely by *A. culicifacies*. The longer the period without rain in these three months, the more prolific is the breeding of *A. culicifacies* in the river pools. And whenever there is an increase in the number of *A. culicifacies* larvae captured, there is a rise in the attendance rate in the hospitals and the death rate of the district. Whereas the numerical prevalence of the other species of Anopheles has no influence whatever on the amount of malaria.

Now 1934 was a year of altogether exceptional drought. The

south-west monsoon failed, and there was widespread drought from May to October. At the end of September the Medical Department of the Government sent round a circular to all the health officers in the wet zone warning them that in view of the prolonged drought there was likely to be a considerable epidemic of malaria, and urging them to see that they had plenty of quinine available and an organization for its distribution. A fortnight later a definite increase in the dispensary attendance was noticed at Polgohowela in the Maha Oya valley on the borders between the malarious and non-malarious regions; and by the second week of November there was a perceptible rise over a wide area extending into the dry zone to the north and the wet zone to the south.

These initial outbreaks occurred on the immediate banks of the rivers. But during October there were occasional days of heavy rain, and even minor floods in some localities. In consequence, innumerable breeding places were created in borrow pits, brick pits, quarries, shallow wells, and such like. This rain, however, was not sufficient to flood the rivers; and it was succeeded by further drought, for November was moderately dry and December unusually so. More perfect conditions for the multiplication and spread of *A. culicifacies* could not have been devised; and by the beginning of December the hospital attendances shot up in an alarming manner.

I arrived in Ceylon towards the end of December, when the first wave of the epidemic was at its peak; and I had the privilege of accompanying Dr. R. Briercliffe, the Director of Medical and Sanitary Services, on a tour throughout the epidemic area. The roads presented remarkable scenes. Everywhere were people trailing to the dispensaries with their bottles; all along the roads were patients carried in litters, on stretchers, or in bullock carts. The dispensaries were surrounded by dense crowds of patients, many of them shaking and vomiting with malaria. At many of the dispensaries were 'side-shows': kitchens at which local philanthropists (and sometimes, it may be added, local politicians) provided free tea, coriander water, or rice congee; and sometimes stalls where enterprising traders offered bottles for sale at five cents a piece.

The hospitals were exceedingly crowded; and temporary wards were being rapidly set up. At Kurunegala hospital, for instance, with 140 beds, there were 405 in-patients, the floors of the wards and the verandahs all being occupied. All the doctors, apothecaries, and compounders in the affected area, almost without exception, had

had malaria. In many places both they and the nursing sisters in the hospitals looked wretchedly ill. All were obviously overworked. The attendances at single dispensaries had gone up from, say 400 per week for October to about 4200 for the third week of December.

The area affected was about 5800 square miles, about one-quarter of Ceylon. To the north it merged gradually into the dry zone where, as we have seen, malaria is highly endemic. To the east it was bordered by the hills. It extended south as far as Kalutara and westwards almost to the coast, affecting even the outskirts of Colombo. There were differences in incidence and in severity in different parts, but in many of the villages every man, woman and child had been knocked down by the disease. Towards its southern limits the epidemic was mild.

Everywhere the rivers were exceedingly low. Residual pools and quiet backwaters along the margins were teeming with *A. culicifacies* larvae, twenty to thirty of which could often be obtained at a single dip with a soup ladle. Often practically the entire bed was occupied by residual pools. On the sand banks, beside the natural depressions, were often elephant hoof marks forming little pools of water, ideal breeding places for *A. culicifacies*. The same thing was to be seen in the smaller tributary streams; they were reduced to a series of rock pools full of *A. culicifacies*. *A. culicifacies* was by far the commonest mosquito in houses. Adult females sent in for dissection to Dr. K. J. Rustomjee, Director of the Malaria Department, showed an average rate of infection of about 14 per cent over the whole epidemic area. In one area 21 per cent of the adults were infected with the malaria parasite! Infection was found in no other species.

It has been estimated that between one-third and one-half of the total population of the island suffered from malaria. The total loss of life attributable to the epidemic was something like 100 000. The mortality during the early weeks was surprisingly low; but in January, 1935, the death rate rose distressingly; and this first wave of mortality had only just come to an end in April when it was succeeded by a fresh outburst of cases associated, fortunately, with a much lower mortality rate. This second wave seems to have been due partly to recurrences in the patients previously infected, partly to new infections.

By the time this widespread epidemic had broken out, it was too late to attempt anti-larval measures of control, even assuming these to have been practicable in any case. The only thing to do was to treat the sick; the main problem was how quinine could best be got to the people. During previous epidemics of malaria in Ceylon the procedure has been for Sanitary Inspectors to distribute quinine in the affected villages; and in the early days of the recent outbreak the same method was employed. But it soon became apparent that this itinerating system would not work in an epidemic on such a scale. No one knew when the Sanitary Inspectors might be expected to reach a given village, and while some villages were well served, others had no help whatsoever. Early in December, therefore, when the magnitude of the epidemic became apparent, the Medical Department changed the entire policy. The Sanitary Inspectors were to travel round their districts and collect information as to what villages were most severely affected, about the number of cases, the deaths, the economic condition of the people, and so forth; they were to explain to the people where to send for medicine, but were to issue quinine themselves only in urgent cases. They were to make daily reports to their Medical Officers of Health, and on the information derived from these reports temporary treatment centres were to be established, the object being that no one should have to go more than a mile or two miles to obtain quinine. Every available man in the Medical and Public Health Service, every medical student, was taken over to man the centres.

This scheme of organization was got going within a few days. It worked remarkably well where it was efficiently carried out; and the requisite efficiency was generally forthcoming. Ceylon was fortunate in having in Dr. R. Briercliffe a Director of Medical Services with the administrative ability, the drive, and the tact needed to meet an unprecedented emergency. Nor could one fail to be equally impressed by the loyalty and devotion shown by all ranks in the Service, in the face, sometimes, of most unjust disparagement. It is perhaps worth while quoting the views of Colonel C. A. Gill, Expert Adviser on Malaria appointed by the Ceylon Government, on the way in which the epidemic was dealt with by the Medical Department; he refers to 'the prompt and thorough manner in which it was tackled . . . the able manner in which the scheme was organized and administered by the Head of the Medical Department, and, it may be added, the splendid response made by all members of the Medical and Sanitary Departments to the heavy demands made upon them'.

The Medical Department was soon faced with the problem of the best routine treatment it should recommend. The tried and standard drug for malaria is quinine, which has always formed the basis of routine treatment in the past. During recent years, as the result of brilliant chemical researches, a number of synthetic drugs have been produced which may be used as substitutes for quinine. Plasmoquine and Atabrine are the best known. To test with an unbiased mind the relative value of these various drugs, and to decide the circumstances where each can best be used, is no easy matter. It is a problem on which physicians have been sifting the evidence for several years. But it is also a problem in which enormous economic interests, as between the growers of quinine on the one hand and the manufacturers of synthetic drugs upon the other, are involved. Early in the epidemic the claims of the diverse drugs were loudly voiced in the Press, and there was a real danger that the Medical Department might be influenced by factors other than scientific evidence in its recommendations. Fortunately for Ceylon the Department kept its head. All the drugs were tested; but they were tested scientifically. When one group of patients was treated with one drug, a second, control, group was treated simultaneously with another. As a result a most valuable mass of data was accumulated, and many fatalities which would certainly have followed the use of the wrong drug in certain types of case were prevented; while the level-headed attitude of the Department has done much to enhance its prestige.

It is clear from the foregoing account of the epidemic that there was nothing mysterious about its origin. Severe epidemics of malaria have occurred in Ceylon in the past. Many of those in the last century were associated with drought and other departures from normal rainfall — often drought followed by excessive rain. The severity of the recent outbreak was due to the simultaneous action of several causes. 1934 was preceded by five exceptionally healthy years in that region where the dry zone merges into the wet zone. Consequently the population in this area had lost all its immunity or tolerance for malaria. Then two successive monsoons failed; and the rice crop failed throughout much of the wet zone. Lack of food thus lowered the resistance of the people still further. The drying of the rivers led to *A. culicifacies* multiplying in vast numbers in residual pools, and the short burst of rain in the autumn provided still more temporary breeding places. Whether there were other less tangible influences at work is not certain. Colonel Gill, for instance, acknowledges the importance of all these factors but believes that there was another, still more important — a direct effect of abnormal climate upon the

91

malaria parasite latent in the people, which caused them to develop a veritable 'epidemic of relapses'. This afforded the mosquito population the opportunity to become infected and so to convey the disease to the young children and the uninfected adults. This is an intriguing hypothesis supported by arguments which cannot be neglected, but it has not yet gained general acceptance.

Such being the causes of the epidemic, could it have been prevented? Before we attempt an answer to that question we must consider the malaria problem of Ceylon as a whole. It should be clear from the foregoing account that there is not one malaria problem in Ceylon but many. There is, first and foremost, the problem of the dry zone; formerly rich cultivated land, now semi-jungle sparsely populated with a people decimated by malaria and kept at their present level only by immigration from the south. The resettlement of these regions which, indeed, comprise most of Ceylon, is impossible until the malaria is controlled. But the existing measures for the control of malaria — by oiling, by draining, and so forth — if applied wholesale to rural settlements, would entail an expense out of all proportion to any possible returns. The only conceivable measure of approach, it seems to me, is to develop methods of agriculture which will automatically limit the breeding of the dangerous species of mosquito. That is probably what the ancient Sinhalese did without knowing it. The return to such a policy now is easily suggested; to put it into practice will require great enterprise and vision, and a degree of co-operation between Medical, Agricultural, and Public Works Departments such as I have seen only in the Netherlands Indies.

Then there is the problem of the larger towns. If they wish to do so, the towns can protect themselves from malaria in Ceylon just as well as elsewhere in the tropics. The methods to be employed are well known. The area over which they would have to operate need not usually extend more than half a mile from the periphery of the town, so that the cost, when set against the value of improved health and lowered death rate, is not unreasonable. All that is needed is an efficient and energetic organization backed by legal powers. That last link is the weak one! It is not only in Ceylon that there have been keen and efficient Health Services whose malaria control work has been frustrated by the indifference of the public on the one hand and the want of legal backing on the other.

The case of the plantations is not very different from that of the towns. The labour force which needs protection is concentrated, so that the area to be controlled is usually of manageable extent. The benefits that come to malarial estates from successful malaria control — in the contentment and competence of the coolies, the facilitation of recruitment, the improved health of the estate managers and their families — can only be appreciated when one has had the opportunity, as I have in Assam and Malaya, of contrasting side by side controlled and uncontrolled estates. The amount of malaria in the different estates in Ceylon varies greatly. Many are perfectly healthy; but others, particularly in the northern parts of the wet zone, are always more or less malarious, and in years of drought suffer severely. The cost of the measures needed to control the breeding of *A. culicifacies* is also very variable. Sometimes control is easy and cheap, often it is very difficult and costly. The least fortunate estates are those contiguous with uncontrolled Government land — often traversed by rivers liable to dry up and become a prolific source of mosquito breeding — into which the estates have no right of entry. This is a common situation in all parts of the tropics, and one not easy to resolve.

There are many towns and estates in the wet zone which suffer so little from malaria in some years that a permanent organization for control seems at first sight scarcely necessary. But that brings us to the last malaria problem of Ceylon: epidemic malaria. The south-western quadrant of Ceylon has been subject to repeated epidemics of malaria in the past, and these will assuredly recur in the future. Towns and estates so managed that *A. culicifacies* cannot multiply within their borders can remain unscathed in the heart of such epidemics: the main parts of Colombo were unaffected in the recent outbreak, and the town of Chilaw, where much control work has been done of recent years, probably suffered less than it would otherwise have done. Malaria control is therefore an insurance against future epidemics as well as a preventive during inter-epidemic periods.

But we have still said nothing about the rural districts and small villages throughout the area that is subject to the epidemics. To have prevented the last epidemic throughout those 5800 square miles of territory by eliminating the breeding places of *A. culicifacies* would have been a far vaster undertaking than has ever been attempted anywhere in the world for the control of rural malaria. The epidemic as it affected the villager could not have been prevented by such means; nor will the epidemics of the future. Yet there is no call to turn defeatist. It may well be that if we had more precise knowledge about the natural history of *A. culicifacies,* we could devise new ways of gaining protection from it: perhaps by killing the adult females in their resting places,* by diverting them to cattle, or by modifying chemically the water in their breeding places so as to make it unattractive to them, or, what is more likely, in ways quite unforeseen. For the moment, efficient treatment of the disease is all that can be offered to the villager.

For all these malaria problems Ceylon needs two things: more research into the fundamental questions of malaria and mosquitoes; and more application of the results of research which already exist. Ceylon is such a magnificent field for research that the lessons learned there would benefit not herself alone, but the whole tropical world.

*See Chapter 1, p. 4.

9

MALARIA IN WAR

Throughout the centuries of European history, from causes that are still subject to dispute, malaria has ebbed and flowed like a fatal tide (Hackett, 1937). During the nineteenth century the disease was in retreat and in 1914 seemed to be hanging on in only a few localities, mostly in the south-east corner. The War of 1914—18 changed all that. With the massing of troops unaccustomed to infection in malarious regions, malaria became rife among the combatant forces. With the return of these to their homes, and the interchanges of peoples which took place after the War, the disease revived among the civil population in all sorts of unexpected places: in the eastern half of England, the north coast of Germany, parts of Italy long free from malaria, up in the Arctic at Archangel; while a terrible epidemic decimated vast areas of Russia.

That malaria would be important to the armies in Europe and elsewhere was foreseen by Laveran, Ross, Nocht, and a few other malariologists; but their warnings were unheeded. How important it proved may be judged from a few figures. In East Africa the average strength of Allied troops was about 50 000. Admissions for malaria in 1916 and 1917 have been estimated at 120 000. In Macedonia in 1916 the French could put into the field only 20 000 men out of a force at least six times this strength. On the same front the British had 30 000 men down with malaria in 1916, 70 000 in 1917. In 1918 more than two million service days were lost on account of malaria.

It is not my purpose, however, to review the whole subject of malaria in war (see Christophers, 1939), but, as part of a discussion on the relation between pure and applied biology, to use the subject of malaria as a text from which to illustrate the ways in which pure biological research can help the practical man, and the almost greater frequency with which empirical results provide the starting point for fundamental work.

Let us first summarize the theories of malaria transmission as they are accepted to-day. Malaria is caused by Plasmodium, of which there are three or four species producing in man clinically different varieties of the disease. The sexual forms of the parasite mature and conjugate in the stomach of the mosquito, giving rise to numerous 'sporozoites' which invade the salivary glands and are injected into man when the mosquito feeds. This cycle takes place only in Anopheles. All the members of this genus, which contains some 150 species, are therefore potential carriers of malaria. But in fact relatively few of these species are important — indeed only a proportion of those which breed near human habitations and feed readily on man. In regions of endemic malaria, the local population, while harbouring plenty of malaria parasites, acquires a certain tolerance to the disease (the existence of a true immunity is a much debated question). Such people are the source of the infection which wreaks such havoc among unseasoned troops quartered in their midst.

To consider now the carriers of malaria in the areas of present or prospective hostilities. The chief carrier of malaria in Europe is *A. maculipennis;* a species which breeds in swamps and grassy pools and slowly flowing rivers. It is the species responsible in the Roman Campagna, and many other coastal regions of Italy, Sicily, and Sardinia; the carrier in the notorious Struma Valley in Macedonia, the low-lying parts of Albania and Greece, the coasts of the Black Sea.

Before the War of 1914—18, malaria in Europe was thought always to be associated with low-lying country of this type. It came as a complete surprise to find that malaria was often most intense in mountainous regions. The Germans discovered this in the Taurus of Anatolia, the Italians in southern Italy, the Allies in Palestine. In the eastern Mediterranean rain falls only in the winter. In the spring the streams from the mountains are raging torrents unsuited to mosquito larvae; but as the summer advances these streams are reduced to broken pools or trickles among stones and provide the breeding places of *A. superpictus,* a species rendered all the more dangerous because during the summer the people concentrate around the few remaining sources of water.

Egypt has commonly been regarded as comparatively free from malaria — because it is not conspicuous in the large towns and military cantonments. But it has recently been realized that there is much malaria, carried probably by *A. pharoensis,* among the rice cultivators of the delta region.

Moving westward into the dry regions of North Africa one would expect malaria to be absent; and that is true enough of the open desert and of the coastal zone of Cyrenaica. But it is not true of the oases. Jarabub and the other oases of the western desert, Kufra and other oases of Fezzan are all intensely malarious. The carrier species is not fully proved but is probably *A. multicolor,* a mosquito that thrives in brackish or highly saline water.

In the coastal belt of Tripolitania the situation is different. Here are streams running into the sea. These have been blocked by settlers to assist in irrigation. Swampy breeding places for *A. maculipennis* have thus been created, and recent years have seen a great increase in malaria.

In Africa south of the Sahara there are some thirty species of Anopheles but only two are really important. *A. gambiae* is a ubiquitous species that breeds in rainwater puddles, borrow pits, river pools or quiet backwaters — any water freely exposed to sunlight. In dry regions like Somaliland its prevalence is related to local rainfall. It is the most dangerous Anopheline in the world — its introduction in 1932 from Dakar to Brazil is one of the major health disasters of recent times. It constitutes a threat to the southern parts of the United States, and has caused America to invoke the principle of 'hemisphere defence'. *A. funestus,* the other dangerous African species, is confined to the grassy edges of slowly flowing streams. Such waters are often perennial, so that this mosquito may keep malaria smouldering in a locality until local conditions of rainfall and temperature favour *A. gambiae* and initiate an epidemic.

That is an over-simplified account of malaria transmission; and particularly so in regard to *A. maculipennis.* For the local abundance of this species bears no relation to the incidence of malaria in Europe. The current explanation of this phenomenon of 'anophelism without malaria' must, in the interests of brevity, be set forth dogmatically (Hackett, 1937). It is that the species *A. maculipennis* is made up of a number of biological races or varieties which differ in their habits and so in their capacity to convey malaria. Morphological differences between these races were at first sought in vain. Systematic entomology, which is often twitted for excessive zeal in subdividing species, proved too superficial for the task. Later such differences were found in the structure and pattern of the eggs. To take a few examples: race *messeae* with richly patterned eggs and race *typicus* the eggs of which have two bars on a white field, breed in fresh inland waters: they feed almost exclusively on cattle and the chances of their taking the necessary two meals from man at the appropriate intervals are so remote that, with few exceptions, areas where these are the prevalent races are free from malaria. Race *labranchiae,* with small egg floats and a more uniform pattern, is a brackish water breeder of the western Mediterranean (Italy, Sicily, North Africa). It is far more prone to bite man, and its prevalence is always associated with malaria. Race *elutus*, with no egg floats or pattern, is a brackish water breeder of the Balkans and the Near East. Precipitin tests on the blood in wild caught females have shown a preference for human blood; and wherever this race occurs it is a dangerous carrier. Race *atroparvus* is more puzzling. Its chief area of distribution is the Atlantic seaboard of Europe. In egg type and breeding habits it is allied to *labranchiae,* but whereas in some localities it attacks man and conveys malaria, in others it seems to be diverted to cattle, and malaria is absent. Perhaps there are differences in the housing of man or animals which will account for this; perhaps there is not one *atroparvus* race but several.

In *atroparvus* regions (around Amsterdam for example) malaria is often a house disease. Instead of going into complete hibernation in the winter (as does *messeae,* for example) *atroparvus* females will continue feeding and so transmitting malaria to the household. But they fail to develop their ovaries, so that they have no call to leave their resting places and fly afield. Here is an attractive problem, presumably of internal secretion (Wigglesworth, 1935), directly connected with the epidemiology of malaria.

What is the zoological status of these mosquito races? Here is a field crying out to be worked by geneticists; particularly geneticists prepared to study the genetics of *behaviour* — for it is the natural history and behaviour of these insects which are important from the malariologist's point of view. A little has been done by the malariologists themselves. Only the *atroparvus* male has so far been persuaded to mate in small cages. Crossed with females of the other races, varying degrees of infertility are revealed, lethality supervening at varying points. With *messeae* most of the eggs are sterile; with *elutus* the larvae die; with *typicus* sterile adults of both sexes result; with *labranchieae* all the resulting females are normal but only a part of the males.

That being the malaria situation, what is the Army doing about it? The general plan (Christophers, 1939) is to establish mobile malaria laboratories. These are commanded by officers with wide experience of malaria in the tropics; their commissioned staff includes malariologists and entomologists; the senior non-commissioned officers will be young graduates in biology or senior laboratory assistants. The function of these units will presumably be to instruct the field hygiene sections in general anti-malarial work; to provide all the necessary local information regarding the incidence of malaria in the local population, and the breeding places, habits and infectivity of the dangerous species; and to advise on specific measures of prevention.

As an organization this seems well conceived. What it will achieve in practice must depend, as in all human enterprises, upon the abilities of the people doing the work. For there is no rule of thumb in malaria control; each problem is a local problem which must be approached with an open mind. It is where the malariologist has applied blindly, in a new locality, methods which he has found successful elsewhere, that the disasters have occurred which have brought the subject into disrepute.

The methods of malaria prevention still call for investigation. Of all the single measures, sleeping under a mosquito net is perhaps the most valuable. That should be practicable in base camps; but is it possible to devise a bivouac net for use by troops in the open and to persuade them to use it (Christophers, 1939)?

In the past, little value has been attached to the destruction of adult mosquitoes; but where semi-hibernating *atroparvus* are the cause of malaria this is a most important measure. Under war conditions there may be times when it is the only practicable measure. It involves the whole subject of insecticidal sprays and the methods for dispersing them.

The abolition of breeding places is often an engineering problem of a special kind. The engineer must turn malariologist or vice versa; or the two must co-operate. That is a vast field beyond our scope. One form of engineering control consists in connecting the breeding places with the sea. What factors — water movement, predators, salinity — are here concerned would repay investigation.

Increasing use has been made recently of 'flushing' to control stream breeding mosquito larvae (Macdonald, 1939). Siphons are built into the stream which periodically release a large volume of water. It is believed that larvae migrating to the margins of the stream are stranded as the flow subsides, but the question merits study.

99

The classical method of killing mosquito larvae is by applying oil to the surface of the water. This does not, as is popularly supposed, suffocate the larvae by preventing their breathing at the water surface. A little of the oil enters the tracheal system of the larva and the oil contains poisons which affect presumably the nervous system. A vast amount of empirical information exists on the preparation and application of oil mixtures, but exact knowledge is scanty. We know almost nothing about the toxic constituents of the oils used.

Oil is usually applied as a spray to form a layer $15-20\,\mu$m thick. Equal in importance with toxicity is the ability of the oil to form a stable film of this thickness on the water surface. As a result of an investigation financed by a group of oil companies and carried out at the London School of Hygiene and Tropical Medicine by D. R. P. Murray (1936, 1939), some light has been thrown on this problem. If an oil contains polar substances such as naphthenic acid or long-chain fatty acids, with a strong tendency to form mono-molecular films on the water, these may spread out ahead of the oil, occupy the water surface, and force the main body of oil into lenses or droplets. Indeed, it has been observed in practice in Malaya that if the coolies waded in the water, an oil which previously spread might be prevented from doing so by oil films coming from their bodies (Hacker, 1925). Such resistance to spreading, or general instability in the oil film, may, however, be overcome by the presence in the oil of 'spreaders'. These are of unknown composition but include 'cracked spirit gum' (derived from polymerization of olefinic hydrocarbons), certain resins, and some constituents of petroleum residues, particularly the undistilled residues of aromatic concentrates. The efficiency of such 'spreaders' in a given oil may be gauged by the direct measurement of their spreading power against surface contamination in the Adam—Langmuir surface pressure trough.

The difficulties of this subject of oils are made greater by the fact that the experimental materials are largely of unknown composition. Mixtures on the market with the same names have often been produced not only from different oil wells but also by different processes. It is clear, however, that a physico-chemical specification for an anti-malarial oil is urgently required. Provisionally we carry out three rough empirical tests: the oil should have a greater spreading pressure than that of castor oil; it should form a fairly complete stable flm when sprayed on water in the customary amounts; and Anopheles larvae below such a film at 24° C should all be dead in two or three hours.

With some types of water, notably where much vegetation is present, 'dusting' is preferred to oiling. This consists in blowing over the water a cloud containing one or two parts per cent of Paris green in a vehicle of dry dust. Anopheles larvae feed at the water surface and are poisoned by the floating particles. Apart from some information about the size of particle ingested by the larvae, knowledge of this subject is at the empirical stage.

The last method of control I intend to mention (there are many more) is known as 'shading'. This has been developed principally and with great success by Ramsay (1930) in Assam and northern Bengal against *A. minimus,* a species closely allied to *funestus,* and which likewise breeds in grassy edged streams. It has been found that if suitable bushes are planted along these streams so that they are densely shaded, *A. minimus* disappears. But the cause of its disappearance has been a matter for speculation. Does the female avoid shaded waters in laying her eggs; or is the shaded water unfavourable for the development of larvae?

During the last three years R. C. Muirhead Thomson (1940), supported by the Royal Society and the London School of Hygiene and Tropical Medicine, has been working on this problem in the tea gardens of Assam. Briefly, he has shown that although the female *A. minimus* lays her eggs during the night she prefers to lay them in the shade. At a light intensity one-quarter of starlight she will still show a preference for deeper shade; below 0·000008 ft candle, about one-tenth of starlight, she becomes indifferent. Yet egg collections in the field show that she does not lay in the shaded streams. Thomson has proved that this is because she will not lay in moving water. Under laboratory conditions she refuses to lay in water flowing at a rate of 0·05 ft/s. Normally she finds both shade and still water among the grass at the margins of the streams. All this vegetation is eliminated by shading.

Shade also exerts an effect upon the larva. Contrary to general belief these stream-breeding larvae have very weak powers of resistance to flowing water. *A. minimus* larvae cannot remain anchored if the rate of flow exceeds 0·29 ft/s. They normally find the still water necessary to their security in the grassy margins. They are kept there, not by an avoidance of moving water but by a reaction to light and shade which is enhanced by flowing water.

In this reaction to light are several elements: (i) a photokinesis or increased activity in bright light. This may be inhibited by thigmo-taxis if the larva is anchored to some object; (ii) an undirected avoiding reaction on passing from shade to light; (iii) a directed reaction or phototaxis towards an area of shade. Under experimental conditions the larva can be made a victim to these responses, and by shading the middle of a stream can be caused to leave the margin where it is safely anchored and swim to the middle, where it is swept away by the current.

This work illustrates well enough how right the malariologist may be in his methods and how completely in the dark as to their mode of action. He has no time and often receives no encouragement to probe deeply into such matters. Here lies a vast and profitable field awaiting the attention of research workers informed on modern biology and unhampered by the need of producing immediate practical results.

REFERENCES

Christophers, S. R. (1939) Malaria in war. *Trans. R. Soc. Trop. Med. Hyg.,* **33,** 277—292.

Hacker, H. P. (1925) How oil kills Anopheline larvae. *F.M.S. Malaria Bureau Reports,* **3,** 1—62.

Hackett, L. W. (1937) *Malaria in Europe. An ecological study.* London: Oxford University Press, 336 pp.

Macdonald, G. (1939) A design of flushing siphon for control of Anopheline breeding. *J. Malar. Inst. India,* **2,** 63—69.

Murray, D. R. P. (1936, 1939) Mineral oils as mosquito larvicides. *Bull. Ent. Res.,* **27,** 287; **29,** 11; **30,** 211.

Ramsay, G. C. (1930) The factors which determine the varying degrees of malarial incidence in Assam tea estates and the fundamental principles governing mosquito control of malaria in Assam. *Trans. R. Soc. Trop. Med. Hyg.,* **23,** 511—518.

Thomson, R. C. M. (1940) Studies on the behaviour of *Anopheles minimus. J. Malar. Inst. India,* **3,** 265—348.

Wigglesworth, V. B. (1935) Functions of the corpus allatum of insects. *Nature,* **136,** 338.

10

THE INSECT AS A MEDIUM FOR THE STUDY OF PHYSIOLOGY

INTRODUCTION

Insects live and feed, move, grow and multiply like other animals; but they are so varied in form, so rich in species, and adapted to such diverse conditions of life that they afford unrivalled opportunities for physiological study. The general problems of physiology are much the same in all groups of animals; and this lecture, which represents, in effect, an apology for the study of insect physiology, is an attempt to show that among the insects may be found material well suited for the solution of many of these problems.

By human standards most insects are small in size, and this brings with it certain features which dominate their physiology. There is the same degree of functional specialization in their organs as there is in mammals; but they are made up of cells of the same dimensions as those in other animals — often, indeed, of cells which are larger than most. Each organ therefore contains far fewer cells, and the organization of their bodies must of necessity appear more simple. It is, however, a deceptive simplicity; for the range of physiological activities of which the single cell is capable is no less and may indeed be greater than it is in larger animals. On the other hand, their small size enables the insects to dispense with many of the physiological elaborations that are needed by mammals. Air-containing tracheae run direct to the tissues; and the high rates of metabolism which active insects develop can be met by the diffusion of gases along these tubes, supplemented in the most active forms by mechanical ventilation of the larger trunks or of the air sacs into which they are dilated.

The needs of respiration being met in this way, the circulatory system may be correspondingly simplified. It is an open circulation, in which the body fluid or haemolymph circulates at about atmospheric pressure. A valved and peristaltic dorsal vessel collects fluid from the abdomen and discharges it into the head. Accessory

103

pumps and vessels, or pulsating membranes, ensure the subsidiary circulation in the wings, legs and antennae.

The respiratory centres in the brain and segmental ganglia, which control the ventilation of the tracheal system and the closure of its spiracular openings, are mainly influenced by the tension of gases in the tracheae and are therefore not dependent on the circulation of a nicely regulated internal medium. The elaborate behaviour of insects seems not to involve the mental processes of reasoning and insight; their judgement is not deranged, as Barcroft has shown ours to be, by minimal disturbances in the internal environment.

For all these reasons the insect is tolerant of much greater insults than can be borne by mammals. Some insects can survive decapitation for a year or more; many can support complete anoxia for several hours; or can be kept narcotized with pure carbon dioxide for long periods. Although temperature plays a very important part in all aspects of their physiology, most species can support a range of body temperature extending over some 30—40 °C — from a reversible chill coma to a reversible heat stupor.

Clearly, insects present some very desirable properties as objects for experiment. They are extremely tolerant of operation; they are so varied in form and habit that some species suited to the problem in hand can surely be found; and their small size makes it possible for the observer to be constantly aware of the whole while focusing his attention upon the part.

THE FATE OF HAEMOGLOBIN IN A BLOOD-SUCKING INSECT

As an example of the ease with which a complex series of changes may be witnessed as a whole, we may consider the fate of haemoglobin ingested by the blood-sucking bug *Rhodnius prolixus* (Wigglesworth, 1943). The adult *Rhodnius* is an insect about 2 cm in length and weighs about 80 mg. At a single meal it may ingest more than twice its own weight of blood. Most of the water in the meal is rapidly eliminated, and the concentrated blood is stored in a capacious 'stomach'. Here some part may remain undigested for a month or more, suffering no change save a partial conversion into methaemoglobin. But blood is passed on little by little to the intestine where it is broken down. Acid haematin is formed, the globin moiety is assimilated and a residue of iron porphyrin is excreted unchanged.

That represents the fate of the bulk of the blood pigment. But a small amount is absorbed without being digested, and circulates in the haemolymph. While circulating it is denatured to produce kathaemoglobin (parahaematin) which gives the body fluid a reddish tinge. Some of this kathaemoglobin is taken up by the salivary glands and converted to a deep cherry red pigment with properties resembling haemalbumen. Some is taken up by the pericardial cells — cells which are nowadays regarded as the equivalent of the reticulo-endothelial cells of vertebrates — and is there converted into biliverdin, which renders the blue-green heart as striking an object on dissection as the bright red salivary glands.

More of the pigment is taken up by the epithelial cells of the gut. Here it is converted to a brown pigment — an altered haematin which gives rise to a pyridine haemochromogen that fails to crystallize and has absorption bands at 546 and 515 nm, as compared with 557 and 526 nm of pyridine protohaemochromogen. Associated with this altered haematin is a green pigment of the verdohaem type, resembling the choleglobin of Lemberg, Legge and Lockwood (1939, 1941), and blue-green droplets of biliverdin. The biliverdin is finally discharged from the cells into the lumen. The iron set free in this breakdown never appears in the excreta, but accumulates throughout the life of the insect in the cells of the gut wall, which become progressively more laden with free iron as the insect ages.

The circulating kathaemoglobin is taken up also by the follicular cells of the ovary and deposited in the yolk of the egg, so that the new-laid egg has a delicate pink tinge. This pigment suffers no further breakdown during the development of the embryo but remains unchanged in the yolk; and, since the residue of the yolk is finally enclosed in the lumen of the stomach, if the newly hatched bug is dissected, its stomach is found to contain a deep red solution of kathaemoglobin, as though it had already taken a meal of blood. The salivary glands are colourless. During the first few days of life this inherited blood pigment is digested and a black residue of haematin appears in the intestine. At the same time a little of the pigment is absorbed and taken up by the salivary glands to produce their cherry red colour; so that when the young bug takes its first meal, a little of this altered haemoglobin is reinjected into the body of its host.

If laked blood is injected into the body cavity of *Rhodnius,* all these processes are exaggerated. The salivary glands become a deeper red. The pericardial cells become loaded with the same altered haematin pigment as occurs in the gut, together with the verdohaem intermediate, biliverdin and free iron. Enormous quantities of free iron accumulate in the cells of the gut wall. The same process occurs on a small scale in the cells of the Malpighian tubes; and the excessive quantities of biliverdin displaced from the pericardial cells are largely excreted by the Malpighian tubes where they fuse in the lumen to form the most beautiful blue-green droplets. The eggs are chocolate or purplish in colour, and the changes in the young bug are correspondingly exaggerated.

The various pigments resulting from the breakdown of haemoglobin do not appear to have any physiological significance in the insect. The normal content of cytochrome and free haematin (parahaematin) in the muscles remains unchanged throughout all these vicissitudes. But the story is of interest as illustrating the freedom with which the haemoglobin molecule may be passed around the tissues, and the ease with which its fate can be followed in the insect.

The extent to which haemoglobin is absorbed, and its subsequent fate, may be quite different in other blood-sucking arthropods. Some preliminary results are summarized in Table 1.

WOUND HEALING IN AN INSECT

The clarity and simplicity with which a physiological reaction can be demonstrated in the tissues of the insect may be illustrated in the phenomena of wound healing (Wigglesworth, 1937). The mammalian integument consists of epidermal cells, the Malpighian layer, continuously producing outer cells which in turn become progressively cornified and scale off. There is therefore a continual growth for maintenance. The integument of the insect, on the other hand, is composed of an epidermis one cell thick which undergoes periods of active growth, secretes a more or less sclerotized cuticle and then becomes quiescent. There is no continuous growth of maintenance; any cell divisions that are seen after injury therefore represent uncomplicated growth of repair. Furthermore, since the epidermis is made up of one cell layer alone it is easy to stain and mount the integument entire and so to observe the behaviour of every epidermal cell around a given injury in a single preparation.

On this material there is no difficulty in reproducing, with a

Table 1

Arthropod species	Haemolymph	Salivary glands	Pericardial cells	Malpighian tubes	Gut wall	Eggs
Anoplura						
Pediculus humanus	nil detectable	?	biliverdin and free iron	nil	biliverdin and free iron (in lumen only)	oxyhaemoglobin
Hemiptera						
Cimex lectularius		haemalbumen	nil	nil	nil	alkaline haematin
Rhodnius prolixus	kathaemoglobin	haemalbumen	biliverdin	nil	altered haematin, 'verdohaem', biliverdin and free iron	kathaemoglobin
Triatoma infestans	nil	nil	kathaemoglobin	biliverdin	protohaematin	nil
T. brasiliensis	nil	nil	biliverdin and free iron	biliverdin and free iron (traces)	altered haematin, 'verdohaem', biliverdin and free iron	nil
Eutriatoma sordida	nil	nil	bilirubin and biliverdin	biliverdin	nil	nil
Diptera						
Aëdes aegypti	nil	nil	nil	nil	nil	nil
Anopheles maculipennis	nil	nil	nil	nil	nil	nil
Siphonaptera						
Nosopsyllus fasciatus	nil	nil	nil	nil	nil	nil
Acarina						
Ornithodorus moubata	alkaline haematin	—	—	nil	protohaematin	alkaline haematin
Ixodes ricinus	? methaemalbumen	—	protohaematin	nil	protohaematin	alkaline haematin

minimum of effort, the results observed on wound healing in the vertebrate — or, indeed, of extending these observations in certain particulars. Incision or excision of the epidermis results in the enlargement and 'activation' of the surrounding cells. These cells appear to be stimulated by the peptones and polypeptides or other products of protein autolysis, and leaving their attachments to the cuticle they migrate to the site of injury. If the gap is a small one they proceed to spread over it, always maintaining contact with their neighbours by means of their cytoplasmic connexions, and cell divisions rarely occur at the actual point of injury. It is in the zone around where the cells have been rendered sparse by the inward migration of their fellows that the cell divisions are most numerous. Sparseness among activated cells seems to be the stimulus to cell division.

Meanwhile there are aggregations of the phagocytic blood cells at the site of injury, but they play no essential part in the fundamental process of repair. If the gap is very small the overcrowded epidermal cells along its margins are many more than are needed for repair. When continuity is restored the excess nuclei dissolve until their normal density is regained. It is possible to produce an abnormal sparseness among the epidermal cells by blocking the anus of the insect with paraffin while it is distended by a recent meal of blood. A wound is then followed by exaggerated cell divisions. By injecting fragments of autolyzing tissue below the intact epidermis, or even applying such material to the intact surface of the cuticle, all these responses can be evoked without any interruption to the continuity of the epidermis.

Autolysis is less evident at the margin of a burn. Here the aggregation of activated epidermal cells scarcely occurs, and the repair of a burn is effected by the cells along the margins, which spread inwards dividing as they go.

The thigmotactic spreading of epidermal cells during the healing process is reminiscent of that which takes place at the margin of a colony of cells in tissue culture. It is seen very strikingly if a cylindrical fragment of a limb, for example, is implanted into the abdomen of the insect; the epidermal cells spread outwards and backwards from the cut ends until they establish continuity with each other in the form of two superimposed sleeves of epidermis — a sort of dermoid cyst (Wigglesworth, 1934).

The chemotactic stimulus which initiates repair is short lived;

within 3 days after making one incision the cells can be attracted away from it to a new incision close by. The stimulus that persists derives from the lack of continuity at the margins of the epithelial sheet. What remains obscure in the insect, as in the vertebrate, is the nature of this continuity, the re-establishment of which brings repair to a standstill and mediates again the 'wholeness' of the organism. But it may well be that the insect can provide material for the hopeful study of this problem — the central problem of biology (Wigglesworth, 1948a).

RETENTION OF WATER BY THE INSECT: THE PROPERTIES OF THE CUTICLE

For the most part insects are terrestrial in habit and live in comparatively dry environments. Their small size renders them particularly liable to lose water by evaporation, and the need for retaining water provides a leading motive throughout their physiology — more dominant even than it is among terrestrial vertebrates. This is evident especially in the integument of insects; and although the properties of the integument are in many ways peculiar to the group, the subject does raise problems of physiology which are not entirely devoid of general interest.

The cuticle, as we have seen, is the product of a single layer of epidermal cells. According to the needs of the case it must be rigid, flexible or elastic, and at the same time it must be waterproof. Typically three layers are recognized: an *endocuticle* of chitin-protein micelles arranged in laminae; an *exocuticle* in which, according to Pryor (1940), the protein is tanned by quinones to form a hard brown or amber coloured 'sclerotin'; and an *epicuticle* which, we have recently come to realize, has a complex structure (Wigglesworth, 1945a, 1947, 1948b). It seems to consist of (a) a basic layer, less than 1 μm thick, of 'cuticulin' — condensed lipoprotein which has probably been tanned along with the exocuticle; (b) a layer of crystalline waxes, which Beament (1945) estimates as having an average thickness of 1·25 μm, responsible for waterproofing; and (c) a layer of 'cement' protecting the wax. Cytoplasmic filaments, fifty or more from each cell, run through the cuticle and end below the wax layer.

At intervals throughout its growth the insect moults; it first lays down a new and larger cuticle and then casts off the remnants of the old. As an illustration of the varied activities of which a single cell

109

may be capable, and of the nice timing with which these activities are co-ordinated, it is interesting to observe the stages in the deposition of the cuticle at this time.

The cells detach themselves from the old skin, multiply, arrange themselves in proper order, and then proceed to lay down the new cuticle. First they secrete the cuticulin layer of the epicuticle. This has the appearance of a somewhat refractile homogeneous sheet upon the surface; but I believe it to be pierced by cytoplasmic filaments from the cells, which will later form the pore canals. The cells next turn over to the deposition of the chitin and protein of the exocuticle. But almost at once there begins to exude from the tips of the pore canals a rather viscid fluid which will reduce ammoniacal silver. This secretion appears to consist of dihydroxyphenols, perhaps associated with protein. The minute droplets enlarge and spread, and gradually unite with one another to form a more or less continuous 'polyphenol layer'. Meanwhile the secretion of protein and chitin goes on, and these layers also, destined as they are to form the exocuticle, are likewise impregnated with phenolic substances.

During this process the epidermal cells are pouring out enzymes into the fluid which separates the two cuticles — a chitinase and a proteinase presumably — which digest the chitin and protein of the old endocuticle. And the same epidermal cells absorb the products of digestion through the substance of the new cuticle.

Then, an hour or so before the old skin is shed, the inner layers of the old cuticle having been absorbed, the new cuticle is rendered waterproof by the outpouring of the wax layer. This, too, is secreted by the epidermal cells and appears to crystallize out over the surface of the polyphenol layer so that ammoniacal silver applied to the surface of the new cuticle at this time has access to the polyphenols at a few points only.

The mechanism of secretion of this wax presents some interesting problems. Chibnall and Piper (1934) suggested that these long-chain waxes might be synthesized *in situ* at the surface of the cell from more diffusible materials. Lees and Beament (1948) have recently studied the secretion in bulk of the wax with which the tick waterproofs its eggs. They suggest that the wax is solubilized by association with protein, and that the protein is detached and perhaps reabsorbed as secretion is completed.

When the old cuticle is cast the surface of the new cuticle is completely hydrophobic. Droplets of water will not leave the tip of a waxed pipette to adhere to it. But within half an hour or so after moulting the surface becomes hydrophilic. That is because the numerous unicellular dermal glands which open on the surface of the cuticle now pour out their secretion of cement. This, too, appears to consist of phenol-tanned protein intimately associated with lipides. Finally, the epidermal cells secrete or activate the polyphenol oxidase and the tyrosinase which lead to the hardening and darkening of the cuticle. That completes what is, I think a rather impressive list of activities for a single cell.*

All the stages in this intricate process are nicely timed and synchronized throughout the body. But almost nothing is known of the mechanism by which co-ordination is achieved. Perhaps hormones, the secretion of which is controlled by the central nervous system, are responsible. Thus Fraenkel (1935) has observed that if the blowfly (*Calliphora*), which normally becomes hard and dark within an hour of emergence from the pupa, is obliged to burrow continuously through the soil, it will remain soft and pale for 6 or 7 h and then proceed to darken when it becomes free. Something of the same sort is seen in the mosquito larva *Aëdes* (Wigglesworth, 1938*b*). When this larva hatches from the egg the tracheal system is full of liquid. The young larva rises to the surface of the water, opens its spiracles to the atmosphere, and after a pause the liquid is slowly absorbed through the tracheal walls and the system fills with air. Absorption may be delayed for 3 days by keeping the larva submerged and yet take place normally on exposure to the air; but after 4 days some change has supervened and filling is never complete. Likewise, if the larvae of fleas are allowed to hatch in water and kept submerged for several days the tracheal system will no longer fill with air when the larvae are dried (Sikes and Wigglesworth, 1931). If the newly hatched mosquito larva is narcotized with chloroform and then placed with its spiracles open to the air, filling does not take place. After recovery from the

---

*Interpretations of cuticle structure, including that of the epicuticle, and details in the process of its deposition, have been modified in some important respects by more recent work. That concerns particularly the nature of the silver binding material (the mis-named 'polyphenol layer') and the incorporation of the waterproofing wax (Wigglesworth, 1975).

anaesthetic there is still a pause of 10 min or so and then the process begins. Clearly the nervous system is involved; yet there is no reason to suppose that the cells bounding the tracheal system are supplied with nerves.

Recent work on the cuticle has emphasized the constant association of chitin and protein. Indeed, in the latest classification of muco-proteins and the like (Stacey, 1943; Haworth, 1946), 'chitin' in the loose sense is referred to the group of mucopolysaccharides. That recalls the fact that, so far as is known, insects do not secrete mucus. In those forms which ingest with their food solid particles that might be expected to injure the delicate epithelium or which, maybe, are derived from ancestors that fed upon such things, the contents of the gut are separated from the wall by a so-called peritrophic membrane. This consists of chitin and protein, closely bound together. In many insects, such as caterpillars, grasshoppers and bees, it is produced as a secretion by the cells of the mid-intestine throughout its length and condenses as a many-layered sheath around the food. In other insects, of which the earwig, muscid flies, or the larvae of mosquitoes are examples, it is produced as a viscid secretion by a special group of cells at the anterior end of the mid-gut. This secretion is passed through an annular press in which it is condensed and moulded to form a cylindrical tube of uniform diameter and consistency in which the gut contents are enclosed. These annular moulds are of varied form and often of very elegant design (Wigglesworth, 1929, 1930a, 1939).

THE ROLE OF WATER IN EXCRETION

Throughout the animal kingdom water is a dominant factor in the excretion of waste nitrogen. The majority of insects, like birds and reptiles, eliminate their nitrogen almost wholly in the form of uric acid. The characteristic organs of excretion are the Malpighian tubes, blind vessels which lie free and independent of one another in the body fluid and discharge into the lumen of the gut where the proctodoeum joins the mesenteron. The Malpighian tubes afford exceptional opportunities for studying the physiology of excretion. In place of the tangled mass of tubules which compose the kidney, the physiologist can observe a single unravelled vessel in which it is easy to see in the living state any histological changes that take place.

In *Rhodnius* there are four Malpighian tubes, some 4 cm in length, each of which consists of an upper and a lower segment (Wigglesworth, 1931*a*). Both segments are lined by a conspicuous striated border the characters of which, as seen in histological sections, appear to be identical throughout. There has been much controversy in the past as to whether the striated border which lines the kidney tubules, for example, is really a 'brush border' made up of independent filaments arising from the cells or a 'honeycomb border' composed of rods or vesicles organically united with their neighbours.

It is interesting to observe that in the Malpighian tubes of *Rhodnius,* examined in the fresh state in the body fluid of the insect itself (very misleading results are obtained if so-called 'physiological solutions' are employed), the upper segment has a honeycomb border and the lower segment a brush border.* There is no gradual transition from one type to the other; the transformation is complete in adjacent cells. The lumen of the upper segment contains a clear fluid; the lower segment is filled with crystalline spheres of uric acid, and the smallest spheres can often be seen to lie in the free space between the filaments. Furthermore, during the early stages of excretion following a meal of blood, these filaments show some remarkable changes. The uric acid granules are first washed out as the excess fluid is eliminated. Then the filaments grow out and extend across the lumen, where they can be seen waving passively to and fro. Later the entire lumen may be filled for a time with these intermingling filaments entangling the granules of uric acid which are held stationary as in a gel. Later still the filaments contract down and the crystalline spheres are left free in the lumen. The interesting point is that I have never been able to recognize these curious changes in fixed material.

Solid uric acid appears in these tubes almost immediately below the change in cell type. The evidence goes to show that uric acid or urate is secreted in solution by the upper segment, while water and perhaps base are reabsorbed in the lower segment, leading to the crystallization of the free acid. For diffusible dyes, such as neutral

---

*More recent studies with the electron microscope (Wigglesworth and Salpeter, 1962) have revealed that the striated border of the upper segment also is actually a 'brush border' — but the microvilli are much more closely packed than in the lower segment.

red, introduced into the body fluid are quickly taken up by the cells of the upper segment, are discharged into the lumen, and only then appear in the cells of the lower segment. Indicators such as phenol red likewise appear first in the lumen of the upper segment; here the contents are faintly alkaline (pH 7·2). In the lower segment the contents are definitely acid (pH 6·6). Finally, it is possible to apply ligatures to the Malpighian tubes, in the form of tiny wax clamps, at a time when the uratic contents have been washed out. If a length of the lower segment is isolated in this way it shows no distension and no uric acid is deposited within it. Uric acid accumulates above and below the ligated section. (That below has clearly come from the other tubes and entered from the proximal extremity.)

One must conclude that there is a continuous circulation of water and perhaps of base carrying uric acid from the system and then being reabsorbed. After ingesting a feed of blood, *Rhodnius* excretes within the first 3 h some 75 per cent of the water in its meal. It may subsist on the remainder for 6 weeks or more, eliminating uric acid, during the first 2 weeks at least, at an average rate exceeding 0·5 mg/day — the weight of the insect being about 80 mg.

Not all insects have such distinct secretory and reabsorptive segments in the Malpighian tubes. In some, such as the mosquito *Aëdes,* uric acid appears in solid form in the lumen throughout the length of the tubes. Perhaps the same cells are concerned in both secretion and reabsorption. That is not known. But it is certain that insects are capable of holding uric acid in solution at concentrations far above saturation. Many insects deposit uric acid in solid form in various cells in the epidermis or in the fat body. In the larva of *Aëdes* (Wigglesworth, 1942*a*), alongside the reserve deposits of glycogen and fat, the cells of the fat body contain watery vacuoles. In the starved insect the reserves slowly disappear and the cells are filled with these greyish watery vacuoles alone, in a few of which a tiny crystal of uric acid can sometimes be seen. It is easy to observe a selected living cell from day to day under the highest powers of the microscope and then to add a fixative and to see that in each vacuole large wheatsheaf crystals of uric acid separate out.

In other insects, such as the louse *Pediculus* or the mealworm *Tenebrio,* the Malpighian tubes contain a clear fluid throughout their length. Uric acid separates only in the rectum, where there are large epithelial cells sometimes aggregated into so-called 'rectal glands'. There can be little doubt that these cells are concerned in reabsorbing water (Wigglesworth, 1932). In the mealworm, which is particularly well adapted to conserve water, the mixed urine and faecal residue is reduced to a bone-dry powder before it is discharged.

The rectum of the mosquito larva also has a lining of large epithelial cells. These too are clearly absorbing water; for it can readily be seen in the living insect that less water is being discharged from the anus than is reaching the rectum from the Malpighian tubes (Wigglesworth, 1933b). The aquatic larva of the mosquito is, of course, under no necessity to conserve water. This reabsorption is probably for the sake of valuable solutes such as chlorides (Boné and Koch, 1942). It may well be that the rectal glands of terrestrial insects are equally concerned in the conservation of chlorides and other salts (Patton and Craig, 1939).

In addition to these enlarged rectal cells, mosquito larvae have conspicuous 'anal papillae' [sometimes referred to as 'anal gills' — although they have almost no respiratory function (Wigglesworth, 1933b)], which are hollow finger-like protrusions made up of large epidermal cells. These are covered by a very thin cuticle which is readily permeable to water and to salts. Indeed, their epidermal cells provide wonderful material for observing the effects of ions on the cell substance — the swelling and dispersive action of monovalent ions, the cohesive action of divalent and trivalent ions (Wigglesworth, 1933a). Water is continually entering through these papillae to be excreted by the Malpighian tubes; but their main function seems to be the active uptake of chloride from the medium (Koch, 1938). A larva, whose blood chloride has been reduced from 0·3 per cent NaCl to 0·05 per cent by keeping for some days in distilled water, can restore its chloride content to the normal level within 24 h if placed in tap water with a chloride content of only 0·006 per cent. This it cannot do if it is deprived of its anal papillae. If larvae are reared in distilled water containing minimal quantities of chloride they show a functional hypertrophy of the anal papillae (Wigglesworth, 1938a). Surely there is material here well suited for the study of some of the more subtle problems of secretory activity.

WATER RETENTION IN RESPIRATION

All terrestrial animals are obliged to make some compromise between the need for holding water and the need for obtaining oxygen. In insects this is achieved by the provision of sphincters at the spiracular openings of the tracheal system. These are held firmly closed most of the time and opened only enough to meet the oxygen requirements (Hazelhoff, 1926). In most insects, indeed, the greater part of the water loss takes place by evaporation through the spiracles, and if these are kept open by exposure to 2 per cent carbon dioxide the insect rapidly dries up (Mellanby, 1934; Wigglesworth and Gillett, 1936).

The regulation of these respiratory movements, the opening and closing of the spiracles, presents some interesting parallels and contrasts with the control of respiratory movements in mammals. The matter can be very conveniently studied in the flea, which is a small insect that can readily be enclosed in a gas chamber and the opening and closing of the spiracles observed by transmitted light under the microscope (Wigglesworth, 1935). There are two pairs of thoracic and eight pairs of abdominal spiracles* of which the thoracic and the 1st and 8th abdominal are the most important in respiration. These spiracles are held closed in the fasting flea at rest. They open within a few seconds after muscular movements commence. When the general rate of metabolism is increased by feeding or by high temperature, they show a regular rhythmic opening and closing every few seconds. During the height of digestion, or during the development of eggs in the female, they are held continuously open.

Both oxygen lack and carbon dioxide excess contribute to the control of the respiratory rhythm. The closed spiracle is caused to open mainly by the exhaustion of oxygen in the tracheal system; but the amount of carbon dioxide which has accumulated in the tissues during the period of closure determines the length of time the spiracle will remain open. The duration of the open period is therefore more or less proportional to the duration of the closed period that precedes it. If the closed period is very short, as it is at high temperatures where the intensity of metabolism is increased or at low oxygen tensions where the oxygen in the system is soon used up, the open period is likewise shortened. Whereas at low tempera-

---

*In the paper quoted the author followed Lass (1905) in regarding the first abdominal spiracle as the third thoracic. It is more likely that the flea, like other insects, has only two pairs of thoracic spiracles.

tures or in pure oxygen, where the closed period is greatly prolonged, the open period is also prolonged.

The solubility of carbon dioxide in the tissue fluids has, indeed, the same effect in slowing up the respiratory responses as is characteristic of this gas as a respiratory stimulant in mammals. But the immediate stimulus to the respiratory centres, causing the spiracles to open, is probably acidity. Traces of lactic acid introduced into the circulation of the flea will shorten the respiratory rhythm; larger amounts will cause the spiracles to remain permanently open; and the same results appear if the flea is enclosed in a bubble surrounded by alkaline pyrogallol, in which both oxygen and carbon dioxide will be removed from the tissues.

The respiratory centres controlling these movements are distributed throughout the ganglia of the nervous system. Removal of the brain has no effect. After removal of the thoracic ganglia the response in the abdomen remains, although the sensitivity is reduced and there is a very slow reaction persisting, the nervous basis of which is not known, even when the entire central nervous system of the flea has been eliminated.

Thus the flea shows several adaptations to diminished concentrations of oxygen. Oxygen want is more quickly felt when the spiracles are closed; hence the centres are stimulated sooner and the spiracles open more frequently. There is an incomplete oxidation of metabolites, which probably lowers the pH towards the threshold level of stimulation of the centres and in this way contributes to the more frequent opening of the spiracles. The accumulation of metabolites indicates that the oxygen tension in the tissues is reduced. By increasing the difference in partial pressures, this will increase the rapidity of diffusion from the spiracle.

There is another interesting phenomenon which results from the incomplete oxidation of metabolites (Wigglesworth, 1930*b*, 1931*b*, 1935, 1938*a*). The tracheae end by breaking up into very fine thin-walled tracheoles. The lining membrane of these is permeable to water, which can thus enter the lumen and be drawn along them by capillarity. The height to which this fluid rises is determined by the balance between the capillarity of the tracheole, which diminishes, of course, as the diameter increases, and the swelling pressure of the cytoplasm bounding the wall of the vessels. The swelling pressure may be influenced by changes in the surrounding tissues or tissue fluids, notably by the changes in osmotic pressure which result from

117

the incomplete oxidation of metabolites, so that in the asphyxiated insect the liquid is absorbed and air extends into the fine endings of the tracheoles. This has the effect of increasing the surface area over which oxygen can diffuse into the tissues and of doing this most rapidly in those tissues which are most active and whose needs are therefore greatest.

In the abdomen of the flea at rest in air the liquid in the tracheoles rises high up the tubes. After violent muscular activity at room temperature, the air extends a little farther down. At 35 °C this downward movement of air after struggling is more extensive; indeed, in many of the tracheoles the meniscus is moving up or down almost the whole time. But in the insect at rest there is no difference in the equilibrium level at 17 or 35 °C. On the other hand, when the oxygen in the air is reduced to say 10 per cent, the equilibrium position in the tracheoles when the flea is at rest is definitely changed; the air extends more deeply into the tissues. In a 5 per cent mixture of oxygen the air extends still further, and in nitrogen containing 0·8 per cent of oxygen the gas reaches such fine tubes that its limit cannot be seen with the microscope.

Clearly there is an accumulation of metabolites that is arrested at a point which depends upon the partial pressure of oxygen in the atmosphere. Equilibrium between oxygen supply and oxygen consumption is then restored, a constant level of oxygen debt remaining. Even in air a certain accumulation exists, which can be removed in oxygen; for on going from air to oxygen the equilibrium point to which gas extends in the tracheoles, retreats appreciably towards the wider part of the tubes.

HORMONES CONTROLLING GROWTH AND REPRODUCTION

Since the days of Brown-Séquard it has been known that growth in vertebrates is largely controlled by circulating hormones coming in part from cells of internal secretion associated with the gonads, in part from special ductless glands. Attempts were early made to repeat these observations on insects. But neither castration nor implantation of gonads had any influence upon their secondary sexual characters, and, quite gratuitously, the general conclusion was drawn, and the dogma became accepted, that insects have no endocrine organs and secrete no hormones.

In recent years this conclusion has been disproved, and the

regulation of growth by chemical means has been demonstrated in many insects. The possibilities of the material may be illustrated from the observations made on *Rhodnius,* which has proved admirably suited to studies of this kind (Wigglesworth, 1934, 1936, 1940*a*, 1940*b*). *Rhodnius* has five larval, or nymphal, stages before it turns into an adult; and in each of these it takes a single gigantic meal of blood. The nymphs have great powers of resistance to starvation and can survive unfed for many weeks. But if they get a meal of blood above a certain size, which distends the abdomen above a certain degree, a nervous stimulus is carried to the brain and causes certain large nerve cells (neurosecretory cells), lying in the dorsum of the protocerebrum, to secrete a 'moulting hormone'.

Under the influence of this hormone, the epidermal cells leave the old cuticle, grow and divide. Mitosis is, indeed, so exuberant that far more cells are produced than will be needed to lay down the new cuticle (Wigglesworth, 1942*b*). The unwanted cells therefore die. Even while still more cells are being produced, scattered everywhere among them are basophil droplets derived from the dissolution of the unwanted nuclei. This fever of growth and decay lasts for several days, but by 10 days after feeding it is almost at an end; the excess nuclei have melted away, and a regular epithelium with nuclei regularly spaced is ready to begin the deposition of the new cuticle. In due time the old skin is cast off; at a fixed interval after feeding the insect moults.

Throughout the five nymphal stages there is comparatively little change in the body form of *Rhodnius.* The abdomen, for example, bears scattered plaques each carrying a bristle between which the epicuticle is thrown into star-shaped folds. In order to accommodate the great meal of blood that is taken in each instar the inner layers of the cuticle stretch, the stellate folds become partially smoothed out. In the adult, on the other hand, bristles are very scanty on the upper surface of the abdomen, there are no plaques, the epicuticle is thrown into folds running transversely across the abdomen, and the outer parts of the cuticle are sclerotized and therefore incapable of being stretched. The distending meals of blood are accommodated in the adult by the provision of a pleat along either side of the abdomen. This first unfolds, and then a part of it, composed of soft elastic cuticle, stretches to a prodigious extent (Wigglesworth, 1933*c*).

These detailed differences in the cuticle of the abdomen provide a useful indication of the degree of metamorphosis achieved when the abdominal cuticle is viewed by itself. But the more closely the general changes that take place at the moulting of the 5th stage nymph are studied, the more striking does the metamorphosis to the adult appear. There are elaborate changes in the thorax with the development of wings: climbing or adhesive organs appear on the tibiae of the first two pairs of legs (Gillett and Wigglesworth, 1932); ocelli are formed for the first time; the colour pattern of the abdomen is quite different; and the complicated external genitalia are developed.

If a *Rhodnius* nymph is decapitated within a day or so after feeding, it is deprived of the source of the moulting hormone in the secreting cells of the brain, and it fails to moult — although such headless insects have remained alive for more than a year. Some 4 to 8 days after feeding there is a critical period which marks the time when sufficient of the moulting hormone has been secreted, and when this period has passed moulting takes place even in the decapitated insect. If the nymph decapitated soon after feeding is joined by means of a capillary tube to a nymph with the head intact or to a nymph that has passed the critical period, so that the blood flows from one to the other, the decapitated nymph is caused to moult. Moulting can likewise be induced in the headless nymph by implanting into its abdomen that region of the brain which contains the neurosecretory cells.

It is characteristic of many insects that from time to time growth ceases and they enter upon a state of 'diapause'. The arrested growth which supervenes in the decapitated *Rhodnius* nymph has much in common with natural diapause; which suggests that the immediate cause of diapause may be a failure in the secretion of the hormones necessary for growth. This idea has been substantiated by the recent work of Williams (1946, 1947, 1948) on the pupal diapause of the giant silk moths. Doubtless many different factors may be responsible in different insects for the arrest of secretion. In *Rhodnius* a natural diapause does not occur — save in those insects which do not ingest a meal large enough to stretch the abdomen to the requisite degree. But the normal *Rhodnius* always harbours in its gut a symbiotic bacterium, *Actinomyces rhodnii*, which is essential for the nutrition of its host (Brecher and Wigglesworth, 1944). Apparently it produces certain vitamins, probably of the B group, which are deficient in blood. If *Rhodnius* is reared under sterile conditions so as to be freed of its *Actinomyces,* it goes into a state of diapause and will not grow beyond the 4th or 5th stage. Perhaps the vitamins synthesized by this micro-organism provide the raw material for the production of the moulting hormone.

This moulting hormone secreted by the brain appears to be the same in each nymphal stage. But the characters developed by the moulting insect, that is, the occurrence or non-occurrence of metamorphosis, are determined by another hormone (or group of hormones) secreted by the corpus allatum. The corpus allatum bears much the same relation to the neurosecretory cells of the proto-cerebrum as the hypophysis of vertebrates does to the neurosecretory cells of the hypothalamus — it is a small ductless gland which appears to derive its nerve supply from that source (Hanström, 1941; Scharrer and Scharrer, 1944). Throughout the early nymphal stages the corpus allatum secretes what may be called a 'juvenile hormone', the function of which is to maintain the youthful character of the insect and to deter it from metamorphosis into an adult before it is fully grown. During the moulting of the first four nymphal stages this secretion is active and nymphal characters are retained; during the moulting of the 5th-stage nymph the corpus allatum no longer secretes the juvenile hormone, the latent adult characters are realized and metamorphosis takes place.

Recently some evidence has been obtained that the corpus allatum of the 5th stage nymph not only ceases to secrete the juvenile hormone but actively absorbs from the blood any traces of the hormone which remain (Wigglesworth, 1948c). If that is confirmed it will represent a new principle in the activity of endocrine organs. Later still, in the adult insect, the corpus allatum begins once more to secrete the juvenile hormone, and this secretion is necessary for the deposition of yolk in the eggs by the female and the full development of the accessory sexual glands of the male.

Thus if any insect of the first four nymphal stages is deprived of its corpus allatum by decapitation and is then induced to moult by transfusion from the moulting 5th-stage nymph it will suffer a premature metamorphosis. Even the 1st stage nymph, transfused from the moulting 5th stage insect, will turn into a diminutive adult. Conversely, if corpora allata from 3rd or 4th stage nymphs are implanted into the abdomen of the 5th stage nymph, when this moults it develops nymphal characters again, instead of transforming into an adult. The experiment may be repeated, and a giant 7th

INSECTS AND THE LIFE OF MAN

stage nymph has been produced. Sometimes the experiment is less successful and, instead of an extra nymphal stage being produced, an adult is developed which has a little patch of nymphal cuticle over the site at which the corpus allatum was implanted. Around such a patch the cuticle is intermediate in character, and gradually this merges into cuticle of adult type.

One must regard the growing insect as a differentiated continuum or mosaic in which there exist two systems, or one system susceptible to two types of development, nymphal and adult. Reaction with the appropriate hormones decides when and which of these shall become manifest. Taking the simplest case of an ordinary epidermal cell of the abdominal wall, one may picture the cell as containing two enzyme systems. One produces adult cuticle and is activated by the moulting hormone. The other produces nymphal cuticle and is activated by the moulting hormone only in the presence of the juvenile hormone — which may perhaps be looked upon as a sort of 'coenzyme'. In the presence of this coenzyme the nymphal system takes precedence over the adult, and nymphal cuticle is laid down.

It is interesting to note that even after metamorphosis to the adult form, the nymphal system may persist latent within the cells. For it is possible, by transfusion with blood from several moulting 5th stage nymphs, to induce the adult *Rhodnius* to moult again and to develop a new cuticle whose characters are wholly adult. But if a number of corpora allata from 3rd or 4th stage nymphs are first implanted into the abdomen, so that juvenile hormone is present in the blood, there is a partial *reversal* of metamorphosis when the adult moults; the cuticle of the abdomen develops plaques and folds approximating to those of the nymph. It shows, in fact, a genuine rejuvenation.

In the converse experiment, when metamorphosis is produced experimentally in the 1st stage nymph soon after hatching from the egg, the epidermis of the miniature adult that results is made up of less than one-hundredth part of the number of cells which compose the normal adult. This simple observation alone shows how limited is the importance of the cells in defining the form of the body. The cells do not 'co-operate to mould the body form', they seem merely to carry and care for a small segment of the continuum which is the organism and of which they are the servants. The movements and secretions which bring about the visible process of growth and metamorphosis are, of course, the products of the cells. But the cells are only the agents of the pervading web which is the organism itself (Wigglesworth, 1945*b*, 1948*a*).

Whether insects will provide good material for the isolation and characterization of hormones by chemical means remains to be seen. But they can unquestionably afford wonderful material for the study of those subtle problems connected with the analysis of growth and its regulation, with the moulding of the body form, and ultimately with the nature of the organism.

CONCLUSION

It has not been possible in the course of one lecture to give a systematic account of what is peculiar in the physiology of insects. It seemed to me, moreover, that it would serve no useful purpose to devote our time wholly to generalities. I have therefore chosen a few specific examples, drawn for the most part from those aspects of the subject with which I happen personally to have been concerned, and have submitted these in the hope of exciting the sympathetic interest of the physiologist. It is scarcely needful to point out that the studies which have been made are of necessity superficial, and the account of them presented in this lecture more trivial still. This is a world in which nuggets in profusion lie upon the surface. But I hope I may have said enough to prove that rich veins of gold await the real specialist who cares to utilize the insect as a medium for the advancement of physiology.

REFERENCES

Beament, J. W. L. (1945) The cuticular lipoids of insects. *J. Exp. Biol.,* **21,** 115—131.

Boné, G. and Koch, H. J. (1942) Le rôle des tubes de Malpighi et du rectum dans la régulation ionique chez les insectes. *Ann. Soc. Roy. Zool. Belg.,* **73,** 73—87.

Brecher, G. and Wigglesworth, V. B. (1944) The transmission of *Actinomyces rhodnii* Erikson in *Rhodnius prolixus* Stål (Hemiptera) and its influence on the growth of the host. *Parasitology,* **35,** 220—224.

Chibnall, A. C. and Piper, S. H. (1934) The metabolism of plant and insect waxes. *Biochem. J.,* **28,** 2209—2219.

Fraenkel, G. (1935) Observations and experiments on the blowfly (*Calliphora erythrocephala*) during the first day after emergence. *Proc. Zool. Soc. Lond.,* 893—904.

Gillett, J. D. and Wigglesworth, V. B. (1932) The climbing organ of an insect, *Rhodnius prolixus* (Hemiptera, Reduviidae). *Proc. Roy. Soc. B.,* **111,** 364—376.

Hanström, B. (1941) Einige Parallelen im Bau und in der Herkunft der inkretorischen Organe der Arthropoden und der Vertebraten. *Acta Univ. lund. N.F., Avd.,* 2. **37,** No. 4, 1—19.

Haworth, W. N. (1946) The structure, function and synthesis of polysaccharides. *Proc. Roy. Soc. A.,* **186,** 1—19.

Hazelhoff, E. H. (1926) Regeling der ademhaling bij insecten en spinnen. Thesis, Utrecht.

Koch, H. (1938) The absorption of chloride ions by the anal papillae of Diptera larvae. *J. Exp. Biol.,* **15,** 152—160.

Lass, M. (1905) Beiträge zur Kenntnis des histologisch-anatomischen Baues des weiblichen Hundeflohes (*Pulex canis* Dugès u. *Pulex serraticeps* Taschenberg). *Z. wiss. Zool.,* **79,** 73—131.

Lees, A. D. and Beament, J. W. L. (1948) An egg-waxing organ in ticks. *Quart. J. Micr. Sci.,* **89,** 291—332.

Lemberg, R., Legge, L. W. and Lockwood, W. H. (1939) Coupled oxidation of ascorbic acid and haemoglobin. *Biochem. J.,* **33,** 754—758.

Lemberg, R., Legge, L. W. and Lockwood, W. H. (1941) Formation and properties of choleglobin. *Biochem. J.,* **35,** 328—338.

Mellanby, K. (1934) The site of loss of water from insects. *Proc. Roy. Soc. B.,* **116,** 139—149.

Patton, R. L. and Craig, R. (1939) The rates of excretion of certain substances by the larvae of the mealworm, *Tenebrio molitor* L. *J. Exp. Zool.,* **81,** 437—457.

Pryor, M. G. M. (1940) On the hardening of the cuticle of insects. *Proc. Roy. Soc. B.,* **128,** 393—407.

Scharrer, B. and Scharrer, E. (1944) Neurosecretion. vi. A comparison between the intercerebralis-cardiacum-allatum system of the insects and the hypothalamo-hypophyseal system of the vertebrates. *Biol. Bull. Woods Hole,* **87,** 242—251.

Sikes, E. K. and Wigglesworth, V. B. (1931) The hatching of insects from the egg, and the appearance of air in the tracheal system. *Quart. J. Micr. Sci.,* **74,** 165—192.

Stacey, M. (1943) Mucopolysaccharides and related substances. *Chem. & Ind.,* **62,** 110—112.

Wigglesworth, V. B. (1929) Digestion in the tsetse-fly: a study of structure and function. *Parasitology,* **21,** 288—321.

Wigglesworth, V. B. (1930a) The formation of the peritrophic membrane in insects, with special reference to the larvae of mosquitoes. *Quart. J. Micr. Sci.,* **73,** 593—616.

Wigglesworth, V. B. (1930b) A theory of tracheal respiration in insects. *Proc. Roy. Soc. B.,* **106,** 229—250.

Wigglesworth, V. B. (1931a) The physiology of excretion in a blood-sucking insect, *Rhodnius prolixus* (Hemiptera, Reduviidae). *J. Exp. Biol.,* **8,** 411—451.

Wigglesworth, V. B. (1931b) The extent of air in the tracheoles of some terrestrial insects. *Proc. Roy. Soc. B.,* **109,** 354—359.

Wigglesworth, V. B. (1932) On the function of the so-called 'rectal glands' of insects. *Quart J. Micr. Sci.,* **75,** 131—150.

Wigglesworth, V. B. (1933a) The effect of salts on the anal gills of the mosquito larva. *J. Exp. Biol.,* **10,** 1—15.

Wigglesworth, V. B. (1933b) The function of the anal gills of the mosquito larva. *J. Exp. Biol.*, **10**, 16—26.

Wigglesworth, V. B. (1933c) The physiology of the cuticle and of ecdysis in *Rhodnius prolixus* (Triatomidae, Hemiptera); with special reference to the function of the oenocytes and of the dermal glands. *Quart. J. Micr. Sci.*, **76**, 270—318.

Wigglesworth, V. B. (1934) The physiology of ecdysis in *Rhodnius prolixus* (Hemiptera). II. Factors controlling moulting and 'metamorphosis'. *Quart. J. Micr. Sci.*, **77**, 191—222.

Wigglesworth, V. B. (1935) The regulation of respiration in the flea. *Xenopsylla cheopis*, Roths. (Pulicidae). *Proc. Roy. Soc.* B., **118**, 397—419.

Wigglesworth, V. B. (1936) The function of the corpus allatum in the growth and reproduction of *Rhodnius prolixus* (Hemiptera). *Quart. J. Micr. Sci.*, **79**, 91—121.

Wigglesworth, V. B. (1937) Wound healing in an insect (*Rhodnius prolixus* Hemiptera). *J. Exp. Biol.*, **14**, 364—381.

Wigglesworth, V. B. (1938a) The regulation of osmotic pressure and chloride concentration in the haemolymph of mosquito larvae. *J. Exp. Biol.*, **15**, 235—247.

Wigglesworth, V. B. (1938b) The absorption of fluid from the tracheal system of mosquito larvae at hatching and moulting. *J. Exp. Biol.*, **15**, 248—254.

Wigglesworth, V. B. (1939) *The Principles of Insect Physiology.* London: Methuen.

Wigglesworth, V. B. (1940a) Local and general factors in the development of 'pattern' in *Rhodnius prolixus* (Hemiptera). *J. Exp. Biol.*, **17**, 180—200.

Wigglesworth, V. B. (1940b) The determination of characters at metamorphosis in *Rhodnius prolixus* (Hemiptera). *J. Exp. Biol.*, **17**, 201—222.

Wigglesworth, V. B. (1942a) The storage of protein, fat, glycogen and uric acid in the fat body and other tissues of mosquito larvae. *J. Exp. Biol.*, **19**, 56—77.

Wigglesworth, V. B. (1942b) The significance of 'chromatic droplets' in the growth of insects. *Quart. J. Micr. Sci.*, **83**, 141—152.

Wigglesworth, V. B. (1943) The fate of haemoglobin in *Rhodnius prolixus* (Hemiptera) and other blood-sucking arthropods. *Proc. Roy. Soc.* B., **131**, 313—339.

Wigglesworth, V. B. (1945a) Transpiration through the cuticle of insects. *J. Exp. Biol.*, **21**, 97—114.

Wigglesworth, V. B. (1945b) Growth and Form in an insect. *Essays on Growth and Form.* Oxford University Press.

Wigglesworth, V. B. (1947) The epicuticle in an insect, *Rhodnius prolixus* (Hemiptera). *Proc. Roy. Soc.* B., **134**, 163—181.

Wigglesworth, V. B. (1948a) The role of the cell in determination. I. Growth changes in *Rhodnius prolixus. Symposia Soc. Exp. Biol.*, **2**, 1—16.

Wigglesworth, V. B. (1948b) The structure and deposition of the cuticle in the adult mealworm, *Tenebrio molitor* L. (Coleoptera). *Quart. J. Micr. Sci.*, **89**, 197—217.

Wigglesworth, V. B. (1948c) The functions of the corpus allatum in *Rhodnius prolixus* (Hemiptera). *J. Exp. Biol.*, **25**, 1—14.

Wigglesworth, V. B. (1975) Incorporation of lipid into the epicuticle of *Rhodnius* (Hemiptera). *J. Cell Sci.*, **19**, 459—485.

Wigglesworth, V. B. and Gillett, J. D. (1936) The loss of water during ecdysis in *Rhodnius prolixus* Stål. (Hemiptera). *Proc. R. Ent. Soc. Lond.* A., **11**, 104—107.

Wigglesworth, V. B. and Salpeter, M. M. (1962) Histology of the Malpighian tubules in *Rhodnius prolixus* Stål. (Hemiptera). *J. Ins. Physiol.,* **8,** 299—307.

Williams, C. M. (1946) Physiology of insect diapause: the role of the brain in the production and termination of pupal dormancy in the giant silkworm, *Platysamia cecropia. Biol. Bull. Woods Hole,* **90,** 234—243.

Williams, C. M. (1947) Physiology of insect diapause. II. Interaction between the pupal brain and prothoracic glands in the metamorphosis of the giant silkworm, *Platysamia cecropia. Biol. Bull. Woods Hole,* **93,** 89—98.

Williams, C. M. (1948) Physiology of insect diapause. III. The prothoracic glands in the Cecropia silkworm, with special reference to their significance in embryonic and postembryonic development. *Biol. Bull. Woods Hole,* **94,** 60—65.

11

THE CONTRIBUTIONS OF
SIR JOHN LUBBOCK (LORD AVEBURY)
TO INSECT PHYSIOLOGY

Dr. Neave's *History of the Entomological Society of London,* published on the occasion of our centenary in 1933, contains, among much other interesting matter, brief biographies of twenty distinguished Fellows. At that time I was a junior member of Council, and, as I well remember, there were naturally some differences of opinion about the selection of the names to be included in this list. Some of us pressed for the inclusion of the name of John Lubbock; but the President, Professor Poulton, was adamant on this point; for he maintained that in his later years Lord Avebury had lost interest in the work of the Society. I am venturing to use the present opportunity to make good what I felt to be an unfortunate omission on that occasion.

The remarkable achievements of John Lubbock in the world of affairs and in the world of science will be well known to most of you. But before touching on his contributions to entomology and, particularly, to insect physiology, I would remind you briefly of his career.

Sir John Lubbock, 4th Baronet, was born in 1834, one year after the foundation of our Society, and he died in 1913. His father was a banker of distinguished mathematical ability, for many years treasurer of the Royal Society. The young John Lubbock was sent to Eton at the age of eleven; but his services were soon required in the bank and he left school before he was fifteen. In banking he soon showed exceptional capacity, and before long he assumed responsibility for an important share in the management, and in due course he became the first President of the Institute of Bankers. At the age of twenty-two he inaugurated two important reforms: the system of Country Clearing, and the publication of clearing house returns, for which measures he secured the agreement of all the

English banks. In the same year he got married, and he did the work on the reproduction of *Daphnia* which earned his election to the Royal Society two years later.

Lubbock was persuaded to enter Parliament as Liberal M.P. for Maidstone in 1870 and remained there until he was raised to the peerage as Lord Avebury in 1900. He never accepted office but he was extremely active and promoted many private bills. His best known effort was his first — the Bank Holidays Act of 1871. It was not apparent from the title that these were to be national holidays and not confined to Bank employees — otherwise the Bill would not have gone through so easily. Certainly that achievement has been a tremendous boon to entomologists; at one time the first Monday in August used to be known as 'St. Lubbock's Day'. By contrast the Early Closing Act of 1904 took 30 years to get onto the Statute Book, and the Act for the Preservation of Ancient Monuments had many failures before it was passed in 1882. Altogether he sponsored some thirty successful bills, aimed at improving social conditions, conservation of nature (for example, the protection of wild birds) and many other matters. His record as a backbencher has never been approached by others and will certainly never be repeated.

But his career in banking and his work in Parliament were only two examples of Lubbock's activities in public life. I do not propose to give you a catalogue of his varied doings. My purpose here is merely to give some indication of the crowded life that formed the background to his contributions to science.

From his earliest years Lubbock had a remarkable capacity for concentration, for the organization of his daily timetable, and for switching his interest at a moment's notice to completely different topics.* After leaving school at the age of fourteen he set himself to make good his uncompleted education by systematic study. He became a prolific author, and as a popularizer of science (who always had some original thoughts to offer) and as an intellectual and moral mentor of the general public, he had a vogue which is almost without parallel — and which has indeed done much to

---

Punch wrote of him as follows:

'How doth the Banking Busy Bee
Improve the shining hours?
By studying on Bank Holidays
Strange insects and wild flowers'

obscure the originality of so many of his own contributions. The moralizing in his writings is out of fashion; the style, packed with quotations, strikes us as Victorian and sententious; but these books sold in hundreds of thousands to the newly educated classes for whom they were written.

Lubbock suffered, also, from being labelled an 'amateur' — the amateur archaeologist who first clearly distinguished the hunting Palaeolithic from the agricultural Neolithic cultures, and gave them these now familiar names; who played a prominent part in discovering the famous early Iron Age burials and cremations of Halstatt in Austria; who saved Avebury, the finest megalithic monument in Europe, by buying it under the nose of the speculative builder, and who saved Stonehenge from a branch line of the London and South Western Railway. He was the amateur paleontologist who (on a walk before breakfast with Charles Kingsley) found the first fossil musk-ox to be recorded in Britain, and concluded that the river gravel in which it was found had been laid down in glacial times. He was the amateur zoologist who discovered and named *Pauropus* from rubbish in his garden and suggested that it was a primitive sort of centipede (and to the present day we have not got very much further than that). He was the amateur entomologist who in 1871 wrote the Ray Society volume on the Collembola and Thysanura. This volume contains much that was new at the time; indeed, it was Lubbock who first recognized that these insects form two distinct orders and who proposed the name Collembola. He was the amateur entomologist who on a holiday in Switzerland in 1862 discovered that the little egg parasite which he named *Polynema natans* uses its wings for swimming under water.

The Lubbocks resided at Down. John was still a small boy when their distinguished neighbour came to live there. At the Darwin—Wallace Celebration, in 1908, Lord Avebury remarked: 'I first heard his name in 1842, when I was just eight years old. My father returned one evening from the City, and said he had a great piece of good news for me. He excited my hopes and curiosity, and at last announced that Mr. Darwin was coming to live at Down. I confess I was disappointed, I thought at least he was going to give me a pony! But my father was right. I little realized what it meant to me, nor how it would alter my whole life.' Darwin persuaded the father to let the boy have a microscope. They became great friends; and in his later years Darwin confessed that he relied on the opinions of three men only: Hooker, Huxley and Lubbock; and of these he inclined to put Lubbock first, on account of 'the course of your studies and the clarity of your mind'. Although T. H. Huxley is usually credited with fighting Darwin's battles for him and breaking down public opposition to the doctrine of natural selection, it is likely, as Pumphrey has pointed out, that Lubbock with his lucid and persuasive writing and his avoidance of polemics really did far more to win men's minds to the acceptance of Darwin's theories.

Lubbock's interest in entomology started when he was very young. He recorded that his earliest outstanding memories were a glimpse of Queen Victoria's coronation procession and 'the sight of a large insect under glass'. He joined our Society in 1850 at the age of sixteen. He served on the Council, and many times as Vice-President. He was President in 1866—67 and again in 1879—80 — but of course one must remember that he was also president of twenty-five other learned societies and at least an equal number of professional and governmental bodies. His portrait hangs in our rooms at the top of the first flight of stairs. Our library catalogue lists 33 entomological items extending from 1853, when he was nineteen, until 1899 when, at the age of sixty-five, he was describing some new Australian Collembola; but this list is certainly far from complete.

It will not serve a useful purpose to catalogue all the minutiae of Lubbock's contributions to entomology. I want merely to demonstrate that he made major contributions in methods and in ideas to entomology and to insect physiology — and that these methods and ideas still play a part in our thought today. His chief claim to fame as a biologist lies in the fact that he was a pioneer in the experimental study of behaviour.

The originality of his approach was very evident in his work on the colour vision of bees. Since the time of Sprengel in the eighteenth century it had been assumed that the colours of flowers served for the attraction of insects; and from this it was inferred that insects can distinguish colours. Lubbock set about testing the matter experimentally. He trained bees to visit honey smeared on pieces of glass which were laid on differently coloured papers. By moving the glasses around he showed that bees always visited the colour to which they had been trained; that they had an inborn preference for blue; and that they were unable to distinguish red from black. He concluded that this colour choice was not a preference for brightness as such because they paid no attention to sheets of glass placed over white paper.

This method of 'training' has been of enormous value in elucidating the sensory perceptions of insects. Under the name of 'Dressur' it has been used extensively by the German school led by v. Frisch. It was the invention of Lubbock.

In the early years of the present century Carl v. Hess was asserting that bees could not distinguish colour qualities: all they were doing was distinguishing parts of the spectrum of different apparent brightness. In 1914 v. Frisch published his classic paper which refuted this point of view. His methods were those which Lubbock had devised forty years earlier: the training of bees to come to feed on syrup placed on glass over papers of different colour. v. Frisch made one addition to Lubbock's experiments: besides plain white paper as used by Lubbock he employed a series of shades of grey arranged as a chequer board with some squares coloured. He showed that the bees could not be trained to come to any particular shade of grey. This was a most useful improvement in dealing with the arguments of v. Hess. v. Frisch, of course, refers to Lubbock's experiments; but subsequent authors have not done so and the experiment of v. Frisch is commonly regarded as the original demonstration of colour vision in the bee.

A very important point, however, was not touched upon by v. Frisch. In a classic experiment in 1876 Lubbock had shown that if a colony of *Formica fusca* or *Lasius niger* was illuminated with the colours of the spectrum they quickly carried their brood to one or other of the dark ends. At the long-wave end they were content to deposit the brood in the infrared, just at the limit of our visible spectrum. But at the short-wave end they carried the brood well beyond the zone in the violet that is visible to our eyes; they appeared to be highly sensitive to ultraviolet. If this zone were shaded by a thin layer of carbon disulphide or quinine sulphate, to absorb the ultraviolet, although this made no difference at all to the human eye, the ants were now prepared to deposit the brood in the shaded zone.

Lubbock realised that he was using ultraviolet rays of very low intensity; he therefore concluded that this was no mere irritant effect of ultraviolet but that 'ultraviolet rays must make themselves apparent to the ants as a distinct and separate colour (of which we can form no idea) . . . white light to these insects would differ from our white light in containing this additional colour'. Since the reflection of ultraviolet by diverse objects must vary just like the colours visible to us he concluded 'that the colours of objects and the general aspect of nature must present to them a very different appearance from what it does to us'.

The possibility therefore remained that the coloured papers used by v. Frisch might be recognised by the bee through their reflecting more ultraviolet than any of the grey papers employed. This was excluded by the experiments of Alfred Kühn (1927) who showed that bees could be trained to visit patches of pure spectral light projected upon a screen. Meanwhile F. E. Lutz (1924) in the United States had followed up Lubbock's suggestion about the differences in ultraviolet reflection of natural objects. He showed that flowers differ greatly in the amount of ultraviolet they reflect. Many which appear uniformly yellow to us appear to have a black centre when photographed through an ultraviolet screen. He showed that many insects are strongly attracted to screens emitting only ultraviolet rays and that bees (*Trigona*) could distinguish process-white which reflects ultraviolet, from Chinese white which does not, although these paints appear alike to the human eye (Lutz, 1933). In more recent years these matters have been explored in detail by Lotmar (1933), Hertz (1939), and Daumer (1958) and Lubbock's conclusions have been fully substantiated — although his work is usually not quoted.

Lubbock's most extensive experiments were carried out on ants. He realized that the way to study their behaviour closely would be to maintain cultures in captivity for long periods. He therefore took great pains in devising the method of setting up ant colonies in earth between sheets of glass. The method proved highly successful and has continued in use unchanged to the present day. The ingenious experiments which he carried out with these cultures occupy a large part of his book on *Ants, Bees and Wasps* first published in 1882. I cannot attempt to summarize this work here; but it is worth while listing some of the familiar methods that we use today, and some of the familiar features of ant behaviour, which were first devised or discovered by Lubbock.

He was the first to mark particular insects and was able to assure himself that workers of *Lasius niger* and *Formica fusca* remained alive at least seven years, and he kept alive two queens of these species for more than thirteen and fourteen years respectively. He showed for the first time that an isolated female ant could rear her young to maturity. He proved that the eggs of aphids were carried by ants into their nests for the winter and that when they hatched in the spring the larvae were taken out and placed on their proper food plants. He formed the opinion (now generally shared) that ants possess the power of developing a given egg into either a queen or a worker. On one occasion only did he rear queens (of *Formica fusca*) in captivity and concluded that this was brought about by the abundant animal protein in their diet — a view often expressed today.

Most of the key discoveries relating to the homing of ants were made by Lubbock. He showed that the methods used are different in different species, and that they vary with the circumstances. He demonstrated the importance of scent trails and proved that ants followed the road marked out by these odours but that they could not distinguish the direction to or from the nest. On the other hand there were times when ants showed a quite uncanny 'sense of direction'. He proved that this was dependent on the direction of the incident light — the so-called 'sun compass' reaction. The sun compass reaction was reinvestigated much later by Santschi (1911) and Brün (1914).

Since then two major advances have been made in this field. Firstly, it was shown by v. Frisch (1950) that bees can steer not only by the position of the sun but by the pattern of polarized light in the blue sky. These observations were extended to ants by Vowles (1954) and by students of v. Frisch (1950). It is now known that the same capacity is widely spread among insects. Secondly, it has been found in recent years that ants and bees and other insects not only steer by the sun but they are able to compensate for the changing position of the sun at different times of the day. By combining this sense of time with the capacity to orientate by the sun, or by the pattern of polarized light in the blue sky, insects are capable of an elementary type of astronomical navigation (Lindauer, 1961). That is a good deal further than Lubbock got; he was not successful in the few studies he made on the homing of bees — but the foundations were his.

Lubbock also discovered a group of chordotonal organs in the upper end of the tibia of the ant *Lasius*. He noted the similarity of these to the tympanal organ of the long horned grasshoppers. This structure, usually called nowadays the 'subgenual organ' was later shown by Graber (1882)* to be widely distributed in insects. It was

---

*Graber refers to Lubbock as 'der ausgezeichnete Experimentator'.

assumed by Lubbock to be an organ of hearing. Electrical recordings made by Autrum (1941) from the tibial nerve in Orthoptera showed that the subgenual organs are sensitive to vibrations of very small amplitude in the substratum. Autrum and Schneider (1948) found that species which possess subgenual organs are far more sensitive to such vibrations than species in which they are absent.

In his studies on insect behaviour Lubbock did not draw a sharp distinction between intelligent behaviour and instinctive behaviour. He did not divide animals, as did Ray Lankester, into 'little brain' types, rich in ready-made instincts but not susceptible to much education, and 'big brain' types with few specialized instinctive capacities but with great powers of rapid learning. It has been charged as a defect of Lubbock's thinking, attributable to the generosity of his temperament, that he failed to separate sharply instinctive and intelligent behaviour. This is a matter which is, of course, still *sub judice* — but I myself see every justification for Lubbock's caution.

In 1873 Lubbock published his small book of 108 pages on the *Origin and Metamorphosis of Insects*. This was reprinted many times and translated into many languages. It is an inspiration to read it even today. Unlike the books on the senses and behaviour of insects it contains rather little original observation and experiment, but is rich in original thought.

'We may almost state it as a general proposition' he writes 'that either before or after birth animals undergo Metamorphoses.' 'The metamorphoses of insects depend then primarily on the fact that the young quit the egg at a more or less early stage of development . . .'. That was not a new idea; it goes back to Aristotle and was developed by William Harvey and by later authors. Since Lubbock's time it has been elaborated by Berlese (1913), and is often called the 'Berlese theory'. Lubbock continues: 'and consequently the external forces acting upon them in this state, are very different from those by which they are affected when they arrive at maturity'. Hence he concludes 'metamorphosis may be divided into two kinds, developmental and . . . adaptive'.

He points out that the metamorphoses of insects form 'one of the greatest difficulties of the Darwinian theory. . . . A clue to the difficulty may, I think, be found in the distinction between developmental and adaptive changes. The larva of an insect is by no means a mere stage in the development of the perfect animal. (That is, it is no mere step in a process of 'recapitulation'.) On the contrary it is subject to the influence of natural selection, and undergoes changes which have reference entirely to its own requirements and condition.

'If an animal which, when young pursues one mode of life, and lives on one kind of food, subsequently, either from its own growth in size and strength, or from any change of season, alters its habits or food, however slightly, it immediately becomes subject to the action of new forces: natural selection affects it in two different, and, it may be, very distinct manners, gradually tending to changes which may become so great as to involve an intermediate period of change and quiescence'.

That is an account of the nature and origin of the pupal stage which accords with views commonly held today. Certainly with the interpretation that I have adopted on several occasions; and Dr. Hinton, after a brief flirtation with the opinions of Poyarkoff, has stated in his most recent paper (1963): 'what is now suggested is in effect a functional subdivision of the larval stages into a series chiefly concerned with feeding and a final larval instar, now a pupa, chiefly concerned with bridging the gap between the specialized feeding stages and an adult specialized for reproduction and distribution'. That differs little from what Lubbock wrote.

Lubbock points out that the mature insect, like other animals, may appear in two or more different forms — the phenomenon of dimorphism or polymorphism. Certain insects, such as the fungus gnat *Miastor,* as discovered by Wagner (1863), undergo an alternation of generations: larvae which reproduce by paedogenesis and larvae which give rise to sexually mature adults. For this successive type of polymorphism he proposed the name 'polyeidism'; and he points out how similar is this phenomenon to normal insect metamorphosis. This idea, that metamorphosis and polymorphism are essentially comparable phenomena, has been much developed in recent years (Wigglesworth, 1954, 1959, 1961); it fits in well with our current ideas on the activation of genes and on the hormonal control of growth.

In discussing the origin of wings in this same book, Lubbock is inclined to derive them from movable branchiae extending to the thorax of some aquatic form. He regards the case of *Polynema natans,* which, as he himself originally discovered, uses its wings for swimming, as a rare phenomenon. He suggests that 'it is possible that the principal use of the wings was, primordially, to enable the

135

mature forms to pass from pond to pond, thus securing fresh habitats and avoiding in-and-in breeding. If this were so, the development of wings would gradually have been relegated to a late period of life.' That would not have been an unhelpful contribution to our discussion on the origin of flight eighteen months ago (Wigglesworth *et al.*, 1964).

If Lubbock had held an academic appointment, had published his biological researches and memoirs (or perhaps just his contributions to the study of insects) and occupied the rest of his time with worthy teaching and other academic duties, he would have been accorded a high place among the biologists of the nineteenth century. But, like Darwin, he was an amateur; and unlike Darwin, he devoted only a minute fraction of his time to scientific pursuits. The extraordinary position that he came to occupy in public life, and in the public esteem, obscured his remarkable contributions to science. A.E.S., writing his obituary notice for the Royal Society* in 1913, could only say this of him: 'Without being a great researcher, Lord Avebury took a prominent part in encouraging the research of others.' The only specific discovery attributed to him was that he first recognized the distinction between the Collembola and the Thysanura.

Now that the banker, the moralist, the practical sociologist, has been dead for fifty years, it is time we gave due credit to the original scientific experimentalist and thinker who was so often far ahead of his time.

REFERENCES

Autrum, H. (1941) Über Gehör und Erschütterungssinn bei Locustiden. *Z. vergl. Physiol.*, **28**, 580—637.

Autrum, H. and Schneider, W. (1948) Vergleichende Untersuchungen über den Erschütterungssinn der Insekten. *Z. vergl. Physiol.*, **31**, 77—88.

Berlese, A. (1913) Intorno alle metamorphosi degli insetti. *Redia*, **9**, 121—138.

Brün, R. (1914) *Die Raumorientierung der Ameisen und das Orientierungs-Problem im allgemeinen.* Jena.

Daumer, K. (1958) Blumenfarben, wie sie die Bienen sehen. *Z. vergl. Physiol.*, **41**, 49—110.

---

*The Royal Society's minutes record that Professor E. B. Poulton was unable to prepare an obituary notice on Lord Avebury and this was eventually undertaken by Sir Arthur Shipley.

Duff, A. G. (1924) Ed., *The Life-work of Lord Avebury (Sir John Lubbock)*. London: Watts & Co.

v. Frisch, K. (1914) Der Farbensinn und Formensinn der Biene. *Zool. Jahrb., Physiol.*, **35**, 1—182.

v. Frisch, K. (1950) Die Sonne als Kompass im Leben der Bienen. *Experientia*, **6**, 210—221.

Graber, V. (1882) Die chordotonalen Sinnesorgane und das Gehör der Insekten. *Arch. mikr. Anat.*, **21**, 65—145.

Hertz, M. (1939) New experiments on colour vision in bees. *J. Exp. Biol.*, **16**, 1—8.

Hinton, H. E. (1963) The origin and function of the pupal stage. *Proc. R. Ent. Soc. Lond.* A, **38**, 77—85.

Hutchinson, H. G. (1914) *Life of Lord Avebury*, 2 vols. London: Macmillan.

Kühn, A. (1927) Über den Farbensinn der Bienen. *Z. vergl. Physiol.*, **5**, 762—800.

Lindauer, M. (1961) *Communication Among Social Bees*. Harvard University Press.

Lotmar, R. (1933) Neue Untersuchungen über den Farbensinn der Bienen, mit besonderer Berücksichtigung des Ultravioletts. *Z. vergl. Physiol.*, **19**, 671-723.

*Lubbock, J. (1873) *The Origin and Metamorphosis of Insects*. London: Macmillan.

*Lubbock, J. (1882) *Ants, Bees and Wasps*. London: Kegan Paul, Trench & Co.

*Lubbock, J. (1888) *The Senses of Animals*. London: Kegan Paul, Trench & Co.

Lutz, F. E. (1924) A study of ultraviolet in relation to the flower-visiting habits of insects. *Ann. N.Y. Acad. Sci.*, **29**, 181—283.

Lutz, F. E. (1933) Experiments with 'stingless bees' (*Trigona cressoni parastigma*) concerning their ability to distinguish ultraviolet patterns. *Amer. Mus. Novit.*, No. 641, 26 pp.

Neave, S. A. (1933) *The history of the Entomological Society of London. 1833—1933*. London.

Pumphrey, R. J. (1958) The forgotten man — Sir John Lubbock, F.R.S. *Notes and Records of Roy. Soc. Lond.*, **13**, 49—58.

Santschi, F. (1911) Observations et remarques critiques sur le mécanisme de l'orientation chez les fourmis. *Rev. suisse Zool.*, **19**, 303—338.

Vowles, D. M. (1954) The orientation of ants to light, gravity and polarized light. *J. Exp. Biol.*, **31**, 356—375.

Wagner, N. (1863) Beitrag zur Lehre von der Fortpflanzing der Insektenlarven. *Z. wiss. Zool.*, **13**, 513—527.

Wigglesworth, V. B. (1954) *The Physiology of Insect Metamorphosis*. Cambridge University Press.

Wigglesworth, V. B. (1959) *The Control of Growth and Form*. Cornell University Press.

Wigglesworth, V. B. (1961) *Insect Polymorphism — a tentative synthesis*. In Kennedy, J. S., Ed., *Insect Polymorphism*, 103—113. *Symp. R. Ent. Soc. Lond.*, No. 1.

Wigglesworth, V. B. *et al.* (1963) The origin of flight in insects. *Proc. R. Ent. Soc. Lond.* C, **28**, 23—32.

---

*References to original papers will be found in these three books and in Duff (1924).

12

FIFTY YEARS OF INSECT PHYSIOLOGY

The first international congress of entomology to be held in this country took place at Oxford just over half a century ago. I did not attend on that occasion. I was too busy collecting insects in the countryside. Born in the North, in Lancashire, my parents had moved South, to Hertfordshire in 1911. For me it was like discovering El Dorado — so rich in insect life were the lanes and woods of Hertfordshire in those days. (How different today, when industry and suburbia are sweeping everything before them.)

I had already been passionately interested in insects for a good many years. Indeed, some years earlier in 1905 while caring for my culture of *Abraxas grossulariata,* I had discovered the metamorphosis of insects. In those days of uncorrupted youth it did not trouble me at all to learn, much later, that the phenomenon had already been described by Aristotle long before and that I could not claim 'priority'.

Before that, I had made an observation which had impressed me even more forcibly. We had in the garden in Lancashire a willow tree; and I was particularly attracted by the red galls of *Pontania* which it always carried in large numbers on its leaves. I opened these galls and found that every one contained a grub — although there was never any hole by which it could have entered. I sought the guidance of my parents about this mystery — but in vain. From that moment I was a committed entomologist.

Time passed; the collecting of insects continued; in 1918 I was able to watch *Papilio machaon* on the slopes of Vimy Ridge. Then in 1919, to Cambridge, with all available time spent collecting on the chalk hills and in the fens. While starting research in biochemistry under Professor Gowland Hopkins I was able, as a side-line, to look again at the pigments in the wings of *Pieris*. At that time Hopkins still believed the white pigment to be uric acid itself. I showed that about half the nitrogen excreted during pupal development was deposited in the wing-scales.

Dr. Erich Becker, whose early death was such a loss to insect biochemistry in Germany, described this work of mine as a 'warnender Beispiel' — because I had estimated as uric acid what was proved a few years later to be the pteridine pigment 'leucopteridine'. But only last year, a colleague of mine, using modern methods was able to prove that in the Pierid butterflies the pteridine pigments are indeed a major medium of nitrogen excretion, which is chiefly deposited in the wings. The pigments are indeed, as Hopkins had claimed, 'waste substances which function in ornament'.

In 1926 Professor P. A. Buxton was appointed head of the Department of Medical Entomology at the London School of Hygiene and Tropical Medicine. Buxton had formed the opinion that the future development of applied entomology required an intensive study of the physiology of insects. At that time I had just qualified in medicine and was invited to join Professor Buxton and work in this field.

My first discovery, in an incubator in the laboratory, was the blood-sucking bug *Rhodnius prolixus,* which had been brought from Venezuela by Professor E. Brumpt a year or two earlier and presented to Col. Alcock, Buxton's predecessor. *Rhodnius* proved to be a most valuable experimental animal; cultures of this insect, nearly all of them from Prof. Brumpt's strain, now exist in laboratories all over the world.

It is not my intention to recall the various lines of research into the physiology of insects which have occupied my time so happily since then. But in the course of these researches I have had to read pretty extensively in the literature of the subject and I have followed pretty closely the developments during the past forty years.

INSECT PHYSIOLOGY IN 1912

People sometimes speak as though almost all that is known of the physiology of insects has been gained in the last fifty years. But at the time of the Congress in 1912 there was a substantial body of knowledge in existence; indeed the main outlines of the subject had been mapped out. In 1910 Paul Marchal had written his admirable account of insect physiology for Richet's *Dictionnaire de Physiologie.* Some of the insect chapters of Winterstein's *Handbuch der vergleichenden Physiologie* and some of the physiological sections of Schröder's *Handbuch der Entomologie* had already appeared. The foundations of our modern knowledge on insect respiration and digestion had been laid by F. Plateau forty years earlier. Early in the nineteenth century George Newport in this country had abandoned surgery to devote himself to insect physiology and in 1837 had published his classic work on the circulatory system of *Sphinx ligustri.* There was much good physiology in *Die Insekten* of V. Graber published in 1877. There are valuable contributions to the physiology of insects in the writings of Henri Fabre. The classic account of the optics of the insect eye, published by Exner in 1891, has begun to be questioned only during the last few years.

The main outlines of the sensory physiology of bees and ants (the perception of ultraviolet light, the training to colours, and the use of scent trails and solar navigation) had been marked out by those two remarkable amateurs of entomology, Sir John Lubbock in this country and, later, Auguste Forel in Switzerland. But Professor v. Frisch was still concerning himself with the behaviour of fishes; he had scarcely discovered his true vocation. Lubbock's classic little book on the metamorphosis of insects, first published in 1869, is still worth reading, but in 1912 the attempts to describe the physiological mechanism of the process were wholly speculative. Genetics had been established as a discipline since 1900; but the link between genetics and development had not yet been forged by Richard Goldschmidt. Entwicklungs-Mechanik of sea urchins and amphibia had been making rapid progress, and in 1908 R. W. Hegner, of the University of Michigan had made the first key discovery in the Entwicklungs-Mechanik of insects by proving the existence of 'germ cell determinants' at the posterior pole of the egg of *Leptinotarsa,* which determine the cleavage cells arriving in that area to become the precursors of the gonads.

ADVANCES IN THE PHYSIOLOGY OF RESPIRATION

The discoveries of the fifty years that have passed since that time have been remarkable indeed. I do not propose to fill up my allotted time in giving you a complete catalogue of those advances. I would rather try to present a picture of the great change that has come about by the description of a few selected examples.

There are certain aspects of the physiology of insects that are peculiar to the Class, or at least to the Arthropoda. The first example that I wish to discuss is the tracheal system of respiration.

It was pointed out by Thomas Graham, when he described the laws of gaseous diffusion in 1833, that insects must depend for their respiration on the diffusion of gases within the tracheal system. But it was not until 1921 that August Krogh in Copenhagen proved this idea experimentally, and by measurement and calculation.

Krogh's treatment of the subject was based on the assumption that the spiracles were always open. It is curious to reflect that at that time the importance of the spiracular valves in preventing the loss of water by the insect was not recognized. We know now that if the spiracles are kept open the insect very soon dies of desiccation. This function was first pointed out by E. H. Hazelhoff in 1926 when studying under Hermann Jordan in Utrecht. In those insects which have no forced ventilation of the tracheal system the opening and closing of the spiracles represents a compromise between the need to obtain oxygen and the need to conserve water.

In the more active insects, as has been known since Plateau and earlier, there is an active mechanical ventilation of the system superimposed on simple diffusion. The directed streams of air, which were argued about during the last century, have been clearly demonstrated. And in the most recent publications the supply of oxygen from the tracheoles to the tissues has been studied quantitatively and it has been proved that here also diffusion is adequate to meet the respiratory needs even in the most active organs.

THE CUTICLE

Following closely upon the realization of the function of the spiracles in retaining water, came the recognition (in the late 'twenties) of the paramount importance of the waterproof properties of the integument. Odier in 1823 had discovered chitin in the insect cuticle. Odier made use of the elytra of *Melolontha* for his researches. He recognized that the horny substance of the elytron was an 'albuminoid' material which had to be dispersed with hot alkali in order to liberate the soft and colourless chitin. But this clear picture of the cuticle became lost in the course of the century, and the horny component itself came to be regarded as a sort of chitin. It was not until 1940 that this brown material was recognized as a proteinaceous polymer in which the protein chains had been tanned and bound together by reaction with quinones.

This remarkable polymer, called 'sclerotin', forms a striking parallel with 'keratin', the corresponding polymer of vertebrates in which the protein chains are linked together through disulphide bridges. The recognition of the nature of sclerotin has added enormously to our understanding of the physiology of insects. And along with the discovery of sclerotin has come the recognition that neither chitin nor sclerotin is responsible for waterproofing the insect, but a third, waxy component, which crystallizes out over the surface of the cuticle and forms a mechanical barrier to the escape of water molecules. It is not possible to claim that the insect cuticle is fully understood. Far from it. But even in our present state of knowledge it has been revealed as a structure of great interest and enormous complexity.

WATER CONSERVATION AND ION RESORPTION

It is a little surprising how slow we were to recognize the over-riding necessity for water conservation in the small terrestrial insect, as reflected in the rigorous closure of the spiracles and the waterproofing of the integument. Likewise, water must be conserved in the excretory and alimentary systems. The 'rectal glands' which had seemed such puzzling structures in the past were obviously concerned, in many insects, in recovering the precious water from the excrement before it was discharged. But rectal glands may be conspicuously developed also in insects with copious watery excreta. That has been proved to mean that they are also actively engaged in recovering valuable inorganic ions.

Thus we have been forced to abandon the simple picture of a process of excretion limited to the vasa varicosa of Malpighi, and to substitute for it an excretory *system,* in which the reabsorptive properties of the rectum are at least as important as the eliminating functions of the Malpighian tubules. This co-operative activity finds its highest development in the cryptonephridial system of beetles from dry environments.

So urgent is the need for inorganic salts, in animals living in fresh water, that, as Krogh discovered, many aquatic species have special organs for extracting chlorides, sodium, and potassium, from fresh water. The equivalent structures in the larvae of mosquitoes and other Diptera proved to be the puzzling anal papillae, working in co-operation with the rectal epithelium.

SENSE ORGANS

I wish to turn now to a totally different side of insect physiology: the sense organs. Although many of the principles involved in the operation of insect sense organs, notably in the generation of electrical nerve impulses, seem to be identical in insects and in vertebrates, there are certain features that are peculiar to the insects.

For nearly a century and a half we have been content with the mosaic theory of vision by the compound eye as put forward by Robert Hooke and by Johannes Müller and later developed by Exner. But during the last few years the theory of image formation by the compound eye has entered once more into a state of flux. I cannot elaborate the matter here, but if I might hazard a guess it would be that the mosaic theory will continue to stand, but at the same time it is becoming clear that this is not the only way in which the compound eye can be used. A certain amount of visual analysis can take place within the single ommatidium — in the flicker created by radial patterns, and in the perception of the plane of polarized light.

It is little more than 15 years ago that Professor v. Frisch astonished us by his announcement that bees could steer their way by the pattern of polarized light in the blue sky. But now we know that all insects can perceive the plane of polarization of light; and the study of the fine structure of the retina of the compound eye with the electron microscope has come very near to demonstrating how it is done.

In the study of insect hearing, as in the other senses, the development of electronic methods of recording nervous disturbances in single cells and axons, has led to a rapid expansion of knowledge in recent years. The most intriguing problem about the hearing of insects was how they are able to recognize the insect songs which we find indistinguishable. It turns out that although insects cannot discriminate pitch, as we can do, their ears have an exceedingly small 'time constant'; they can easily separate sounds which follow one another at intervals of less than 1/100th of a second. They are therefore extremely sensitive to changes in 'frequency modulation', that is, in the frequency with which pulses of sound succeed one another — a type of music to which we are almost completely deaf.

Lastly smell. Since the insect is covered by a continuous layer of cuticle, it was problematical how the organs of smell, the tiny hairs on the antennae, could operate. Now we know, from studies with the electron microscope, that these little hairs are perforated by hundreds of minute pores in which the terminal dendrites of the sensory neurones are freely exposed to the atmosphere.

VITAMINS AND SYMBIONTS

A large part of the study of insect physiology consists in repeating on the insect what has already been done on other animals. The ubiquity and uniformity of the basic processes of biochemistry, and the main elements in cellular structure, in all the living organisms on this planet are among the most significant biological discoveries of this century. The insects fall into this scheme, but they do show minor variants here and there.

At the time of the 1912 Congress, Gowland Hopkins had recently demonstrated the existence of essential 'vitamins', and essential amino-acids, necessary for the nutrition of mammals. The requirements of insects for both these groups of substances are remarkably similar to the needs of vertebrates. But my former colleague, the late R. P. Hobson, showed many years ago that for the insects cholesterol is in effect a vitamin. Carnitine and unsaturated lipids are other substances, essential for some insects, which mammals can manufacture for themselves.

There are many insects which feed on restricted diets, incomplete diets, or food devoid of micro-organisms. They cope with this situation by an intimate association with hereditary micro-organisms carried in special cells (the mycetocytes). These had been first described in ants and cockroaches by Blockmann in 1884 and later in Anobiids by Escherich in 1900. The symbiotic organisms are transmitted from one generation to the next in an amazing variety of ways — the unravelling of which will always be associated with the name of Professor Paul Buchner and his school in Munich.

These organisms were long believed to assist in digestion; but during the past thirty years their main significance has been proved to lie in the provision of those components, vitamins of the B group, and certain essential amino-acids, that are deficient in the diet. This has been proved in the blood-sucking insects, in insects feeding on plant juices, beetles in dry seeds, and most recently in the cockroaches. But the colonies of flagellates and bacteria, in the hindgut of termites and the larvae of Scarabaeid beetles, do play an important part in the digestion of cellulose for their hosts.

HORMONES

At the turn of the century, many different people had conceived the idea that the gonads of insects might influence the secondary sexual characters, as do the gonads of vertebrates. But all the experiments of excision or transplantation gave negative results, and thus the belief grew up that insects do not secrete hormones. It was not until 1917 that Kopeč carried out his simple but convincing experiments on *Lymantria* and showed that the brain is the source of a hormone which induced pupation in the full-grown caterpillar and continued development in the pupa. Experiments in other Lepidoptera raised doubts about this conclusion; for in them pupal development seemed to be controlled by a centre of some kind in the thorax.

It was not until the nineteen-thirties that detailed studies of the hormonal control of moulting and metamorphosis were undertaken. As the result of these studies (which are still being actively continued in many parts of the world at the present time) we know that insects have a well-defined endocrine system which controls their growth, metamorphosis and reproduction. The source of the hormone that induces growth and moulting is the gland of internal secretion named the 'ventral gland' of the head, or the prothoracic or thoracic gland, according to its situation in different species. This gland is activated by a second hormone produced by neurosecretory cells in the dorsum of the brain and apparently discharged into the bloodstream from the corpus cardiacum. The 'moulting hormone' (named 'ecdysone') exists in a number of closely related chemical forms; it appears to be a steroid derived from cholesterol. The nature of the brain hormone is a subject of active study at the present time.

The moulting hormone may lead to larval moulting, to pupation, or to adult development. The course taken depends partly on the stage of development of the insect, but chiefly on the presence or absence of the secretion of the corpus allatum, the so-called 'juvenile hormone'. If the juvenile hormone is present in sufficiently high concentration, the moulting larva develops into a larva again; if the hormone is absent it undergoes metamorphosis to the adult.

The chemical nature of the juvenile hormone is subject to debate

145

at the present time. The isoprenoid alcohol 'farnesol', which can be synthesized by insects, and can be extracted from them, will give precisely the same effects as the juvenile hormone if it is suitably formulated and administered. It looks as though the natural hormone is very closely related to substances of this type.

In the adult insect, another hormone from the neurosecretory cells, and the juvenile hormone from the corpus allatum, are responsible in varying degrees in different insects for the sexual maturation of both sexes.

But these are not the only processes that we now know to be controlled by hormones: colour change, diurnal rhythms of activity, diuresis, the rate of heart-beat, and the movements of other viscera, are all regulated by hormones, many of them derived from neurosecretory cells. Indeed the wheel has gone full circle; we seem to be returning to the views of the Ancients, which were supposedly discredited during the last century; more and more of the activities of the body seem to be regulated by humours from the brain. It is interesting to recall that the demonstration of hormone secretion by the neurosecretory cells in the dorsum of the insect brain was the first definite function for the neurosecretory cells to be proved in any animal.

MUSCLES AND FLIGHT

One of the puzzles of insect physiology in 1912 was the performance of the flight muscles. The way in which the indirect muscles of flight deform the thorax and indirectly cause the wings to rise and fall, was well understood. It had been shown by Marey in the last century, by the use of the kymograph and by other means, that flies can beat their wings at a frequency of several hundred times a second. Subsequent studies in biochemistry and electron microscopy have shown that the flight muscles of insects differ very little in essentials from the muscles of vertebrates — but no vertebrate muscle will contract and relax at a rate exceeding about twenty to thirty times per second.

In fact, the indirect flight muscles of insects do not contract and relax in response to nervous stimuli. The thorax, with the wings articulated to it, undergoes a high-speed oscillatory movement which alternately stretches the indirect muscles and then releases them at a rapid rate. The course of this movement is determined by the structure of the thorax. The muscles must be kept in a state of activation by the nerves. What is peculiar about the insect flight muscle is that, provided it is kept activated in this way, it is caused instantly to contract when stretched and instantly to relax when released. Given the capacity to respond in this way there seems to be almost no limit to the speed at which the muscles can operate. The midge *Forcipomyia*, with its wings cut short, will vibrate them at the rate of more than 2000 times a second.

CYTOCHROME

Apart from these interesting peculiarities, what has the study of insect physiology contributed to general biology? Fifty years ago the biochemical study of oxidation in the living body had only just begun. Much was done during the next ten years. Otto Warburg produced evidence for the existence of an enzyme which catalysed the combination of hydrogen with oxygen, the so-called 'Atmungs-ferment' — but the nature of this agent remained undiscovered. In 1925, when David Keilin was studying the haemoglobin that is found in the larva of *Gasterophilus* he observed a series of absorption bands in insect muscles which he recognised as the bands of haematoporphyrin.

These bands had been seen many years before by McMunn who could never gain acceptance of his observations. But what Keilin saw was entirely new. He saw that in the flight muscles of the bee and of the wax moth, the pigments responsible were alternately oxidized and reduced within the living insect. He at once realized that here was the universal oxidizing system that everyone had been looking for: the chain of cytochromes through which electrons were transferred to molecular oxygen so that this became 'activated' and caused to unite with the hydrogen detached from the body fuels.

To-day everybody knows about cytochrome; but I suspect that there may be many biochemists who do not realize that the discovery of cytochrome was a product of the study of insect physiology.

BIOCHEMICAL ACTION OF GENES

My other example goes back to the middle 'thirties, when German, French and American workers were studying the eye-colour mutants of *Ephestia* and *Drosophila*. In both insects, the amino-acid trypto-

147

phane was converted by a series of enzymes through kynurenine and oxykynurenine to the ommochrome pigments of the eye. The mutants 'vermilion' and 'cinnabar' resulted from defects in this metabolic chain. Each link in the chain was controlled by a specific enzyme which was the product of a specific gene.

This classic story was the first clear-cut example to support the 'one gene, one enzyme' hypothesis. It provided the foundation for the *Neurospora* work that has since formed the main basis for this theory which is now generally accepted.

I hope you will agree that these are impressive examples of the potential contribution of insect physiology to general biology. But I believe that the great era of insect physiology is yet to come. As Crick has pointed out, anyone who sat down and thought at any time during the past fifty years could have inferred that inheritable characters must be enshrined or as we say nowadays 'encoded' in some really stable molecule; and the nucleic acids were the only possible candidates. Now this is accepted, and the orderliness of development is seen as the result of the step-wise activation of particular components of the genetic code.

We have long realized that metamorphosis is a genetic switch or transformation of just this kind; the controlling factor being the presence or absence of the juvenile hormone. Environmentally directed polymorphism among the individuals of a species, and cellular differentiation within the tissues of the individual, are commonly regarded as comparable phenomena.

But these are largely general ideas and impressions. They must be given substance and detailed biochemical proof. There is certainly no more important problem in biology to-day; and I submit that there is no more promising medium than the insect, in which this problem can hopefully be studied.

13

THE EPIDERMAL CELL

The objective of the biochemist is commonly defined as the description in chemical terms of all the activities of the cell. If we are to form some estimate of the magnitude of this ambition it is instructive from time to time to survey the range of these activities. For the biochemist 'the cell' is a somewhat abstract concept, a sort of disembodied liver cell. But cells are of many kinds, and they differ greatly from one another in their capabilities. In this essay we shall be concerned only with the epidermal cell of an insect, the blood-sucking bug *Rhodnius prolixus*.

The epidermal cell of the insect is interesting because it combines within itself so many functions, actual and potential. Some are social functions, in which the activity of the cell can be considered only in relation to the whole community of cells of which it forms a part. Others are individual functions, in which the cell seems to be concerned primarily with its own affairs. But even the individual functions, which are much more amenable to study, are closely integrated with the activities of neighbouring cells.

THE RESTING CELL

We may first consider the ordinary epidermal cell of the abdominal wall of the 4th or 5th instar larva. In the resting state this cell is not a very impressive object (Fig. 1). It is exceedingly flattened and attenuated (not more than 3 μm in thickness), the nucleolus is small, the scanty cytoplasm contains only traces of ribonucleoprotein, a few scattered spheres of red pigment, and relatively few mitochondrial filaments and granules. It rests upon a basement membrane, but is not intimately attached to this. Its outer surface is adherent to the cuticle which is traversed by fine canals, the pore canals, which presumably contain cytoplasmic filaments.

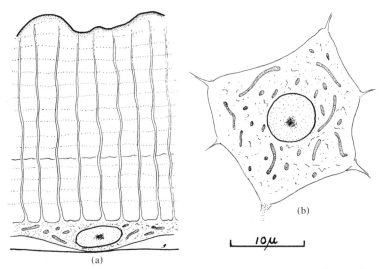

Fig. 1. (*a*) Transverse section of resting epidermal cell in 5th-stage larva of *Rhodnius,* showing the cuticle and pore canals; (*b*) surface view of the same showing mitochondria.

THE HEALING OF WOUNDS

If an incision or a small excision is made in the integument, the dormant epidermal cells are stimulated to activity. The cells that are actually cut by the wound die and give rise to autolytic products of some undetermined nature which diffuse outwards and 'activate' the surrounding cells up to a distance of some 350 μm. Activation is characterized by a great increase in the size of the nucleolus, an increase in the quantity of cytoplasm, and a large increase in the ribonucleic acid content. At the same time the mitochondria become swollen and far more numerous. These changes are well advanced within 12 or 24 h after the injury.

Meanwhile the activated cells leave their attachments to the cuticle and migrate by amoeboid movement to the margin of the wound, where they become densely aggregated, and then proceed to spread over the gap (Fig. 2*b*). This cellular migration leaves a peripheral zone in which the activated cells are exceedingly sparse. But no parts of the cuticle are left devoid of cells, for the epidermal cells never let go of one another; all are connected, though sometimes only by the most slender filaments.

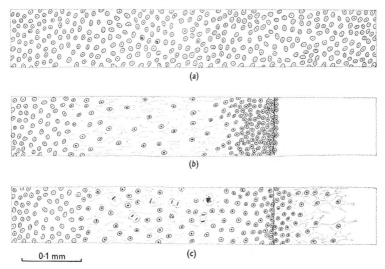

Fig. 2. (*a*) Surface view of the epidermis in normal adult *Rhodnius*; (*b*) the same 24 h after an excision about 1 mm square; (*c*) the same 4 days after the excision.

Mitosis is uncommon among the cells that spread over a small wound. It is in the sparse zone of activated cells that cell divisions begin about 3 or 4 days after the injury (Fig. 2*c*). The process continues until migration in the centre and division at the periphery have restored the normal density of epidermal cells (Wigglesworth, 1937).

THE SEARCH FOR OXYGEN

This response of the epidermal cell to the products of injury is strikingly different from the response to lack of oxygen. The epidermis of the insect receives a very rich tracheal supply — a measure of its importance in metabolism. Indeed the tracheal supply to the integument is often the most prominent in the whole body. That may explain why the metabolic rate of insects is often approximately proportional to the body surface. The small tracheae penetrate the basement membrane and break up into tracheoles which run a convoluted course between the epidermal cells. These tracheoles are rather evenly distributed, so that no cell, as a rule, is separated from an air-filled tracheole by more than 30 μm, that is, at the most by three cell widths.

151

It so happens that each abdominal tergite receives a single tracheal branch from the lateral trachea of each side, and there is no anastomosis between the branches on the two sides or between those of one segment and the next. If, therefore, the tracheal branch is cut through near its origin, one-half of that abdominal tergite will be deprived of its tracheal supply. If that is done during an intermoult period, when no growth is taking place in the tracheal system and no new tracheal branches can be formed, the tracheal deficiency is made good by the movement of tracheoles from the adjacent segments into the region that has been deprived of its tracheal supply.

It was earlier supposed that the active agents in this migration were the tracheoles themselves, and that the cytoplasm investing these tracheoles sent out amoeboid processes — as indeed happens during the development of new tracheae and tracheoles (Wigglesworth, 1954a). But it has recently been shown that the active agents are in fact the epidermal cells themselves. These do not leave their initial sites (as they do in response to injury) but they send out filamentous processes which converge upon the tracheoles, attach themselves to these, and then pull (Fig. 3). These filaments may be

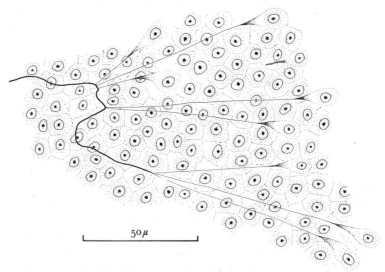

Fig. 3. Epidermis of *Rhodnius* 4th-stage larva in surface view. The area to the right has been deprived of its tracheal supply by section of a trachea. The epidermal cells show contractile filaments attached to an air-filled tracheole to the left.

152

as much as 125—150 μm long. They are evidently contractile structures* under the control of the cells from which they arise, and by their united action the tracheoles may be dragged half way across the segment, perhaps half or three-quarters of a millimetre (Wigglesworth, 1959a).

Presumably it is this activity of the epidermal cell which is responsible for the normal regular distribution of the tracheoles. That can be demonstrated, without any injury to the tracheal system, by exposing the insect for 24 or 48 h in 4 per cent oxygen. Everywhere the epidermal cells can be seen reaching out and attaching themselves to the tracheoles.

THE SECRETION OF THE CUTICLE

The chief function of the epidermal cell is the provision for growth; that is, the complex series of changes which lead up to the formation of a new and larger cuticle and the moulting of the old cuticle. The growth process in *Rhodnius* is initiated by the meal of blood; only one meal is needed for each moult. The distension of the abdomen provides a nervous stimulus to the brain, and leads to the discharge by the neurosecretory cells of the hormone which activates the thoracic gland and causes this to secrete the growth and moulting hormone (ecdysone) (Wigglesworth, 1934, 1940b, 1952). The consequent changes in the epidermis may be summarized as follows.

The effects of the moulting hormone are closely similar to those which follow injury (Wigglesworth, 1957a). Within a few hours the cells are 'activated'. The nucleolus enlarges, the mitochondria become swollen and soon begin to increase in number, ribonucleoprotein increases in the cytoplasm. Within 2 days the epidermis forms a cubical epithelium (Fig. 4b), the nuclei are enlarged with highly lobulated nucleoli, the extensive cytoplasm is filled with swollen mitochondria. By 4 days cell division has begun (Fig. 4c), and may be so active that many more cells are produced than are needed to lay down the new cuticle. The unwanted cells die and their

---

*Examination of these epidermal cells with the electron microscope shows that the fine filaments contain closely packed bundles of microtubules. This modification is comparable with that which takes place in the epidermal tendon cells, whose function is to resist tension where muscles are attached to the cuticle.

nuclei undergo dissolution, with the production of Feulgen-positive droplets ('chromatic droplets') (Wigglesworth, 1942) which are eventually assimilated by the adjacent cells, until, by about 7 or 8 days after feeding, the epidermis forms a regular columnar epithelium ready to begin the deposition of the new cuticle.

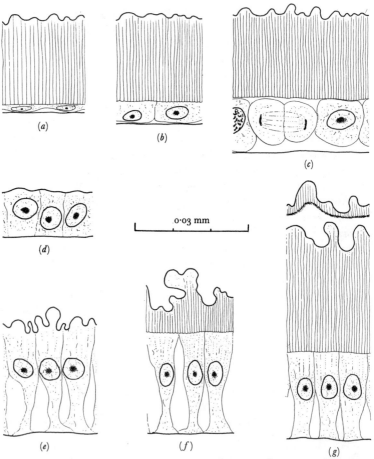

Fig. 4. Stages in the formation of the cuticle during moulting in *Rhodnius* 4th-stage larva. (*a*) Immediately after feeding; (*b*) 2 days after feeding; (*c*) 4 days after feeding; (*d*) 6 days: smooth epicuticle laid down; (*e*) 8 days: epicuticle thrown into folds; (*f*) 11 days: endocuticle being laid down; (*g*) 13 days: day before moulting; the inner layers of the old cuticle visible above are almost completely digested.

The epidermal cell now first lays down a smooth thin layer of lipoprotein which will become the 'cuticulin layer' of the epicuticle (Fig. 4d). It is probable that this material is the product of the large 'oenocytes' which lie between the epidermis and the basement membrane, and is passed on to the epidermal cells for rapid secretion on the surface (Wigglesworth, 1933, 1947). This layer expands, perhaps by the uptake of water from the fluid in which it is bathed, and is thrown into star-shaped folds (Fig. 4e).* The epidermal cells then proceed to secrete the inner layers of chitin and protein which compose the main substance of the cuticle (Fig. 4f).

CYTOLOGY OF THE EPIDERMAL CELL

At this stage, the most active phase in the life of the epidermal cell, the cytological structure is complex. It is not possible to represent this in a single preparation, since different procedures are necessary to reveal the various components. Some of these are shown in Fig. 5a—e; and a partial image of the cell will be obtained if these five figures are superimposed in the imagination.

Fig. 5a shows the droplets of red pigment (probably a pteridine) as seen in the unstained cell. These droplets often show a linear arrangement, normal to the cuticle, suggesting the presence of a vertical structure† in the cell (Wigglesworth, 1933).

In Fig. 5b the cell has been fixed with osmium tetroxide and stained with ethyl gallate to reveal mainly the lipid components (Wigglesworth, 1957b). It shows a dark spherical nucleolus, and nuclear membrane; the cytoplasm contains granular, rod-like and filamentous mitochondria; the sites of the pigment droplets appear as small vacuoles. The cytoplasm itself is rather darkly staining in the distal half of the cell; sections examined with the electron microscope show that this is due to the presence of innumerable closely packed double membranes of endoplasmic reticulum (Wigglesworth, 1957a). The transition from cytoplasm to cuticle is not very sharp;

---

*The electron microscope has revealed more details of the structure of the epicuticle and the mechanism of the process by which it is thrown into star-shaped folds (Wigglesworth, 1973).

†The 'vertical structure' consists of bundles of microtubules, as seen with the electron microscope (Wigglesworth, 1973).

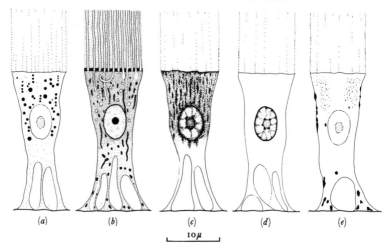

(a)   (b)   (c)   (d)   (e)

⊢___ 10μ ___⊣

Fig. 5. The epidermal cell in *Rhodnius* at the height of cuticle secretion. (a) Unstained showing red pigment droplets; (b) osmium and ethyl gallate showing mitochondria and other lipid components; (c) alcoholic Bouin and gallocyanin at pH 1·6 showing total nucleic acids; (d) the same after treatment with ribonuclease, showing desoxyribonucleic acid; (e) alcoholic Bouin and periodic acid—Schiff test, showing glycogen.

the boundary zone is characterized by a deeply staining layer traversed by the clear unstained pore canals. The pore canals often extend beyond this band for a variable distance into the epidermal cell. Sometimes they dilate in a funnel-shaped manner and appear to end in clear vacuoles. Sometimes they will coil round in a loop. Sometimes, bounded by darkly staining cytoplasm, they follow a straight course and may extend almost to the nucleus.

Fig. 5c shows the distribution of nucleic acid (RNA and DNA) as revealed by gallocyanin or pyronin and methyl green. Fig. 5d represents the desoxyribonucleic acid after removal of RNA with ribonuclease.

Fig. 5e shows the distribution of glycogen, which is most evident at the base of the cell where this is attached to the basement membrane. There are commonly very fine dust-like deposits of glycogen towards the distal apex of the cell.

In addition to the components shown in Fig. 5, certain enzymes have been demonstrated in the epidermal cell. Succinic dehydrogenase appears to be associated with the mitochondria. An 'esterase' capable of hydrolyzing 5-bromoindoxyl acetate is present in the form of slender filaments most commonly applied to the surface of the nucleus (Wigglesworth, 1958). And alkaline phosphatase occurs in the form of rounded granules distributed throughout the cytoplasm particularly in the outer half of the cell.

THE FINAL STAGES OF CUTICLE FORMATION*

The subsequent activities of the epidermal cell during the process of cuticle secretion are summarized in Fig. 6. As we have seen, it first lays down the 'cuticulin' layer. Then the micelles of chitin and protein are deposited in laminae around the cytoplasmic filaments which form the pore canals. When the new cuticle is nearing completion the cells produce and discharge into the moulting fluid, between the old cuticle and the new, the enzymes protease and chitinase. These are passed through the substance of the new cuticle, perhaps by way of the pore canals. They digest the inner layers of the old cuticle (sometimes as much as 90 per cent may be dissolved) and the products of digestion are then reabsorbed by the epidermal cell through the substance of the cuticle (Wigglesworth, 1933).

About this time another product of the epidermal cell appears on the surface of the epicuticle. This is a viscid proteinaceous material which actively reduces ammoniacal silver hydroxide. It is commonly referred to as the 'polyphenol layer' on the assumption that the reducing properties may be due to phenolic groups. This material seems to exude from the ends of the pore canals and then to spread and unite to form a thin continuous layer (Wigglesworth, 1947).

Shortly before moulting the epidermal cells give rise to yet another most important substance. This is the wax that crystallizes out to form a thin waterproof film on the surface of the silver-reducing layer (Wigglesworth, 1947). Meanwhile those regions of the chitin-protein substance of the cuticle which will later become hard and horny have been impregnated with more protein and phenolic substances.

It is at this stage that the undigested residue of the old cuticle is shed. The final layer of the cuticle, the protective layer of 'cement',

---

An updated account of this process, some important details of which have been modified, has recently been published (Wigglesworth, 1975).

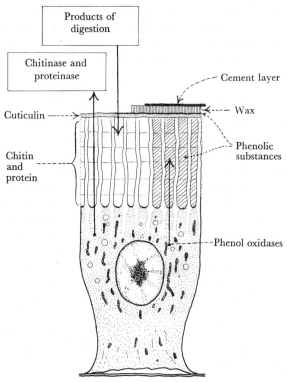

Fig. 6. Schematic figure summarizing the activities of the epidermal cell during cuticle formation.

is now poured out over the surface of the wax. This alone of all the components of the cuticle is not a product of the epidermal cell, but is discharged on to the surface by the dermal glands (Wigglesworth, 1945, 1947). It still remains for the epidermal cell to secrete into the cuticle the phenoloxidase which will oxidize the phenolic substances to the quinones that tan and harden the horny parts of the cuticle, and the tyrosinase that will yield the melanin pigment of the blackened regions (Pryor, 1940).

Nothing has been said of the basement membrane which is sometimes regarded as a product of the epidermal cells. It seems more likely that this is in fact a mesodermal structure, the product of the haemocytes (Wigglesworth, 1956).

THE CAPACITY FOR DIFFERENTIATION

It is evident from this brief summary that the epidermal cell is a functional cell with an amazing range of chemical and physiological activities. But at the same time it is an embryonic cell; it retains a considerable capacity for differentiation. The three most familiar pathways of differentiation it may follow are summarized in Fig. 7.

(1) During each moulting stage, cell pairs, the daughter cells of single epidermal cells, detach themselves from the general epidermal sheet and come to lie between the epithelium and the basement membrane (Wigglesworth, 1933). In the course of the next ensuing moult, these cells enlarge enormously until they develop into the active oenocytes, measuring sometimes as much as 80—100 μm in diameter, which are probably the source of the hydrocarbons composing the waxy lipids of the cuticle (Diehl, 1975).

(2) Other epidermal cells remain in groups of four. One of these grows to form the main gland cell of a dermal gland, enclosing a distensible reservoir; the other three cells are presumably concerned in the formation of the sheath and duct (Wigglesworth, 1933, 1953). These are the glands which secrete mucopolysaccharide to form the so-called 'cement layer' on the outermost surface of the cuticle (Wigglesworth, 1975).

(3) Other groups of four cells are indistinguishable from the dermal glands when they first appear. But two become extremely large and form respectively the trichogen of a tactile hair and the tormogen of the socket, while the other two form the sense cell and its neurilemma cell (Wigglesworth, 1953). The sense cell gives off a distal process which grows to the base of the hair to form the scolopale, and a proximal process which grows inwards, allies itself with the first small nerve it meets, and accompanies this through the basement membrane and ultimately to the central nervous system to form the sensory axon. The neurilemma cell provides the sheath for this structure.

With respect to the formation of sensory hairs and dermal glands the epidermal cell is undetermined. Its determination is controlled by the environment. Every sensillum appears to exert an inhibitory effect around it which prevents the differentiation of other sensory hairs in its immediate vicinity. This influence seems to diminish with distance in a graduated fashion. It has, indeed, been suggested that there may be some essential substance in the epidermis which is

159

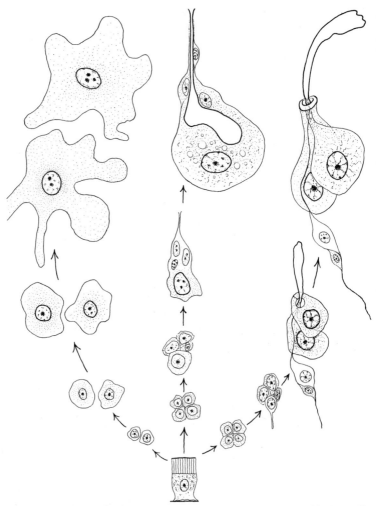

Fig. 7. Three types of differentiation available to the epidermal cell in *Rhodnius*. To the left, formation of oenocytes; in the centre, formation of dermal gland; to the right, formation of tactile sense organs.

necessary in order that an epidermal cell may become determined to form a sensory hair, and that each developing sensory hair drains off this material from the surrounding cells and so deprives them of the ability to differentiate (Wigglesworth, 1940a). There is evidence that

160

the dermal glands and sense organs are homologous structures. The dermal glands are more closely spaced than the sensory hairs. It may be that the same essential factor is required for the determination of both — but that there is a quantitative difference, and a higher concentration of the material is necessary for the evocation of a sensory hair (Wigglesworth, 1953).

Around each sensory hair on the abdomen of *Rhodnius* is a small rounded plaque. That means that the epidermal cells in the immediate vicinity of the hair are themselves subject to some determining influence which causes them to become distended with vacuoles during the early stages of moulting. They are thus raised above their fellows to form a dome-like structure, and then lay down a smooth and somewhat hardened cuticle to form the plaque (Wigglesworth, 1933).

POLARITY AND PATTERN

When a new sensory hair with its plaque is developed in the course of growth and moulting it shows the same orientation as all the existing structures, with the hair directed backwards. The same orientation is apparent when plaques are regenerated after an extensive burn in the epidermis. Plaques and hairs do not appear in the first moult after a burn, but they are formed at the normal intervals and with the normal orientation at the second moult (Wigglesworth, 1940a). If a piece of the integument is excised, rotated through 90° or 180° and reimplanted, the bristles show a corresponding change in orientation at the next moult (Wigglesworth, 1940a).

One must, therefore, conclude that some sort of polarity already exists within the cytoplasm of the undifferentiated epidermal cell; with the result that when they divide to produce the tormogen and trichogen cells, these are so placed in respect to one another that the bristles grow out in the predetermined direction.

The gradients around an existing sense organ which control the appearance of other sense organs, and the polarity of the cells which controls the orientation of the sensory hairs, are examples of the social functions of epidermal cells. Indeed, the different epidermal cells form elements in a social pattern which is the basis of the body form.

Certain parts of this pattern become apparent when the cuticle is laid down. Some cells in the surface of the abdomen, for example, are contributing to the formation of plaques; others are forming the intersegmental membranes; and yet others are forming the black pigment spots at the sides of the abdomen, or the serried rows of plaques along the margins. Other elements in the pattern are not normally apparent. But they become detectable as a gradient in the mutual relations between the epidermal cells; when excised areas of the integument are implanted in different regions of the abdomen it is found that cells at the anterior part of a body segment unite more readily with other cells coming from this level than they do with cells from a more posterior part of a segment. There is evidently an invisible gradient of some kind (Locke, 1959).

When the epidermis over an extensive area is killed by burning and the surrounding cells multiply and spread inwards to repair the injury, they carry with them the potentiality to form their specific component of the body pattern (Wigglesworth, 1940*a*). That is most obvious when the margin of the burn passes through the lateral pigment spots. At the ensuing moult, when a new cuticle is laid down, the migrating cells and their daughter cells are found to have carried with them their capacity to form pigmented cuticle. A centripetal displacement of the pattern is the result (Fig. 8). Other elements, such as the crowded marginal plaques, or the intersegmental membranes, can be similarly extended and displaced.

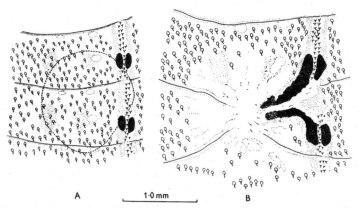

A   1·0 mm   B

Fig. 8. (*a*) Lateral region of the dorsal surface of two segments of the abdomen in a 3rd-stage larva of *Rhodnius*. The broken line shows the approximate extent of the epidermis killed by burning; (*b*) the corresponding region in the 4th-stage larva after healing and moulting.

THE LATENT ADULT PATTERN AND METAMORPHOSIS

The pattern of the abdomen in the adult *Rhodnius* is very different from that of the larval stages. One obvious difference is in the arrangement of the black pigment spots. During the larval stages there is an oval spot lying at the postero-lateral angle of each segment. In the adult there are trapezoidal spots occupying the antero-lateral angles. If a small burn is inflicted between two lateral pigment spots in the 3rd instar larva (Fig. 9a, a), these will be found united to form a continuous spot in the fourth and fifth stages. Or, if one pigment spot is burned out (Fig. 9a, b), its place will be taken by unpigmented cuticle at the next instar. But in the resulting adults these effects are reversed (Fig. 9c); where two black pigment spots had united in the larva, there is an unpigmented zone in the adult; and where a pigment spot had been eliminated in the larva, two adjacent pigment spots of the adult have become fused.

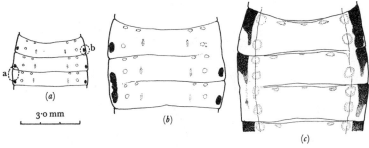

Fig. 9. (a) Three abdominal segments of a normal 3rd-stage larva of *Rhodnius*. The broken lines at 'a' and 'b' show the regions burned; (b) corresponding segments in the 5th-stage larva resulting; (c) corresponding segments in the adult resulting.

These results serve to emphasize that the adult pattern is already latent within the larval cells; and that when these cells divide, the capacity to form particular elements in this pattern is transmitted to the daughter cells. They carry their properties with them through their divisions and wanderings, but these properties remain latent and unrealized until metamorphosis occurs.

Metamorphosis is controlled by hormones. Throughout the larval stages the corpus allatum, which lies immediately behind the brain, secretes the so-called 'juvenile hormone' or 'neotenin'. In the presence of this hormone, which is probably a quite simple substance, the epidermal cells all lay down cuticle of larval type. Their capacity for forming adult cuticle remains latent. But if growth and moulting take place in the absence of the juvenile hormone, either experimentally, or normally, as in the 5th-stage larva, the latent adult characters are realized (Wigglesworth, 1954b).

The same cells persist from larva to adult. In the normal insect they lay down either adult or larval cuticular structures, but never structures with intermediate characters. However, under experimental conditions, by varying the timing of the hormone supply, or the amount of hormone present, it is possible to produce intermediate forms. Fig. 10a shows a sensory hair and plaque in a 4th-stage larva, and Fig. 10e shows a bristle from a normal adult. Fig. 10b, c and d show intermediate bristle types produced by decapitating 3rd-stage larvae and so depriving them of juvenile hormone at different points in the moulting cycle. These figures show clearly the progressive

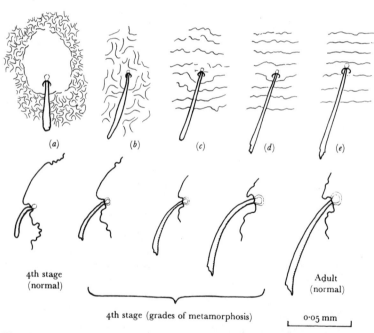

(a) (b) (c) (d) (e)

4th stage (normal)   4th stage (grades of metamorphosis)   Adult (normal)   0·05 mm

Fig. 10. Above, series of sensory hairs on the surface of the abdomen; below, sensory hairs from the margin of the abdomen in the same insects. (a) Normal 4th-stage larva; (b, c and d) 4th-stage larvae produced by decapitating 3rd-stage larvae and showing various grades of precocious metamorphosis; (e) normal adult.

assumption of adult characters in both the sculpturing of the cuticle surface and the form of the bristles as the amount of juvenile hormone available becomes less.

It is impossible not to be impressed by the general similarity between the effects of the juvenile hormone, a product of the endocrine system, in controlling the realization of the adult characters latent in the epidermal cell, and the effects of the components in the local gradient systems in the epidermis in controlling the latent capacity to form different elements in the body pattern. If these locally acting factors, which control the realization of the various genetic potentialities of the epidermal cell, should prove to be of a chemical nature (as indeed seems probable) then the analogy between metamorphosis and differentiation becomes very close (Wigglesworth, 1959*b*).

CONCLUSION

The purpose of this essay has been to illustrate the wide range of the physiological functions with which the epidermal cell of an insect is endowed.

The epidermal cells will migrate to the site of a wound and repair the injury. They can look after their own oxygen supply by giving out slender contractile filaments which become attached to the air-filled tracheoles and pull these closer.

During the moulting process the epidermal cell secretes the lipoprotein (cuticulin) of the epicuticle, and then lays down the inner layers of chitin and protein. It secretes and discharges the enzymes protease and chitinase which digest the inner layers of the old cuticle, and it reabsorbs the products of digestion. It produces the phenolic compounds which will later be responsible for hardening and darkening, and then the long-chain waxes to waterproof the surface. Finally, it produces the phenoloxidase enzymes which lead to melanization and tanning. All these processes are integrated and timed so that they follow one another in orderly sequence, and synchronously in all parts of the body.

The epidermal cell is at the same time an embryonic cell. It can differentiate, for example, to produce oenocytes, dermal glands or sensilla. In the production of a sensillum one of the four daughter cells of the epidermal cell becomes a primary sense cell whose axon process grows into the central nervous system. Local chemical gradients probably control this differentiation.

Thus the epidermal cells, as members of the whole community which makes up the surface of the body, have certain social functions. They are indeed the prime agents responsible for the form and pattern of the insect. This form changes strikingly at different stages in the life cycle. In the larval insect, besides the visible larval pattern, there is an invisible adult (and sometimes pupal) pattern which is equally determined, but which does not become apparent until metamorphosis. The realization of this latent pattern is controlled by the growth hormones (ecdysone and neotenin) acting directly upon the epidermal cells.

A study of the epidermal cell thus illustrates well enough what James Gray (1931) has called 'the complexity of ideas which arise from a study of the simplest of morphological units'.

REFERENCES

Diehl, P. A. 1975) Synthesis and release of hydrocarbons by the oenocytes of the desert locust, *Shistocerca gregaria. J. Insect Physiol.,* **21,** 1237—1246.

Gray, J. (1931) *Text-book of Experimental Cytology.* Cambridge University Press.

Locke, M. (1959) The cuticular pattern in an insect, *Rhodnius prolixus* Stål. *J. Exp. Biol.,* **36,** 459—477.

Pryor, M. G. M. (1940) On the hardening of the cuticle of insects. *Proc. Roy. Soc.* B, **128,** 393—407.

Wigglesworth, V. B. (1933) The physiology of the cuticle and of ecdysis in *Rhodnius prolixus* (Triatomidae, Hemiptera); with special reference to the function of the oenocytes and of the dermal glands. *Quart. J. Micr. Sci.,* **76,** 269—318.

Wigglesworth, V. B. (1934) The physiology of ecdysis in *Rhodnius prolixus* (Hemiptera). II. Factors controlling moulting and 'metamorphosis'. *Quart. J. Micr. Sci.,* **77,** 191—222.

Wigglesworth, V. B. (1937) Wound healing in an insect (*Rhodnius prolixus* Hemiptera). *J. Exp. Biol.,* **14,** 364—381.

Wigglesworth, V. B. (1940a) Local and general factors in the development of 'pattern' in *Rhodnius prolixus* (Hemiptera). *J. Exp. Biol.,* **17,** 180—200.

Wigglesworth, V. B. (1940b) The determination of characters at metamorphosis in *Rhodnius prolixus* (Hemiptera). *J. Exp. Biol.,* **17,** 201—222.

Wigglesworth, V. B. (1942) The significance of 'Chromatic Droplets' in the growth of insects. *Quart. J. Micr. Sci.,* **83,** 141—152.

Wigglesworth, V. B. (1945) Growth and form in an insect. *Essays on Growth and Form.* Oxford University Press.

Wigglesworth, V. B. (1947) The epicuticle in an insect *Rhodnius prolixus* (Hemiptera). *Proc. Roy. Soc.* B, **134,** 163—181.

Wigglesworth, V. B. (1952) The thoracic gland in *Rhodnius prolixus* (Hemiptera) and its role in moulting. *J. Exp. Biol.,* **29,** 561—570.

Wigglesworth, V. B. (1953) The origin of sensory neurones in an insect, *Rhodnius prolixus* (Hemiptera). *Quart. J. Micr. Sci.,* **94,** 93—112.

Wigglesworth, V. B. (1954*a*) Growth and regeneration in the tracheal system of an insect *Rhodnius prolixus* (Hemiptera). *Quart. J. Micr. Sci.,* **95,** 115—137.

Wigglesworth, V. B. (1954*b*) *The Physiology of Insect Metamorphosis.* Cambridge University Press.

Wigglesworth, V. B. (1956) The haemocytes and connective tissue formation in an insect, *Rhodnius prolixus* (Hemiptera). *Quart. J. Micr. Sci.,* **97,** 89—98.

Wigglesworth, V. B. (1957*a*) The action of growth hormones in insects. *Symp. Soc. Exp. Biol.,* **11,** 203—227.

Wigglesworth, V. B. (1957*b*) The use of osmium in the fixation and staining of tissues. *Proc. Roy. Soc.* B, **147,** 185—199.

Wigglesworth, V. B. (1958) The distribution of esterase in the nervous system and other tissues of the insect *Rhodnius prolixus. Quart. J. Micr. Sci.,* **99,** 441—450.

Wigglesworth, V. B. (1959*a*) The role of the epidermal cells in the 'migration' of tracheoles in *Rhodnius prolixus* (Hemiptera). *J. Exp. Biol.,* **36,** 632—640.

Wigglesworth, V. B. (1959*b*) *The Control of Growth and Form.* Ithaca, N.Y.; Cornell University Press.

Wigglesworth, V. B. (1973) The role of the epidermal cells in moulding the surface pattern of the cuticle in *Rhodnius* (Hemiptera). *J. Cell Sci.,* **12,** 683—705.

Wigglesworth, V. B. (1975) Incorporation of lipid into the epicuticle of *Rhodnius* (Hemiptera). *J. Cell Sci.,* **19,** 459—485.

14

PREFORMATION AND INSECT DEVELOPMENT

JAN SWAMMERDAM AND THE NATURE OF METAMORPHOSIS

I was exceedingly impressed to read the names of the nine previous recipients of the Swammerdam medal since this award was established in 1880. It is indeed an honour to have one's name included in such distinguished company. I will say only one thing in support of my claims: that there has perhaps been no recipient before whose work has followed so closely and so sympathetically upon that of Jan Swammerdam. There are many discoveries of fundamental interest to the insect physiologist set out in the *Biblia Naturae* or *Historia Generalis Insectorum;* but I am thinking particularly of Swammerdam's contribution to the understanding of growth and metamorphosis.

The scientific study of insect metamorphosis goes back to Aristotle who first put forward the idea that the insect 'larva while it is yet in growth is a soft egg' and that in fact the embryonic life of insects really continues until the formation of the adult, the 'perfect insect' or 'imago'.

William Harvey, in his second great work, *De Generatione Animalium* published in 1651, extended his interests beyond the mammals and the vertebrates and devoted much attention to the generation of insects. We do not know to what extent Harvey's conclusions on this subject were based upon his own observations, for all his records have been lost. Extending the argument of Aristotle, Harvey developed the theory that the insect egg contains so little yolk that the embryo is forced to leave it before completing its development. It then goes through a more or less prolonged larval stage during which it stores up food reserves before resuming the egg form or pupa and completing its embryonic growth.

Harvey recognized quite rightly that the substance of the full-grown larva furnished the material for the production of the adult

168

insect. But he supposed that under the action of some mysterious influence this material suffered a 'metamorphosis' and was rebuilt in an entirely new form: 'like wax bearing the impress of a seal', as he wrote.

It was this miraculous element in Harvey's conception of insect 'metamorphosis' that Swammderdam was out to challenge. The *Biblia Naturae* was completed in 1669, some eighteen years after Harvey's work. In his courteous refutation of some of the opinions of 'this great philosopher' he excused the mistakes of Harvey on the grounds that insects are difficult to study 'unless by persons accustomed to experiments of this kind; it is no wonder that the most happy geniuses, the immortal Harvey, for example, and many others should have fallen into an error'.

For Swammerdam 'epigenesis', a gradual and natural growth, is the only way in which all animal form is fashioned. He stripped away the skin of the caterpillar before it was cast off and found the wings and other parts of the adult butterfly already in process of growth. He inferred that every structure arises by a process of continuous growth from an existing structure; that everything is already preformed in some state, some invisible state that we are unable to appreciate, from the earliest stages of growth. As growth proceeds, the parts become visible and differentiated.

We have in English a familiar invocation: 'may heaven protect us from our friends!' Unfortunately the followers of Swammerdam adopted the crude and exaggerated idea that all the future structures of the body were actually 'preformed' in a literal sense in the egg, and that all growth and development consisted in the unfolding of these structures as successive covering shells were discarded. The height of absurdity was reached when observers claimed to have seen 'homunculi', diminutive outlines of the human form, within the spermatozoon! It was excesses such as these which brought the very reasonable views of Swammerdam into disrepute.

Swammerdam was trying to express ideas for which there was as yet no adequate foundation in physiology. One must realize that at the time he was writing, chemistry was virtually nonexistent; cells were unknown; the foundations of histology were only just being laid by Malpighi; genetics lay two and a half centuries ahead. The best idea he could suggest was that the unformed organs were in a sort of dissolved state and that the evaporation of water caused them gradually to separate out.

Harvey's theory, that the insect egg cannot complete its development because it is deficient in yolk, was shown by Swammerdam to be untenable — because, in the more primitive insects such as silver fish (*Lepisma*) or grasshoppers the creature that emerges from the egg has the same general form as the adult. It is in the higher insects, such as beetles, butterflies, bees and flies, that the most striking examples of metamorphosis are found; yet the eggs of these higher insects are not notably more deficient in yolk.

EMBRYOLOGY AND DIFFERENTIATION

When it comes to the understanding of metamorphosis we are still very much in the dark. But the great advantage over Swammerdam that we enjoy is our knowledge of genetics. The insect begins its development as the fertilized egg cell or zygote. The chromosomes of the zygote carry encoded within them the blueprint for every structure and every function of the future organism. The daughter nuclei of the germinal vesicle, as they migrate to the periphery and enter the different regions of the germ band zone of the cortical plasma (in the mosaic type of insect egg) become committed to form the different regions of the body: the head, thorax, abdomen or gonads.

We see here an example of 'polymorphism': the segmentation nuclei seem to be moulded by the environment in which they find themselves. As they migrated through the yolk they still retained the capacity to form any and every part of the organism. Now they can build only the structures characteristic of some particular region of the body.

This progressive polymorphism of the parts of the body is called 'differentiation'. It seems that local chemical differences or gradients of one sort or another call forth particular elements or capabilities in the chromosomal blueprint; and when that has happened there is generally no return; 'particular powers have been evoked, more generalized potency has been lost' — as Spemann has said.

We do not know precisely the nature of this chemical transformation; but there is some evidence that the characteristic effects which the different regions of the cortical plasma exert upon the nuclei that enter them, may depend upon differences in the nature of the RNA content of each zone.

In these, and other examples that I could quote, it is the

cytoplasm which seems to be exerting the determining influence. It is for this reason that it has been customary in the past to ascribe to the cytoplasm the responsibility for differentiation. But in recent years the tendency has been to put the onus for the developmental changes upon the genes in the nuclei and to describe the cytoplasmic changes as controlling the activation of the relevant parts of the gene system.

The development and differentiation of the embryo is an immensely complex matter: a single cell, the zygote, differentiates in a few days (or even a few hours) into a complex organism, with sense organs and nervous system, muscles, alimentary canal, circulatory system and the rest. The whole process is so bafflingly complex that it seems to defy physiological analysis.

THE EPIDERMIS AS A MODEL OF THE EMBRYO

But, as Swammerdam realized, embryonic development continues in the insect right up to the adult stage. What we need is to isolate a suitable part of this process and so to provide a simpler system that will be more amenable for experimental study. Such a system is to be found in the epidermis of the insect. As was originally shown by Haeckel, this consists of a single layer of cells which lay down a more or less inert cuticle. Each cell is responsible for producing its own tiny area of cuticle, which thus consists of a mosaic made up of the contributions of individual epidermal cells. The epidermis is the chief agent in the control of the body form of the insect. The pattern of the cuticle reflects the differentiation of the cells below, and provides a permanent record of that differentiation.

Here we have a system in which we can observe differentiation at work. I propose to take a very simple example: the epidermis of the abdomen in the blood-sucking bug *Rhodnius*. Over a small area of the surface the integument consists of cubical or flattened epidermal cells with their overlying cuticle. The obvious function of each epidermal cell is, as I have said, to secrete its little area of cuticle — and that is an exceedingly complicated chemical and physiological process which I do not propose to describe (see p. 157). But at the same time the epidermal cell is an embryonic cell: it retains a considerable capacity for differentiation.

When the insect grows it first lays down a new and larger cuticle;

and then it moults and casts off the old cuticle. During this process a given epidermal cell may divide and give rise to daughter cells of the same character which secrete the new cuticle.

Alternatively the cell may divide to produce a group of four cells. Of these one becomes a trichogen cell and gives rise to a tactile hair or bristle; one forms a socket for the hair; one becomes a primary sense cell which gives off a distal process running to the base of the hair and a proximal process or axon which grows inwards and ultimately finds its way to the central nervous system; and finally the fourth cell becomes a neurilemma cell which spreads itself over the axon to provide a sheath for it. Thus the epidermal cell has become differentiated to form a little sense organ or sensillum.

How is this process of differentiation determined? Sensory hairs, each surrounded by a smooth dome-like area or 'plaque' of cuticle are scattered fairly evenly over the surface of the abdominal segments. A certain number of new sensory hairs are formed at each moult; and it is often possible to predict where they will appear — for they always develop where the spaces between the existing hairs are greatest. They are never developed close to the site of an existing hair.

If the epidermal cells below an area of the cuticle are killed by touching the cuticle with a heated rod, the cells from the surrounding zone migrate inwards, dividing as they go, and thus restore the continuous epidermal sheet. When the insect moults the new cuticle laid down by this sheet of cells shows no sensory hairs and plaques. But when the insect moults a second time new sensory hairs appear — and they are scattered at regular intervals just as in the normal insect.

Thus it seems that each sensory hair exerts an inhibitory influence around it, which prevents the appearance of a new hair in its immediate neighbourhood. There are a number of possible explanations for this; the idea that I favour is that some chemical material in the cytoplasm of the epidermal cells is necessary to the development of a sensory hair. When a hair develops it drains the hypothetical substance from the surrounding cells and thus prevents these cells from differentiating to form sense organs. But beyond a certain distance the cells are not deprived of the hypothetical substance. Development of a sensillum begins and this in turn drains away the active substance from the surrounding zone.

What is the meaning of these observations? It would seem that there is a gradient of some kind around each little sensillum. Perhaps this is a concentration gradient of some chemical substance. When the substance exceeds a threshold level the gene system in some epidermal cell is activated and it begins to develop into a sensillum, drains off the active substance and thereby inhibits this development in the surrounding cells.

Now the epidermal cells may undergo another type of development. After dividing to form a group of four daughter cells, one of them may become a large glandular cell and the remaining three cells cooperate to form a sheath and a duct, to give rise to a dermal gland. These dermal glands are scattered evenly over the surface of the integument; but they are more closely spaced than the sensilla. At the first moult that takes place after burning an area of the epidermis, although, as we have seen, no sensilla appear, yet dermal glands become differentiated at regular intervals.

It may be that the same inducing substance that is necessary for the production of sensilla, when it is present at a lower threshold level, will activate that part of the gene system which leads to the development of a dermal gland.

This idea, that an inducer substance evokes different characters, which are latent in the gene system, when it is present at different levels of concentration, is an important one for understanding the nature of growth and differentiation. There is evidence that in each segment of the abdomen of an insect there is a similar gradient which is responsible for determining the polarity of the sensory hairs as they grow out. And it has been shown by Marcus (1962) and recently confirmed by Stumpf (1968) that in the pupae of the wax moth *Galleria,* each level along this gradient evokes a characteristic type of cuticle, and if a minute piece of the integument is transplanted to a new point in this gradient, it develops new characters accordingly.

METAMORPHOSIS IN THE EPIDERMIS

Of course the epidermis of the abdomen, which we are using as a model of embryonic growth, has already undergone a large amount of differentiation. In the larva of *Rhodnius* it is not only divided into a series of segments connected to one another by intersegmental membranes, but each segment bears certain black pigment spots and shows a characteristic pattern in the distribution of sensory

173

hairs with their surrounding plaques. In particular it may be noted that the pigment spots lie at the postero-lateral angle of each segment.

There are five of these larval stages and the pattern of the abdomen remains constant throughout. But when the fifth-stage larva moults to become adult it undergoes a striking metamorphosis: large membranous wings are formed, the genitalia are differentiated, and there is a complete change in the structure and pattern of the cuticle of the abdomen. Sensory hairs are almost absent except at the margins of the abdomen and there are no plaques. The black pigment spots now form trapezoidal patches at the antero-lateral angles of each segment.

We saw earlier that if the epidermis below the cuticle is killed by heat, the epidermal cells from the margins of the burn divide and migrate inwards until the deficiency is repaired. As these cells grow inwards they carry with them the characters for which they have been determined. So that if the margin of the burn passes through a couple of pigment spots, then, when the wound is healed and the larva moults to the next larval stage it is found that there has been a centripetal displacement of the pigment pattern (see p. 162).

Now it is possible to inflict a burn of this sort between two pigment spots of a young larva (see p. 163, Fig. 9). In the next larval stage, as was to be expected, these spots are found to be united. Or the burn may be applied to a single pigment spot. In the next larval stage this spot has disappeared because the wound has been repaired by cells which have been determined to lay down unpig-mented cuticle.

But, as we have already seen, the position of the pigment spots in the larva and the adult is reversed: what were black pigment spots in the larva become colourless areas in the adult. So that when these larvae undergo metamorphosis to the adult the apparent effect of the injuries inflicted in the young larva are quite different. Where the two pigment spots had fused in the larva, the pigment spot of the adult has almost vanished. And where the pigment spot of the larva was eliminated by burning, two adjacent adult spots have joined together (see p. 163, Fig. 9c).

Swammerdam would have appreciated this experiment, for it illustrates his point extremely well. It shows that even in the larva with its characteristic pattern of the body, the totally different pattern of the adult is already laid out — but in an invisible form.

The cells, actively engaged in forming some element of the larval pattern have already been determined to form some quite different element in the pattern of the adult. The adult pattern is 'preformed'.

This brings us to the question of metamorphosis. What brings about the switch from larva to adult? We have known for many years now that this is brought about by a change in the circulating hormones. The process of growth which leads on to moulting is set going by a secretion from neurosecretory cells in the dorsum of the brain. This secretion passes down the axons of the neurosecretory cells and is discharged into the circulating blood from the corpus cardiacum. This 'brain hormone' activates a gland in the thorax, the so-called 'thoracic gland' and causes this to liberate the 'moulting hormone', ecdysone.

JUVENILE HORMONE

Another glandular organ close behind the brain is the corpus allatum, which secretes another hormone, the so-called 'juvenile hormone'. So long as this hormone is present in the circulating blood at the time of moulting the insect retains its juvenile or larval characters.

But in the 5th-stage larva of *Rhodnius* the corpus allatum no longer secretes the juvenile hormone. And when the growing cells are exposed to the moulting hormone alone, in the absence of juvenile hormone, they develop the latent adult characters and the insect is said to undergo metamorphosis.

If the corpus allatum, removed from a young larva, is implanted into the abdomen of a 5th-stage larva, this duly moults again, but instead of becoming adult it turns into a giant 6th-stage larva. Sometimes the experiment is not so successful as this: the larva may moult to an adult with a little area of larval cuticle immediately overlying the implanted gland.

Clearly the juvenile hormone acts directly on the epidermal cells themselves. Carroll Williams (1956) found that the lipid extracted from adult males of the cecropia silkmoth is an active source of juvenile hormone. If this material is applied locally to the integument of the 5th-stage larva of *Rhodnius* a localized effect is produced so that one can obtain adult insects with one larval wing; or adult insects with one larval segment in the abdomen. It is even possible to engrave the abdomen of an adult with initials in larval cuticle.

We saw that there is some evidence that graded concentrations of inductor substances can lead to *qualitative* differences in the characters produced. The same is true of the juvenile hormone. In such insects as Lepidoptera in which there is a pupal stage interposed between the larva and the adult, there is evidence that when the cells of the moulting insect are exposed to a large amount of juvenile hormone, larval characters are retained; when only a small amount of juvenile hormone is present, pupal characters appear; and in the complete absence of juvenile hormone, adult characters are developed (Piepho, 1951).

These morphological effects are spectacular; and of course the details of the effect are quite different in each part of the body. And yet the whole transformation can be brought about by a simple chemical compound. The chemical nature of the natural juvenile hormone is not yet known. But materials with juvenile hormone activity are widespread in nature and can be extracted from a wide range of invertebrates, from the tissues of vertebrates, including man, from many protozoa, plants, bacteria and yeasts. Peter Schmialek (1961) examined two of these sources: the excreta of the mealworm *Tenebrio* and yeast. In both cases the active material proved to be a mixture of farnesol and its oxidation product farnesal. Schmialek showed that if the stability of these compounds was increased, as in farnesyl acetone or farnesyl methyl ether, the activity was greatly enhanced and Law, Yuan and Williams (1966) have shown that chlorinated derivatives of farnesoic acid are even more active. The insect can synthesize farnesol (Schmialek, 1963) and it may be that in producing the natural hormone it makes use of some farnesol derivative.*

But the point of interest at the moment is that these farnesol derivatives in minute doses will reproduce all the morphogenetic effects of the juvenile hormone. That is because all that the juvenile

---

*The chemical nature of the juvenile hormone in the cecropia silk-moth was shown by Röller *et al.* (1967) to be the methyl ester of a farnesoic acid homologue, in which there is an epoxy ring, and in which two of the methyl side-chains are replaced by ethyl groups; along with this is a second homologue in which only one ethyl group replaces a methyl group (Meyer *et al.,* 1968). And in some other insects a third type has been found which is just the methyl ester of farnesoic acid itself with an epoxy group.

hormone is doing is switching the gene system and thus controlling the manifestation of one or other of its inborn or 'preformed' characters. That is the link which Swammerdam had not got. But when it comes to saying exactly how the hormone exerts this discriminative effect we are not in a position to give a clear-cut answer.

We may summarize our conception of embryonic growth in the insect by saying that when the daughter cells of the zygote are exposed to different chemical environments, sometimes perhaps merely to different concentrations of one chemical, they are induced to follow special lines of development leading to the formation of different parts of the body. Each of these parts of the body can appear in larval form, in pupal form or in adult form — and these differences are known to be controlled by different concentrations of the juvenile hormone.

POLYMORPHISM

Metamorphosis is clearly an example of gene-switching brought about by a controlling hormone. There is increasing evidence to suggest that differentiation is likewise brought about by gene-switching due to chemical differences in the cytoplasm to which the chromosomes are exposed. And there is yet another type of polymorphism which is controlled in the same way.

I refer, of course, to those examples of 'environmental polymorphism' in which there are striking differences in form between different individuals of a species, although their genetic constitution is believed to be identical. Environmental factors of many kinds are responsible in deciding the form that a given individual shall take. But it is interesting to note that circulating hormones are very commonly the agents that are used to bring about this switch. In some cases, such as the change among termites from the worker larva to the soldier, or the switch from the winged aphid to the wingless form, it seems to be the juvenile hormone itself that is used as the hormonal agent to regulate the change.

The 'preformation' that Swammerdam postulated has thus been driven back into the gene system. The next step will be to describe exactly how these genetic switches are brought about. We already have some highly suggestive ideas developed by Jacob and Monod and others to account for the adaptive synthesis of enzymes in bacteria that can be induced by the substrates in the environment. Perhaps these ideas will eventually provide the mechanism we are seeking.

In conclusion I must return to the theory of Aristotle as developed by Harvey: that the insect larva is a walking embryo which builds up reserves of nutriment before it reverts once more to the egg stage or pupa and completes its development to the adult.

This theory gave a satisfying interpretation of metamorphosis which held the field for two hundred years after Harvey's day. But close study of the caterpillar of the butterfly, or of the maggot of the fly, at once reveals that the resemblance of these creatures to embryos is only superficial. These larvae are, in fact, exceedingly complex organisms, each closely adapted to the environment in which it lives.

It is this adaptation which provides the key to the problem. It was pointed out by Darwin that when a larva feeds on different foods and lives in a different environment from the adult, it will be subject to quite different selection pressures, and its characters will evolve quite independently of the adult. The greater the difference in the way of life of the two stages, the wider will the structural differences become — until an intermediate pupal stage must likewise be evolved to bridge the gap between them.

In some degree those elements of the gene system that determine the characters of the larva are independent of the elements that control the characters of the adult. In the end we almost seem to have two (or three) separate forms locked up in the same animal. It was Sir Thomas Browne, in writing of the silkworm three hundred years ago, who expressed his amazement at the existence of 'two souls in those little bodies'.

There is nothing here that is different in principle from what we are familiar with in mammalian physiology. We accept the idea that male and female characters are latent in every embryo. The balance of genes and the endocrine constitution of the individual dictate which of these latent forms shall become evident.

What is peculiar about the insect is the spectacular nature of the changes in form, the clear-cut character of the hormonal regulation of these changes, and the fact that the system is so arranged that the forms which are latent in the embryo are regularly manifested in succession during the life of the individual.

The whole story illustrates the point which Malpighi and

Swammerdam tried to bring home to their contemporaries: that one of the most promising ways of advancing knowledge of human physiology is to study the workings of the body in these simpler organisms.

REFERENCES

Law, J. H., Yuan, C. and Williams, C. M. (1966) Synthesis of a material with high juvenile hormone activity. *Proc. nat. Acad. Sci. U.S.A.*, **55**, 576—578.

Marcus, W. (1962) Untersuchungen über die Polarität der Rumpfhaut von Schmetterlingen. *Wilhelm Roux Arch. Entw. Mech. Org.* **154**, 56—102.

Meyer, A. S., Schneiderman, H. A., Hanzmann, E. and Ko, J. H. (1968) The two juvenile hormones from the cecropia silk moth. *Proc. nat. Acad. Sci. U.S.A.*, **60**, 853—860.

Piepho, H. (1951) Über die Lenkung der Insektenmetamorphose durch Hormone. *Verh. dt. zool. Ges.* Wilhelmshaven, 1951, 62—75.

Röller, H., Dahm, K. H., Sweely, C. C. and Trost, B. M. (1967) The structure of the juvenile hormone. *Angew. Chem. (Int. Ed.)*, **6**, 179—180.

Schmialek, P. (1961) Identifizierung zweier in Tenebriokot und in Hefe vorkommender Substanzen mit Juvenilhormonwirkung. *Z. Naturf.* **16b**, 461—464.

Schmialek, P. (1963) Über Verbindungen mit Juvenilhormonwirkung. *Z. Naturf.* **18b**, 516—519.

Stumpf, H. F. (1968) Further studies on gradient dependent diversification in the pupal cuticle of *Galleria mellonella*. *J. Exp. Biol.*, **49**, 49—60.

Williams, C. M. (1956) The juvenile hormone of insects. *Nature, Lond.*, **178**, 212—213.

15

EXPERIMENTAL BIOLOGY,
PURE AND APPLIED

There are those who really believe that the purpose of science is to increase human welfare. That was the vision which inspired Francis Bacon, writing of the 'Novum Organum' at a time when modern science scarcely existed, and advocating a scientific procedure, which, by and large, has proved unproductive. It was the vision, also, which inspired Joseph Priestley, writing 150 years later when experimental science was really getting under way. Priestley predicted the profound effects that the new knowledge was going to have on human affairs.

That has duly come to pass; and the process is still going forward at an ever-increasing pace. But it is my object in this lecture to assert that that is not the *purpose* of science. The purpose of science is to increase knowledge. Science is the formulation of our knowledge about natural phenomena in a co-ordinated fashion by the establishment of principles and theories which epitomize that knowledge and thus provide enduring tools for thought. Scientific knowledge so formulated becomes common property and can be drawn upon for the solution of practical problems of every kind.

Sometimes, in effect, it is the scientific investigator who himself turns to apply new knowledge to practical ends; so that the boundary between these totally different kinds of activity becomes blurred. Moreover, as everyone knows, scientific research depends on asking the right questions; and some of the most pregnant questions arise from the field of practice. For centuries the problems for the physiologist sprang from the experiences of clinicians. It seems a pity that today academic physiologists tend to cut themselves off from this source.

I do not myself find the distinction between 'pure research' and 'applied research' a good one. The important distinction is between 'useful research' and 'futile research'. Useful research adds effectually to knowledge; research may be futile because the wrong questions are being asked, because it has gone on too long on set lines in one direction, and for many other reasons. But it is not my intention in this lecture to regale you with profound generalizations of this kind. I shall offer you only a personal saga; and first I must explain how it is that I have any claims to speak about applied biology.

TRAINING IN APPLIED BIOLOGY

After a brief experience, of a couple of years, in academic research in biochemistry under Gowland Hopkins, I was trained in medicine, an art based largely upon applied science; and then for twenty years I was occupied in teaching medical entomology. I travelled extensively, and in some of the less healthy places of the world: in the rat-infested shanties that made up much of Lagos during the plague outbreak of 1928; and the areas of Northern Nigeria where epidemics of sleeping sickness were rife; in some of the most malarious areas of India, such as the tea gardens of the northern foothills of Bengal and Assam and in the so-called 'Valley of Death' in the Anamallai Hills of South India. I visited many of the less salubrious locations in Malaya, Burma and Java; and was present in Ceylon during the great malaria epidemic of 1934 in which some 100 000 persons died.

Then, in the early nineteen-forties I switched from medicine to agriculture and entered the employ of the Agricultural Research Council. I travelled throughout the United Kingdom to visit all the main centres where research in agricultural and veterinary entomology is done; and I followed this up with an intensive tour in which I visited some sixty of the corresponding centres in all four corners of the United States and Canada. More recently I have been able to travel in agricultural and in medical entomology in Egypt, in East Africa (where one could witness the transformation in outlook since the pre-DDT days and the advent of modern anti-malarial drugs) and in Japan; and, only last year, throughout the Commonwealth of Australia.

I can therefore claim to have covered a varied practical course in applied entomology — including also forest entomology, stored-product entomology and veterinary entomology. I am not, of course, an applied entomologist; it would be most unwise for any of you to commission me to handle an actual problem in either the medical or agricultural field. But I know the people who do this work, I understand their language and their way of thinking, and have the greatest respect for their achievements.

PURE AND APPLIED SCIENCE IN THE UNITED STATES

Now as you must all be aware, there is alarm and despondency among scientists in the United States because Congress has issued a fiat demanding concentration upon practical problems; and the grant-giving bodies are all being pressed to favour and support only projects that are likely to lead to practical results. There is widespread fear for the ruin of American science and the downgrading of all the outstanding fundamental research that is being carried out.

But let us look a little more closely at this matter. Widespread interest in basic research in the United States is something new. There was, of course, a long tradition of good academic research in the American universities. But, by and large, the United States looked to Europe for the fundamental discoveries of science. What caused the change in outlook? The answer is: the needs of applied science. If you look up the *Atlantic Monthly* for the summer of 1945 you will find an article by Dr Vannevar Bush, then President of the Carnegie Institute in Washington, who held the position of Director of the Office of Scientific Research and Development from 1941 to 1947 and was one of the chief scientific advisors to President Roosevelt during the war years. It was Vannevar Bush and J. B. Conant who advised Roosevelt to proceed with the project of the atomic bomb. The thesis developed in the article to which I refer was that the war had revealed the deficiency of the United States in basic science. The extent to which physicists had necessarily been recruited from Europe for the development of the atomic bomb was stressed, and the need to make good this deficiency was emphasized.

These thoughts bore fruit. The National Institutes of Health were established in the early post-war years; the Atomic Energy Commission was set up; in 1950 the National Science Foundation was formed; in the same year, with the election of D. W. Bronk as President of the National Academy of Science, that august body entered vigorously into the political arena of science; and as part of the general enthusiasm for basic research the armed services in the United States distributed largesse in the way of research grants for almost any scientific topic — not only within America but overseas as well. Support from these sources expanded for nearly twenty years; but now a reaction has set in. Support for foreign research began seriously to be cut in 1964. Now retrenchment is hitting the home market; and pessimists in the United States feel that they are witnessing the beginning of the end of the 'U.S. age of science'. What will the future be? I shall return to that question a little later.

DDT AS AN ILLUSTRATIVE EXAMPLE

It happens that in the same volume of the *Atlantic Monthly,* in the December number (1945), there appeared another article which is relevant to my argument. At that time I had recently returned from the United States, where I had been humbly sitting at the feet of the American agricultural entomologists, trying to learn the elements of their trade, and was taking part in an autumn meeting in Cumberland to discuss problems of sheep dipping, when I was called to the 'phone at our inn in Eskdale. It was a call from the Central Office of Information who had received a request from the United States that I be invited to contribute an article on DDT to the *Atlantic Monthly.* Such indeed was the dependence of the United States on European science! The article was entitled 'DDT and the Balance of Nature'. It appeared under the editorial caption: 'A scientist looks at tomorrow' — but I am afraid that my prophetic perspicacity was not of a very profound order (p. 13).

'DDT', I wrote, 'is a valuable supplement to hygiene and cleanliness. It will not take their place . . . When strong solutions, such as are used for spraying forests from the air, fall on water, not only are all the acquatic insects . . . killed, but . . . fish are destroyed and the streams rendered practically devoid of animal life . . . Only careful experiments can prove whether birds will suffer or not . . . It is obvious enough that DDT is a two-edged sword. We can see how seriously it may upset the balance locally between insect enemies and friends . . . It can bring about within a single year a disturbance that it would take other chemicals a good many years to produce.'

The manner in which insects develop 'resistant races' was described — with the implication that this would surely happen with DDT; and a plea was made for increased study of insect ecology and the search for insecticides of a more selective type. All this has a terribly familiar ring today.

At that time there seemed to be an immense amount of work to be

183

done in the study of DDT and its use. But it was all accomplished within a year or two years at the most. That is my point. 'Applied science' consists mainly in doing useful jobs with the help of scientific knowledge. Nearly always some local adaptations are necessary, sometimes quite difficult ones, so that highly intelligent investigation is required. Indeed the formidable difficulties of applied science are commonly greatly underestimated by the academic scientist. But in a broad sense it is true that the amount of thoroughgoing research is relatively limited. When new ideas or new methods emerge there will be a burst of activity as they are tried out under all varied conditions — and then the cry is for more knowledge. The knowledge that is used for some practical purpose lies at the apex of a pyramid that represents the corpus of Science. The deeper strata of this pyramid represent the accumulated knowledge of the basic sciences.

THE NATURE OF THE CONTRIBUTION OF PURE SCIENCE

My own real interests lie some way up this pyramid, but not at the apex. How did it come about that I should get caught up in the applied sciences — first in medical and then in agricultural entomology? It was the demand from the applied people for more knowledge. In 1926 when Patrick Buxton was appointed head of the Department of Entomology at the London School of Hygiene and Tropical Medicine he wrote a letter to *Nature* in which he pointed out that medical entomology was being held up by lack of knowledge of the physiology of insects. He sold this idea to Morley Fletcher, then Secretary of the Medical Research Council and an influential member of the Board of Management of the School, who believed ardently in 'watering the roots' of science. After a memorable interview with Fletcher, and backed by his friend and former collaborator Gowland Hopkins, I was recruited to enter this field; and so started on some 45 happy years of 'experimental biology' — 'pure', and on the insect.

During the war years, in the time off from crash courses for service medical officers and War Office committees, this work still continued. I became involved in an inquiry, initiated by W. W. C. Topley, then Secretary of the Agricultural Research Council, into insecticides and what could be done to improve them. Much evidence was taken and the outcome was that more *knowledge* was needed — particularly about the physiology of insects. In that way the A.R.C. Unit of Insect Physiology came into being.

That, in principle, is what will happen in the present crisis of science in the United States. Cut off the continuing supply of new basic scientific knowledge and the applied sciences quickly run out of steam. They set up such a call for help that the whole vast machine of fundamental research has to be set going again.

At the outbreak of war in 1939 everyone felt that they ought to do some science that would help the war effort. Even the Council of this Society set going a search for seaweeds to yield agar, and for brambles or briars that would furnish an improved source for gunpowder. And at the London School of Tropical Medicine we all became more self-consciously 'applied' in our outlook. But by the end of the war it was realized that the main shortage was of *knowledge*. War Office committees were funding all kinds of basic pieces of research; and in 1945 when I visited the United States I found that precisely the same thing was happening there. Insect physiology was a word to conjure with.

At a luncheon in Winnepeg during my tour I was invited by B. N. Smallman to speak (off the cuff) on 'The contribution of insect physiology to medical entomology'. To the alarm of my hosts I started by saying that it made 'no contribution' — that is, no *direct* contribution. As I had written earlier (April, 1944) in *Discovery:* 'Lip service is often paid to the importance of pure science as an aid to practice. But even the loudest advocates sometimes fail to make out a convincing case. That is because it is rare for the results of research in pure science to have an immediate practical application.* It is only when the intervening links are interposed that the connexion becomes apparent. It is then seen that the practical measures directed against an insect, for example, depend first upon an accurate recognition of that insect species; then upon a thorough knowledge of its habits. As soon as its habits are closely studied, problems in its physiology arise for solution. These wait upon a knowledge of the physiology of insects in general; and so in turn on general physiology, chemistry and physics.' I propose now to illustrate the point by reference to the physiology of the insect cuticle.

---

*DDT was synthesized by O. Zeidler in 1874; it was nearly 80 years before it found a use as an insecticide.

FORTY YEARS RESEARCH ON THE INSECT CUTICLE

I first became interested in the insect cuticle in the early 1930s. During the previous decade two important points had come to be realized. Firstly, that the hard and horny component of the cuticle was something quite different from the chitin of Odier (as, in fact, Odier himself in 1823 had clearly recognized), and secondly, that the cuticle was not to be regarded solely as an external skeleton, but that its waterproof properties were of equal importance in the life of the insect.

Cuticle hardening

The hardening or 'sclerotization' of the cuticle was attributed to impregnating substances or 'Inkrusten' considered by the German authors to be probably carbohydrate in nature. Working on the cuticle of the blood-sucking bug *Rhodnius*, I suggested that the sclerotizing material was a mixture of lipid and protein that I called 'cuticulin'. This mixture by itself was believed to form the 'epicuticle'; and in the deeper horny layer (the 'exocuticle') it was believed to impregnate the chitinous framework. Cuticulin was supposed to be hardened by lipid polymerization — due perhaps to an oxidative condensation of unsaturated chains, as in the formation of a varnish. Physically the substance resembled shellac in hardness; and shellac is now known to be a lipid polyester (Cockeram and Levine, 1961).

The deposition of this lipid-containing material ran parallel with the secretory activity in the oenocytes which were at their maximum size when the deposition of new cuticle was about to begin; they were completely exhausted at the time of ecdysis when the exocuticle was complete. The bulk of the cuticle (the unimpregnated endocuticle) is laid down after moulting when the oenocytes are inactive. Moreover the oenocytes are very rich in bound lipid. These cells, whose function is usually regarded as enigmatic, are to be thought of, I believe, as ectodermal cells (they commonly continue to arise from the epidermis throughout post-embryonic development) which have become specialized for this one function among many that reside in the epidermis: the secretion and storage of structural lipids or lipoprotein (Wigglesworth, 1933).

Then in 1940 Mark Pryor put forward his illuminating theory that the horny component of the cuticle, which he named 'sclerotin', is just protein that is tanned by quinones produced from the oxidation

186

of diphenols secreted into the cuticle at the time of moulting. In my enthusiasm for this new interpretation I unwisely abandoned my belief that lipids were involved — though Dennell and Malek (1955) firmly maintained that there was a large element of truth in the cuticulin theory.

There is now a very extensive literature on the nature of the tanning process in the cuticle. Notably the work by Karlson and Sekeris and others (Karlson and Sekeris, 1962) in Germany, by Brunet (1967) in this country and by Hackman (1964) in Australia. The enzyme chemistry of the process, notably in the öotheca of the cockroach and in the puparium of blowflies, has been extensively studied. It appears that the proteins are linked directly to the benzene ring of the quinone and are irreversibly bound by what must be a somewhat violent reaction. But very recently a much more gentle form of phenolic polymerization has been described by S. O. Andersen (1970) in which acetyl dopamine seems again to be the precursor; but the proteins are linked to the β-carbon atom of the side-chain and the two phenolic groups on the benzene ring survive intact.

Structural lipids

But this is not the whole story. Quinone-tanned protein is not the same thing as sclerotin. Moreover there is refractile semi-hardened cuticle which shows no evidence of the presence of phenolic substances and is not regarded as being tanned — such as the 'mesocuticle' which lies below the tanned exocuticle in the cockroach, or the 'taenidia' which form the stiffening threads of the tracheae, or the walls of the wing scales of Lepidoptera. Reinvestigation has shown that all these structures are in fact heavily impregnated with lipid. That has been shown histochemically by Sudan-black staining after the oxidative fission of the protein in the cuticle with dilute hypochlorite (Wigglesworth, 1970).

These observations are in agreement with the chemical analyses of the cuticle of various insects that have been carried out in recent years. Far more lipid can be extracted by prolonged treatment with hot chloroform and methanol than is likely to exist in the invisible layer of free wax on the surface. The following are a few of the results reported for total extractable lipids on a dry-weight basis: mealworm, *Tenebrio molitor,* cast larval skins, 5 per cent (Bursell and Clements, 1967); Mormon cricket, *Anabrus simplex,* whole abdominal cuticle, 4·3 per cent (Baker *et al.*, 1960); blowfly, *Lucilia cuprina*, empty puparia, 2·6 per cent; the same, cast pupal skins, 31·4 per cent (Gilby and McKellar, 1970); and the following are some preliminary results obtained recently by Dr J. T. Martin (personal communication): *Dermestes maculatus*, cast larval skins, 9 per cent; *Oncopeltus fasciatus*, cast larval skins, 15 per cent.

There is no doubt that phenolic or quinone tanning is of prime importance in the sclerotization of the hardest parts of the cuticle, but quite firm cuticle can be produced in the absence of tanning or before tanning takes place. The nature of this process is not known. I suggested in a recent paper (Wigglesworth, 1970) that the lipid might be a polyester comparable with the plant cuticle or with shellac; but hydroxy fatty acids are not common among the lipids that can be extracted from the cuticle. Perhaps the change is merely a physical one: a denaturation of protein by interaction with lipid and the consequent exclusion of water.

Waterproofing properties of the cuticle
The importance of the waterproofing properties of the cuticle in the life of insects was appreciated much later than its skeletal function. This appreciation goes back I think only to the theory put forward in 1927 by Hazelhoff that the function of the spiracular valves on the tracheal system of insects is to prevent the loss of water by evaporation. This theory carried with it the assumption that the cuticle itself is highly waterproof. In 1935 I extended Hazelhoff's observations to the control of respiration in the flea and Mellanby (1934) confirmed that if the flea is obliged to keep its spiracles open (by exposure to carbon dioxide) it rapidly loses moisture. It had been pointed out by Kühnelt (1928) that soft-skinned insects, such as larvae of the clothes moth *Tineola*, are just as successful in retaining water as are sclerotized insects, such as larvae of the mealworm *Tenebrio*. Clearly the waterproof layer must be at the surface of the cuticle.

The first indication of the nature of the waterproofing system was obtained by Ramsay (1935), who observed that minute droplets of water sprayed on the surface of the cuticle of the cockroach *Periplaneta*, instead of evaporating in a few moments, remained unchanged for hours. They had been covered by a waterproofing lipid film which had spread over them from the cuticle. When the temperature was raised above about 35 °C there appeared to be a phase change in the lipid coating and the droplets evaporated immediately. Likewise when the whole insect was exposed to a temperature above 35 °C there was a more or less abrupt increase in the rate of transpiration. Thus a thin layer of lipid, perhaps a mono-molecular layer in the case of the water droplets, was highly effective in preventing transpiration.

Abrasive and absorptive dusts

It had long been known that fine inert dusts were lethal to insects. Indeed the protection of stored grain against insect attack by the addition of fine road dust had been practised in North Africa since Roman times. In the early 1940s it was found that certain refined dusts, notably of silica and of crystalline alumina (synthetic sapphire powder) were exceedingly effective. It was generally agreed that the insects died from desiccation, but, as was noted by Alexander, Kitchener and Briscoe (1944), in many species the dust was active only when applied to the living insect. The explanation of this curious observation proved quite simple. Experiments on *Rhodnius* (Wigglesworth, 1945) showed that in many parts of the body the waterproofing layer is quite superficial, but it is not broken down by simple contact with the fine dust — that is, by adsorption; it can be interrupted only by superficial abrasion. When the insect is alive and moving the dust gets into the joints and elsewhere and rubs away a part of the waterproof covering (Wigglesworth, 1945, 1947b).

In the recently engorged larva of *Rhodnius* the distended abdomen is drawn along the surface as it runs. If it is moving on filter paper lightly dusted with alumina, the surface of the cuticle is abraded at the point of contact and within 24 h in a dry atmosphere the larva is completely dried up and dead. The abraded areas are readily detected by immersing the insect in ammoniacal silver hydroxide; the exposed diphenols in the epicuticle produce deep brown areas of silver reduction. But if, under these same conditions, the abdomen is held away from the surface with a little knob of paraffin wax, the larva survives with very little loss of moisture (Wigglesworth, 1945). In certain other insects, such as the cockroach and some termites, the waterproofing material is quite mobile and is readily removed by adsorption in the dead and motionless insect (Wigglesworth, 1945; Ebeling, 1961; Collins and Richards, 1966).

Waterproofing waxes

These superficial waterproofing waxes vary in character from a soft mobile grease as in the cockroach, through soft waxes as in caterpillars and sawfly larvae, to waxes of increasing hardness in the mealworm, in *Rhodnius,* in the honey bee, and finally in the pupae of Lepidoptera (*Pieris*) which must withstand exposure for many months. All these insects show the same phenomenon as the cockroach: there is a more or less abrupt increase in the rate of transpiration when the temperature is raised — but the transition temperature at which the break occurs rises from about 33 °C to about 58 °C as the waxes increase in hardness (Wigglesworth, 1945). And Beament (1945, 1961) using the wax extracted from the cast skins of these same insects, applied to artificial membranes, got comparable results.

Even when the waterproofing wax is a solid crystalline material on the surface of the cuticle it is a very fragile barrier against the drying power of the environment; it is indeed invisibly thin. It turned out that in most insects, just at the time of moulting, a further protective layer, the so-called 'cement layer', is poured out by numerous dermal glands and spreads evenly over the entire surface of the waterproofing wax (Wigglesworth, 1947*a*, 1948). In the cockroach the 'cement layer' seems to be of a sponge-like nature and to be permeated by the waterproofing grease (Kramer and Wigglesworth, 1950).

The cuticular grease of the cockroach is readily obtained by dripping chloroform over the surface of the living insect. I found that when it was stored in contact with the air for some months this grease changed into a hard wax. With my prejudice in favour of the polymerization of unsaturated lipids in the cuticle I was inclined to regard this as the result of autoxidation. At my suggestion the nature of the change was looked into by Beament and he obtained some evidence that it resulted from the evaporation of volatile solvents (he suggested a mixture of short-chain paraffins and alcohols) (Beament, 1955). Gilby and Cox (1963), however, using gas chromatography were unable to confirm the presence of such solvents. The major component proved to be the unsaturated hydrocarbon *cis-cis*-6,9-heptacosadiene (Beatty and Gilby, 1969). Atkinson and Gilby (1970) have recently shown that when the grease is isolated and exposed to the air this unsaturated hydrocarbon undergoes autoxidation, with the formation of the waxy solids stearal and stearic acid. Polymers formed by free-radicals may also contribute to the hardening. In the living insect the free protocatechuic acid, which is believed to be the primary source of the o-quinone involved in tanning (Brunet, 1967), has the additional function of serving as an antioxidant which prevents the oxidative degradation and polymerization of the cuticle lipid (Atkinson and Gilby, 1970).

Of course the 'cement layer' is not proof against gross abrasion. Insects in the soil (wireworms, chafer beetle larvae, etc.) become so scratched by abrasive particles that if they are exposed in a dry atmosphere they lose water rapidly. But if a larva of the wireworm *Agriotes,* for example, is taken from the soil and kept in a moist atmosphere, and allowed to moult under conditions where it does not come into contact with abrasive particles, it lays down a good waterproof cuticle which has a sharp 'critical temperature' and it does not suffer rapid desiccation under dry conditions (Wigglesworth, 1945).

Wax secretion

Where does the wax in the cuticle come from? Until very shortly before the old skin is shed the new cuticle is not waterproof. Indeed the digested product of the inner layers of the old cuticle are being absorbed through it. Only in the last hour or so does the surface of the new cuticle become dry and hydrophobic and waterproof. The wax is exuded through the substance of the new cuticle, which has no visible ducts. It was observed in the 1830s that the cuticle is traversed by fine canals, named by Leydig in 1855 the 'pore canals', which extend outwards from the epidermal cells. But the pore canals, which are only a fraction of a micrometre in diameter, end blindly below the epicuticle, which is usually rather less than a micrometre in thickness.

In 1942 I noted that if any small insect is immersed in a drop of oil, such as medicinal paraffin, covered with a coverslip and observed under the microscope, minute droplets of water soon begin to exude from the cuticle into the oil. This happens both over areas covered by soft cuticle, such as the intesegmental membranes, and, more slowly, over areas with horny cuticle (Wigglesworth, 1942). This was a highly suggestive observation because it implied that there must be a connexion between the pore canals and the surface.

Further evidence of this was obtained by exposing the surface of the new cuticle to ammoniacal silver hydroxide at different stages during the time when the wax layer is being formed. The medium which carries the wax or its precursors forms a precipitate with the silver solution. This blackened precipitate spreads radially from points overlying the pore canals. And it is often possible to see that the precipitate is penetrating the substance of the epicuticle and connecting up with a pore canal (Wigglesworth, 1947a, 1948).

The explanation was ultimately found by Michael Locke (1961) in an electron-microscope study of the cuticle. Locke showed that beyond the distal endings of the pore canals, and connected with the tips of these canals, there are excessively fine tracks, no more than 100—130 Å in diameter in *Tenebrio,* which spread out fan-wise to penetrate the epicuticle and lead to its free surface. These tracts doubtless provide the looked-for outlets from the epidermal cells. In the wax-secreting epithelium of the honey-bee there is the same arrangement in more exaggerated form. The cytoplasm of the epidermal cells contains whorls of filaments which become bundled together and form a sort of rope in the pore canal and then continue into the individual tracts to the surface. Locke calls them 'wax canal filaments'.

At the light-microscope level one cannot see these structures. But with nitric acid and potassium chlorate it is possible to dissolve away the rest of the newly formed cuticle to liberate the contents of the pore canals as fine strands which are rich in lipids. These lipids are set free and become stainable with Sudan black on oxidation with dilute sodium hypochlorite (Wigglesworth, 1970).*

Locke (1961) also showed that the pore canals contain an esterase. This could well be a protease (for most proteases, such as trypsin and many peptidases, have esterase activity) and may perhaps be concerned with liberation of the fluid medium that spreads over the surface of the cuticle and from which the waterproofing wax crystallizes out. It seems likely that this is a continuing process in the life of the insect, and that the pore canals provide a constant reservoir of waterproofing wax. In *Rhodnius,* if the surface of the cuticle is lightly abraded with alumina dust and the powder is then washed off and the insect kept in a humid atmosphere to avoid

---

*Recent studies with the electron microscope, using a new method for visualizing lipid in tissue sections, have shown that although, at times, the pore canals do contain lipids, the lipid-rich strands described above represent the lipid-impregnated *walls* of the pore canals (Wigglesworth, 1975).

desiccation, new wax is secreted and forms a white bloom over the scratched area, and the impermeability of the cuticle to water loss is restored (Wigglesworth, 1945).

Many other interesting things have been discovered about the insect cuticle in recent years: on the interrelations of protein and chitin by Hackman (1964) and by Rudall (1963); on the rubber-like protein 'resilin', which occurs in all those regions where a high degree of elasticity is required, by Andersen and Weis-Fogh (1964); on the reversible plasticity of the soft cuticle, by Bennet-Clark (1962); on the nature and variety of lamination in the chitin-protein micelles of the cuticle by Neville (1965, 1967); and much more besides. I have confined my remarks to those aspects of the subject in which I happen to have been involved.

Conclusions

No one can be concerned in thinking deeply about contact insecticides or about the ecology of insects in adverse climates without constantly reflecting on the properties of the cuticle. In that sense what we have learned in the past forty years is a great contribution to applied entomology: it has provided essential tools for thought. But one would find it difficult to point to a *single* discovery, taken by itself in this field, and claim that *this* has been of practical value.

Besides joining in these investigations of the cuticle, I have been engaged in studying insect digestion, respiration, excretion, and water conservation, ionic and osmo-regulation, the nervous system, sense organs and behaviour, the control of growth and form and various other matters. As with the insect cuticle, the general body of knowledge that has been built up about all these topics by a small army of insect physiologists now forms part of the intellectual armoury of the applied entomologist.

Perhaps the last item on my list, the control of growth and form, is the most academic of the lot, with the least bearing upon applied science. And yet, curiously enough, this is the only topic that has hit the headlines in respect to insect control. When the chemical nature of the juvenile hormone was finally established by Röller and his colleagues (1968) it turned out to be a terpenoid. And many other terpenoids, more or less related, had already been found to have similar effects on growth and reproduction; or abnormal effects, causing malformation or sterility. As a result a new potential field for the synthesis of new kinds of insecticides is being opened up with tremendous energy at the present time. And yet, when I described the hormonal control of moulting and metamorphosis in 1934, and demonstrated the existence of the hormone which we later called the juvenile hormone, I was unable to persuade Patrick Buxton to include a reference to these discoveries in the annual report on the work of the Department of Entomology at the London School.

Man is an arrogant animal. In the euphoric state engendered by her Centenary in 1969, even *Nature* was betrayed into claiming that 'the directions of scientific advance are no longer left to chance but, rather, are charted almost deliberately in advance'. In his famous address to the combined Darwin Centenary and International Congress of Zoology in the Albert Hall in 1958, Julian Huxley assured us that man was no longer subject to natural selection. As one who does not believe any of these things I hold that there are still unexpected discoveries to be made, and that there is still room for the enquiring mind and the untrammelled researches of the experimental biologist.

REFERENCES

Alexander, P., Kitchener, J. A. and Briscoe, H. V. A. (1944) Inert dust insecticides. I. Mechanism of action. *Ann. Appl. Biol.,* **31,** 143—149.

Andersen, S. O. and Barrett, F. M. (1971) The isolation of ketocatechols from insect cuticle and their possible role in sclerotization. *J. Insect Physiol.,* **17,** 69—84.

Andersen, S. O. and Weis-Fogh, T. (1964) Resilin: a rubberlike protein in arthropod cuticle. *Adv. Insect Physiol.,* **2,** 1—66.

Atkinson, P. W. and Gilby, A. R. (1970) Autoxidation of insect lipids: inhibition on the cuticle of the American cockroach. *Science, N.Y.,* **168,** 992.

Baker, G., Pepper, J. H., Johnson, L. H. and Hastings, E. (1960) Estimation of the composition of the cuticular wax of the Mormon cricket *Anabrus simplex* Hald. *J. Insect Physiol.,* **5,** 47—60.

Beament, J. W. L. (1945) The cuticular lipoids of insects. *J. Exp. Biol.,* **21,** 115—131.

Beament, J. W. L. (1955) Wax secretion in the cockroach. *J. Exp. Biol.,* **32,** 514—538.

Beament, J. W. L. (1961) The water relations of insect cuticle. *Biol. Rev.,* **36,** 281—320.

Beatty, I. M. and Gilby, A. R. (1969) The major hydrocarbon of a cockroach cuticular wax. *Naturwissenschaften,* **56,** 373.

Bennet-Clark, H. C. (1962) Active control of the mechanical properties of insect endocuticle. *J. Insect Physiol.,* **8,** 627—633.

Brunet, P. C. J. (1967) Sclerotins. *Endeavour,* **26,** 68—74.

Bursell, E. and Clements, A. N. (1967) The cuticular lipids of the larva of *Tenebrio molitor* L. (Coleoptera). *J. Insect Physiol.,* **13,** 1671—1678.

Cockeram, H. S. and Levine, S. A. (1961) The physical and chemical properties of shellac. *J. Soc. Cosmet. Chem.*, **12**, 316—323.

Collins, M. S. and Richards, A. G. (1966) Studies on water relations in North American termites. II. Water loss and cuticular structures in eastern species of the Kalotermitidae (Isoptera). *Ecology*, **47**, 328—331.

Dennell, R. and Malek, S. R. A. (1955) The cuticle of the cockroach *Periplaneta americana*. III. The hardening of the cuticle: impregnation preparatory to phenolic tanning. *Proc. R. Soc. B*, **143**, 414—426.

Ebeling, W. (1961) Physicochemical mechanisms for the removal of insect wax by means of finely divided powders. *Hilgardia*, **30**, 531—585.

Gilby, A. R. and Cox, M. E. (1963) The cuticular lipids of the cockroach, *Periplaneta americana* (L.). *J. Insect Physiol.*, **9**, 671—681.

Gilby, A. R. and McKellar, J. W. (1970) The composition of the empty puparia of a blowfly. *J. Insect Physiol.*, **16**, 1517—1529.

Hackman, R. H. (1964) Chemistry of insect cuticle. In *The Physiology of Insecta*, vol. 3. Ed. M. Rockstein, pp. 471—506. New York: Academic Press.

Hazelhoff, E. H. (1927) Die Regulierung der Atmung bei Insekten und Spinnen. *Z. vergl. Physiol.*, **5**, 179—190.

Karlson, P. and Sekeris, C. E. (1962) N-Acetyl-dopamine as sclerotizing agent of the insect cuticle. *Nature, Lond.*, **195**, 183—184.

Kramer, S. and Wigglesworth, V. B. (1950) The outer layers of the cuticle in the cockroach *Periplaneta americana* and the function of the oenocytes. *Q. Jl. Microsc. Sci.*, **91**, 63—72.

Kühnelt, W. (1928) Über den Bau des Insektenskelettes. *Zool. Jb.* (Abt. Anat.), **50**, 219—272.

Locke, M. (1961) Pore canals and related structures in insect cuticle. *J. Biophys. Biochem. Cytol.*, **10**, 589—618.

Mellanby, K. (1934) The site of loss of water from insects. *Proc. R. Soc. B*, **116**, 139—149.

Neville, A. C. (1965) Chitin lamellogenesis in locust cuticle. *Q. Jl. Microsc. Sci.*, **106**, 269—286.

Neville, A. C. (1967) Chitin orientation in cuticle and its control. *Adv. Insect Physiol.*, **4**, 213—286.

Odier, A. (1823) Mémoire sur la composition chimique des partes cornées des Insectes. *Mém Soc. Hist. nat. Paris*, **1**, 29—42.

Pryor, M. G. M. (1940*a*) On the hardening of the oötheca of *Blatta orientalis*. *Proc. R. Soc. B*, **128**, 378—393.

Pryor, M. G. M. (1940*b*) On the hardening of the cuticle of insects. *Proc. R. Soc. B*, **128**, 393—407.

Ramsay, J. A. (1935) The evaporation of water from the cockroach. *J. Exp. Biol.*, **12**, 373—383.

Röller, H. and Dahm, K. H. (1968) The chemistry and biology of juvenile hormone. *Recent Prog. Horm. Res.*, **24**, 651—680.

Rudall, K. M. (1963) The chitin/protein complexes of insect cuticles. *Adv. Insect Physiol.*, **1**, 257—313.

Wigglesworth, V. B. (1933) The physiology of the cuticle and of ecdysis in *Rhodnius prolixus;* with special reference to the function of the oenocytes and of the dermal glands. *Q. Jl. Microsc. Sci.*, **76**, 269-318.

Wigglesworth, V. B. (1934) The physiology of ecdysis in *Rhodnius prolixus* (Hempitera). II. Factors controlling moulting and 'metamorphosis' *Q. Jl Microsc. Sc.*, **77**, 191—222.

Wigglesworth, V. B. (1935) The regulation of respiration in the flea *Xenopsylla cheopis* Roths. (Pulicidae). *Proc. R. Soc.* B, **118**, 397—419.

Wigglesworth, V. B. (1942) Some notes on the integument of insects in relation to the entry of contact insecticides. *Bull. Ent. Res.*, **33**, 205—218.

Wigglesworth, V. B. (1944) Medical entomology. *Discovery*, April 1944, 115—119.

Wigglesworth, V. B. (1945) Transpiration through the cuticle of insects. *J. Exp. Biol.*, **21**, 97—114.

Wigglesworth, V. B. (1947a) The epicuticle in an insect, *Rhodnius prolixus* (Hemiptera). *Proc. R. Soc.* B, **134**, 163—181.

Wigglesworth, V. B. (1947b) The site of action of inert dusts on certain beetles infesting stored products. *Proc. R. Ent. Soc. Lond.* A., **22**, 65—69.

Wigglesworth, V. B. (1948) The structure and deposition of the cuticle in the adult mealworm, *Tenebrio molitor* L. (Coleoptera). *Q. Jl Microsc. Sci.*, **89**, 197—217.

Wigglesworth, V. B. (1970) Structural lipids in the insect cuticle and the function of the oenocytes. *Tissue Cell*, **2**, 155—179.

Wigglesworth, V. B. (1975) Distribution of lipid in the lamellate endocuticle of *Rhodnius prolixus* (Hemiptera). *J. Cell Sci.*, **19**, 439—457.

16

WORDSWORTH AND SCIENCE

> To the solid ground
> Of nature trusts the Mind that builds for aye;
> Convinced that there, there only, she can lay
> Secure foundations.

For seventy-five years the first lines of this quotation have appeared on the cover of *Nature*. For long enough the quotation was inaccurate; not until 1929 and 1934 were the errors brought to the notice of the Editor and put right. When the lines first appeared in this setting, Wordsworth had been dead for nearly twenty years. Had he been alive he could scarcely have approved the use to which his words were put. To the scientific reader of *Nature* (after he has permitted himself perhaps a fleeting smile at the *double entendre*) the words may well convey a sentiment gratifying to his self-esteem. But there is little in the sonnet from which they are taken to justify that feeling, and less in Wordsworth's writings as a whole.

In a moment of enthusiasm in 1833, writing of 'Steamboats, Viaducts and Railways', Wordsworth cries:

> Nature doth embrace
> Her lawful offspring in Man's art; and Time,
> Pleased with your triumphs o'er his brother Space,
> Accepts from your bold hands the proffered crown
> Of hope . . .

By 1844, when the railway threatens Kendal and Windermere, the tone has changed:

> Is then no nook of English ground secure
> From rash assault?

He 'scorns a false utilitarian lure'.

But it is Wordsworth's abstract reflections on science, when writing at the height of his powers, that we shall take more seriously.

His attitude to science is almost uniformly hostile. 'All *heaven-born* instincts shun the touch of vulgar sense.' In 1806 he writes of the 'Star-gazers', the public in Leicester Square who, for the price of one penny, are permitted to glimpse the heavens through a telescope. It is a parable on the ultimate dissatisfaction of those who 'pry and pore'. The same feelings about science find their most unbridled expression in 'A Poet's Epitaph' (1799), where men of many sorts in turn approach the poet's grave. The man of science is greeted thus:

> Physician art thou? — one, all eyes,
> Philosopher! a fingering slave,
> One that would peep and botanise
> Upon his mother's grave?

He is besought to take his 'ever-dwindling soul, away!'

A more considered variant on this recurrent theme is to be found in Book IV of 'The Excursion' (1810—20). Shall those 'ambitious spirits' who 'have solved the elements, or analysed the thinking principle . . . prove a degraded Race?' — 'Oh! there is laughter at their work in heaven!'

> . . . go, demand
> Of mighty Nature, if 'twas ever meant
> That we should pry far off yet be unraised;
> That we should pore, and dwindle as we pore,
> Viewing all objects unremittingly
> In disconnection dead and spiritless;
> And still dividing, and dividing still,
> Break down all grandeur . . .
> . . . And if indeed there be
> An all-pervading Spirit, upon whom
> Our dark foundations rest, could he design
> That this magnificient effect of power,
> The earth we tread, the sky that we behold
> By day, and all the pomp which night reveals;
> That these—and that superior mystery
> Our vital frame, so fearfully devised,
> And the dread soul within it — should exist
> Only to be examined, pondered, searched,
> Probed, vexed, and criticised?

His spirit revolts at the ways of men of science, who prize the human soul and the transcendent universe

> No more than as a mirror that reflects
> To proud Self-love her own intelligence.

In one passage only, of which I am aware, and that still later in 'The Excursion', does Wordsworth admit that science may find 'its most noble use . . . in furnishing clear guidance to the mind's *excursive* power' and 'then, and only then, be worthy of her name':

> For then her heart shall kindle; her dull eye,
> Dull and inanimate, no more shall hang
> Chained to its object in brute slavery.

Ought we then:

> To reinstate wild Fancy, would we hide
> Truths whose thick veil Science has drawn aside?

No! No matter how high we rate 'the thirst that wrought man's fall' . . . 'the universe is infinitely wide' and reason will ever meet 'some new wall or gulf of mystery' which nothing but 'Imaginative Faith' can overleap.

The fact is that Nature for Wordsworth has so deep a meaning.

> The sounding cataract
> Haunted me like a passion: the tall rock,
> The mountain, and the deep and gloomy wood,
> Their colours and their forms, were then to me
> An appetite.

Perhaps that is as far as most votaries of Nature get. But in these lines Wordsworth, 'so long a worshipper of Nature' (and if Wordsworth says 'worshipper' he means it) is looking back to his 'thoughtless youth' before he had learned to hear in Nature 'the still sad music of humanity' and had gained 'a sense sublime of something far more deeply interfused . . .', the 'soul of all my moral being'. Indeed, he goes on almost to reproach his sister that 'in the shooting lights' of her 'wild eyes' he can read only those more superficial joys. She lacked as yet:

> . . . the spirit of religious love
> In which I walked with Nature.

It is true that, for a time, depressed and bewildered by the excesses of the Revolution in France and the reactions it provoked, he 'turned to abstract science' and there sought

> Work for the reasoning faculty enthroned
> Where the disturbances of space and time,
> . . . find no admission.

But he was soon recalled by Dorothy and 'preserved a Poet' to 'seek beneath that name alone' his 'office upon earth' and to derive 'genuine knowledge' from 'sweet counsels between head and heart'.

Such is a fair picture of Wordsworth's view of science. Whether the poet would have deemed it an act of piety to con and sift his writings in this way, to the sorry detriment of his grand use of words, is open to doubt. He might well have cried:

> Our meddling intellect
> Mis-shapes the beauteous forms of things:—
> We murder to dissect.

Today, when physics ends in the mists of mysticism, it may be that science might claim kinship with Wordsworth the poet. But science now claims all society as her province, and Wordsworth the prophet and reformer would fit less awkwardly into the pages of *Nature*. The Wordsworth who, standing at the threshold of the Industrial Revolution, with a mind not warped by politics, can compare with truly scientific objectivity, though with all a poet's feeling, the evil of the factory child with the grinding penury of rural England and the ignorance and degradation of the children on the land. The Wordsworth who can describe the factories wherein 'little children, boys and girls' enter and

> where is offered up
> To Gain, the master idol of the realm,
> Perpetual sacrifice,

and who can yet rejoice

> (Measuring the force of those gigantic powers
> That, by the thinking mind, have been compelled
> To serve the will of feeble-bodied Man)

in the conviction that late or soon man will learn that 'physical science is unable to support itself' and that

> . . . all true glory rests,
> All praise, all safety, and all happiness
> Upon the moral law.

The Wordsworth who, surveying all these evils present and to come, finds a solution and a hope (this in 1810) in 'a System of National Education established universally by Government' and urges that such a system be begun at once even 'when oppression, like the Egyptian plague of darkness' is 'stretched o'er guilty Europe'. For then

> Change wide, and deep, and silently performed,
> This Land shall witness.

It had to wait sixty years.

17

THE RELIGION OF SCIENCE

Our Association has severely practical aims. But science itself, in many of the domains where its achievements have been most conspicuous, has been inspired likewise by wholly practical objectives. Joseph Priestley, who foresaw the prospects for science more clearly than most, wrote in 1768 in his *Essay upon the Principles of Government:* 'Nature, including both its materials and its laws, will be more at our command; men will make their situation in the world absolutely more easy and comfortable; they will probably prolong their existence in it, and will daily grow more happy.' I need, therefore, make no apology for devoting my address to some reflexions on what it is that makes science tick.

I must first reassure you on two matters. First, I am not going to tell you anything original, or indeed anything that you do not know already: you need have no fear that I shall be obscure. (I was once invited by the BBC to prepare a contribution to their Third Programme; but they sent my script back asking whether I could not let them have something more profound. I replied that I could not promise to write a script that was profound, but if that would be more acceptable, I could easily make it more obscure.)

Secondly, it is well known that when we can no longer get our experiments to work we may turn to philosophy in despair — as the unsuccessful thief may turn thief-taker. I may myself be happy one day to enter that particular pathway to decrepitude — but that is not my intention at the moment. I propose in this address to devote myself not to philosophy but to 'common sense' — a subject that is indeed anathema to the philosopher.

PHILOSOPHY AND REASON

When I was an undergraduate in this university more than forty-five years ago I sat through a course of one year's duration entitled an 'Introduction to the Study of Philosophy' given by J. E. McTaggart of Trinity. I believe there was one other member of the class who stayed the course until the end — but certainly not more than one. I think I can claim to have survived that experience unscathed. We used to be invited to remain behind after any lecture that we wished and seek guidance on any question we desired; and when we had been told on one occasion that no discoveries in science could influence the conclusions of philosophers, I stayed behind to challenge this assertion — but without avail. McTaggart did tell us that 'Science is common sense systematized'. You might feel that that was fair enough — but you must remember that 'common sense' is almost a dirty word among philosophers. 'Nothing', he said, 'is an ultimate reality which *can* be made more certain by any proof.'

I came away with the feeling, as expressed by Bertrand Russell that 'philosophy, from the earliest times, has made greater claims, and achieved fewer results, than any other branch of learning.' Even the great Bradley himself once wrote in his notebook that 'metaphysics consists in finding bad reasons for what we know by intuition.' I imagine that that was intended to be a piece of derogatory cynicism directed against his own subject — but there have been moments when I have felt it was unduly complimentary.

I ought, however, in fairness, to point out that what we were being indoctrinated with was an idealist philosophy. The enthusiasm for idealism and classical philosophy is not what it was; and I am told that philosophers today do in fact spend a great deal of their time in trying to fit into their metaphysics the theories of modern science.

The trouble started with the Greeks, who laid the foundations of philosophic thought. The Greeks discovered geometry and were so fascinated by the results that could be got in that study by methodical reasoning that they developed an unbounded faith in the powers of human reason, and became convinced that logical thought could explain all things. Plato was not alone in using logic to discredit common sense — a device that is part of the stock in trade of philosophers to this day.

Later, in Western Europe throughout the Middle Ages, logical disputation, developed as a fine art, became the pathway to academic distinction. And when Galileo and his followers refused to play this game according to the rules and rebelled against this servitude to reason, refused to argue, and based their conclusions on simple experiments with limited objectives — it was exceedingly provoking to the scholastics of that time.

Galileo and his successors won the day, and scholasticism became discredited, only because the new experimental methods and measurements gave results which all the argumentation and classifications of the preceding two thousand years had failed to give. We are still living at the height of this Renaissance revolt against reason, which is the special character of our scientific age.

SCIENCE AND ABSTRACTION

The objective in the Middle Ages had been the all-embracing synthesis that would embody all knowledge and all truth. The new method, the method of science, was to abandon the exaggerated belief in the powers of reason, and to abandon the attempt to reach ultimate truth; but just to study by observation and experiment certain limited aspects of the phenomena around us.

This scientific approach may perhaps best be illustrated by a specific example — such as this lecturer's reading table. The philosopher will consider this table as an essential whole. In the first place he will argue far into the early hours of the morning whether it exists at all. (Russell described the 'common-sense belief' in the existence of tables and chairs as 'a piece of audacious metaphysical theorizing'.) The philosopher may concede that you and I can see the table and feel it; but does it still exist when we look the other way and put our hands in our pockets? Furthermore, since it is obvious that each of us sees a different table (for we each see it from a different angle and in a different light) does not the table exist solely in our mind? Galileo pointed out that, apart from eyes, ears and noses, there would be no colours, sounds, or smells. These sensations are projected by the mind so as to clothe appropriate bodies in the external world. Dr. Samuel Johnson would have said that if he were to give this table a kick he would stub his toe: therefore it indubitably exists.

This remark by Dr. Johnson has always been provoking for the philosopher; from his point of view it is utterly irrelevant. But for the scientist it is entirely satisfying. The scientist does not worry about whether the table 'really' exists or not; the fact that he can detect it and specify its qualities by his senses, aided or unaided, is all he cares about. Nor is he in the least concerned about the 'essence' or intrinsic nature of the table; he is interested only in its *aspects,* and these he separates and studies one by one.

That is the key to the scientific approach. The botanist will observe that it is made from oak; and he considers whether it may be from the *Quercus robur* of Linnaeus (that is, the *Q. pedunculata* of Ehrhart); or from the *Q. petraea* of Lieblein (that is, the *Q. sessiliflora* of Salisbury) — or, perhaps more likely, from the *Q. borealis* of François Michaux, or some other of the Canadian oaks. The chemist may be led to reflect upon the probable composition of lignin and the nature of its association with cellulose. The physical chemist may try to analyse the basis of the strength and toughness of this association. The electron microscopist may hope to relate the fine structure of the cellular walls with these physical properties. The technologist will discourse upon the nature of the joints: are these keyed mitre joints, lap-dovetail joints or mortise-and-tenon joints? The nature of the adhesive will be subject to scrutiny; and the character of the surface finish will come under study. The engineer will consider the impact of the stresses and strains that it is called upon to bear and the safety factors that have been incorporated into its design. The Freudian psychologist will look deeply into the shady corners of his mind to discover any associations with the sexual experiences of his babyhood which it may recall. And, finally, the applied biologist may cast an inquiring eye upon these small holes; are they due to the workings of *Anobium punctatum* picked up perhaps from wormy furniture? Or are they the handiwork of *Lyctus* and a reminder of the starch-containing kiln-dried timber that we had in the years between the wars?

You will have noted several points about this brief and superficial survey. It is said that scientists are not interested in people; you will have noted that the scientist is not even interested in things, in themselves. He is not interested in this table, as such. He is concerned only with limited aspects of it or with *abstractions* that he isolates from it. Bertrand Russell has defined the 'things' in which science is interested as 'those series of aspects which obey the laws of physics'. Moreover, and most importantly, each of these scientific aspects enjoys a large degree of autonomy: the theses of the chemist are largely independent of those of the botanist. Each scientist can work away, in ant-like fashion, adding his little grain of knowledge at a single point of the edifice of Science. He may gain an international reputation by his studies on the hind tarsus of the cat flea. The philosopher cannot operate in this way: his house of cards has to be built as one whole; if a card is out of place the whole edifice falls.

You may have noted also that I made no mention of the mathematical approach. Mathematics is the most abstract of all the sciences, it is closely allied to logic and so philosophy. Philosophers spend much time in discussing whether mathematics and logic are the same thing or not. In his younger days Bertrand Russell was immensely enthusiastic about the development of mathematical logic; and was confident that mathematical logic, which could be built up step by step as science is, was going to provide a solid foundation for the philosophy of the future. But in his later years, in his autobiographical writings, he declares himself disillusioned: after immense application he finally reached the conclusion that 'mathematics was just another way of saying the same thing in different words' — that the raw materials of mathematics were the models and ideas that had been reached by ordinary thought and speculation; and that even in the most purely logical realms, it is insight that first arrives at what is new.

Our scientific conception of the universe is unbelievable for the philosopher. It is made up of abstractions — and there is no denying that many of us get into the habit of mistaking these abstractions for concrete realities. Whitehead has underlined the confusion that has arisen from ascribing 'misplaced concreteness' to the scientific scheme of things: 'thought is abstract, and the excessive use of abstractions can be a major vice of the intellect'. But the world of science has 'always remained perfectly satisfied with its peculiar abstractions. They work, and that is sufficient for it.'

SCIENCE AND FAITH

At this point I should perhaps say a word to justify my choice of title: 'The religion of science'. Religion was defined by Whitehead as 'the vision of something which stands beyond, behind, and within, the passing flux of immediate things'. The belief of the scientist in natural laws is not so very different from that. But I am prepared to admit that 'faith' might have been a better word to use in place of 'religion'. Faith is really what I am talking about. The philosopher has no use for faith; that is why he speaks a totally different language from the scientist, whose entire system of thought is based on faith.

It is curious to note how long it took for philosophers to recognize this obvious fact. It seems to have been first clearly pointed out by

David Hume (1711—76) who wrote of science: 'Our holy religion is founded on faith' — a simple faith, that is, in the order of nature. The curious paradox is that for the clergy and for the church this was not sufficient: for them God is rational; and they continued to seek a rational explanation for all things.

Faith has been variously defined. A definition I have heard from the pulpit is that 'faith' is 'that on which a man is prepared to act'. That certainly goes for scientific faith. Every time we travel in a jet plane it is an act of faith in the computations of an army of scientists. It is well known that in the case of the early 'Comets' that faith was misplaced; a number of them fell apart in the sky. But such an occurrence does not weaken scientific faith (any more than it would weaken religious faith). It is at once accepted that the scientific analysis has been incomplete and in this case our understanding of metal fatigue had been inadequate.

We are all familiar with the small boy's definition of faith as 'believin' wot yer know ain't true!'. That certainly applies to scientific faith. For the laws of science, which are the immediate objects of our faith, are not regarded by the scientist as for ever true. They are temporary, provisional, or partial truths. The lives and venturings of seamen are sustained by a complete trust in the nautical almanac. But the almanac is based on Newton's theory of gravitation — and that we know to be untrue.

It is part of the robustness of the scientific faith that it can stand up to rebuffs of this kind. For 250 years we had accepted Newton's theory. Leibnitz, it is true, had chided Newton for introducing magical qualities into science in postulating his miraculous 'force of gravity'; but the idea became universally accepted. And yet, when Einstein, in our own times, pointed out that we can dispense with this idea completely, if we assume that the space surrounding matter is modified and distorted in such a way that other matter, as it approaches, is diverted in the same manner as if gravitation existed — this revolution in thought was not regarded as a disaster but as a triumph. And for everyday use within the solar system Newton's laws are still regarded as true: we still believe in them although we know that they are not true for the universe as a whole. (The strange thing is that if changes of this sort, which might be regarded by some as 'advances', are made in religious beliefs on another plane, they are regarded, not as triumphs, but as disasters.)

In formal logic a contradiction is a sign of defeat; but in science it is often the first step towards victory. You will recall that Lord Rayleigh and Sir William Ramsey encountered samples of 'nitrogen' with different atomic weights. This discrepancy was soon explained by the discovery of argon — and the chemists could breathe again. But it was not so long before Aston revealed the existence of elements which really did have more than one atomic weight — and the idea of isotopes had to be accepted.

The moral is a simple one: to practise the maximum degree of toleration towards different opinions. We were adjured in the parable of the tares to 'let both grow together until the harvest' — but that, I am afraid, is a counsel of toleration that is rarely followed either in religion or in science.

SCIENCE AND TRUTH

According to the teachings of logic a proposition must be either true or false; there is no middle term. That is not accepted by the scientist: he works continually with propositions whose truth is subject to all kinds of limitations and qualifications — many of them not yet defined. You will recall that Galileo fell out with the Inquisition as to whether it is the sun or the earth that is at rest, and which is in motion. That would be an instructive exercise in discussion: which party to this dispute was most nearly right? Certainly they were both wrong.

Science started, as we have seen, with the organization of ordinary experiences. It was not asking for ultimate meanings, but confined itself to investigating the connexions which regulate the succession of occurrences that were observed. All these happenings, both great and small, were conceived as the outcome of general principles that reign throughout the natural order.

These general principles or laws of causation were arrived at by a process of induction from the observation of particular cases. But the theory of induction is the despair of philosophy. As Hume pointed out there are no logical grounds for believing that successions of events that appear to have been consistently repeated in the past will continue to take place in the future — or even that we shall continue to expect them to take place. That the sun has always risen each morning in the past affords no reason for supposing that it will rise tomorrow.

John Stuart Mill (1806—73) likewise emphasized that inference depends on the law of causation; and the best he could do for the law of universal causation was what he called 'induction by simple enumeration' — which means that 'we regard as general truths all propositions which are true in every instance that we happen to know of'. When one is pressed one has to admit that that seems a fallible sort of procedure. It is indeed only the profound faith of the scientist which makes it acceptable.

Where did this faith come from? It is generally supposed to have been derived from the medieval assertion of the rationality of God and the tidiness of the universe. Empiricists such as Thomas Hobbes (1588—1679) maintained that all knowledge is derived from the senses and is dependent upon them; and that all thought is based solely on the memory of past sensations. This interpretation is probably acceptable to the scientist; indeed, the first chapter of the *Leviathan* (1651) has for the scientist a remarkably modern ring.

But empirical evidence deals with *particular* truths; knowledge of *general* truths cannot be derived from the data of sense. By pointing this out philosophers claim to have refuted the beliefs of the empiricists. The scientist, however, is impervious to this refutation — because (for the purpose of his science) he believes by faith in the existence of general truths. The theory of induction is the despair of philosophy — and yet all our activities, in science and in daily life, are based upon it.

THE RELIGION OF THERMODYNAMICS

No account of the religion of science would be complete without reference to the laws of thermodynamics — particularly the second law, which enjoys a degree of reverence among scientists that is a quasi-religious phenomenon. I have known distinguished candidates excluded from election to the Royal Society for years because their results, though well-founded and repeatable, appeared to contravene the second law of thermodynamics.

The first law, the principle of the conservation of energy, was formulated in 1842 almost simultaneously by Mayer and by Helmholz in Germany, by Joule in England and by Colding in Denmark. It has had an extraordinary history in the relations between science, philosophy and religion. Writers in the 1860s such as Herbert Spencer and the American Edward L. Youmans (and many others) became lyrical, almost hysterical, on the subject; and this hysteria persisted almost to the end of the nineteenth century. To quote a single specimen by Youmans writing on the first law of thermo-dynamics in 1865 and including a quotation from Spencer: 'It has been shown that a pure principle forms the immaterial foundation of the universe. From the baldest materiality we rise at last to a truth of the spiritual world, of so exalted an order that it has been said "to connect the mind of man with the Spirit of God".'

At the end of the century the discovery of radioactivity led to experiments that clearly contradicted this most fundamental law of nature. The explanation of radioactivity given by Rutherford, namely the disintegration of matter, provided the key; and henceforth the law of the conservation of energy has had to be combined with Lavoisier's law of the conservation of matter — as had been done, curiously enough, by the zoologist Ernst Haeckel in 1892 when he set down his 'law of substance' (that is, combined matter and energy) as the basis for what he called the 'monistic religion of reason'.

The second law of thermodynamics as formulated by Clausius, Kelvin, Boltzmann, and others in the middle of the last century, that 'the entropy of the universe tends towards a maximum', has likewise had a large impact on the relations between science, philosophy and religion. Dean Inge and others showed that it led to the traditional doctrine that God created the world out of nothing. J. B. S. Haldane used it to prove the contrary. Sir Arthur Eddington, and many others, went into print on this topic. It lies outside the scope of this address; we are not concerned here with the relations between science and religion. I propose to quote only two writers whose remarks are certainly relevant to the subject of this address.

E. N. Hiebert reviewing the subject of 'Thermodynamics and Religion' wrote recently: 'All kinds of private metaphysics and theology have grown like weeds in the garden of thermodynamics. . . No matter how good, how secure, or how elegant a scientific theory is, it is never immune to being used in ways that transgress the limits of credulity to the point of sheer ridiculousness.'

Pierre Duhem (French scientist, philosopher and historian), writing in 1905, expressed the view we are adopting in this lecture, that: 'physics proceeds by an autonomous method, absolutely independent of any metaphysical opinion'. Scientific theories have no grounds

'to penetrate beyond the teachings of experiment or any capacity to surmise realities hidden under data observable by the senses. . . . Thermodynamics employs arbitrary theories that are adequate to the job in hand. The predictions of such theories merit a certain degree of confidence, but their logic gives no grounds on which to assert that the forecasts of these theories alone would be in conformity with reality. In respect to any long-term prediction, the principles of thermodynamics have no special claims to ultimate truth'.

We are back at the point where we arrived before: that science is concerned with 'verifiability'; it is not concerned with ultimate 'truth'.

SCIENCE AND LIFE

We know that 'faith will move mountains'. How far will our scientific faith take us? We do not know; but we do know that the power of science has been grossly underestimated by the scientists of the past. I am not going to recite to you a list of the triumphs of science in our day. But our Association is devoted to biology. How far are we going to get in the understanding, that is, in the causal description, of vital phenomena? The answer is: a great deal further than we think.

Descartes (1596—1650), as we all know, looked upon living organisms as no more than pieces of physical mechanism; and this point of view was maintained by Kant (1724—1804) — in so far as he was concerned solely with the 'phenomenal world' of science. But early in the eighteenth century Stahl (1660—1734) developed the theory of 'vitalism': the idea that in living organisms some active principle was constantly interfering with the physical tendency for organic structure to disintegrate. Vitalism became the standard attitude of men of science until the middle of the nineteenth century. It was then realized that when the influence of the so-called 'vital principle' was investigated in detail its action was always found to depend on what the vitalists themselves admitted to be physical and chemical influences. Thus in the latter part of the last century sentiment swung once more in favour of a mechanistic theory of life; and most biologists came to believe that life must ultimately be regarded as no more than a complicated physico-chemical process.

Physicists are apt to have a strange attitude towards biology, not unlike the attitude of savages towards magic. Lord Kelvin excluded living things from the operation of the second law of thermodynamics. Sir Oliver Lodge endowed the living body with a sort of little

Maxwellian demon which 'through the mysterious intervention of the brain' could liberate energy with 'no "work" at all'. Even some biologists have a streak of mysticism in their scientific make-up. The physiologist J. S. Haldane (the father of J. B. S. Haldane) was one of the most thoughtful philosophers of biology. He demonstrated the philosophical inadequacy of the theory of vitalism — but like so many physiologists he was overwhelmed by the apparent mysteries of embryology and differentiation and the integration of living structure and activity. He allowed himself to write: 'there is not the smallest reason for believing that however far we carry physical and chemical investigations we shall get any nearer to understanding these facts.' We cannot pretend to understand the developmental process even today, forty years after Haldane was writing. But we certainly do not regard this process as for ever beyond the reach of scientific analysis and description.

If we accept the principle that the gene system in the chromosomes of the zygote contains all the coding instructions for the synthesis of all the nucleic acids, and hence, in turn, of all the enzymically active proteins that are needed to produce all the structures and activities that the organism may be called upon to provide (and this 'house-that-Jack-built' is the current teaching of molecular biology): and if we assume (and there is good evidence for this) that the greater part of this potential genetic activity is latent and inactive at any one time or in one given part of the organism: and if we assume (and there is good evidence for this also) that these latent components of the gene system can be brought into activity by circulating hormones produced elsewhere in the body; by the influence of the environment at defined points of the body; or by local chemical factors, themselves in some cases the product of environmental stimuli — we have a system that, in principle at any rate, would manifest the properties of a developing living organism.

This conception is the product of genetics, of molecular biology, of endocrinology and experimental morphogenesis, and, to a modest extent, of insect physiology. In detail it is not yet firmly established; it is still no more than a rough sketch. But it provides the basis for a conception of the 'living organism' that can be expressed in purely scientific terms. And there is no reason in principle why these terms should not be reduced to those of physics and chemistry.

It comes naturally to the biologist to speak and think about the living *organism*. Even while he still does not understand many of the ways in which that organism is held together, he accepts as given that it operates as a whole; and that all its parts are subservient to the needs of that whole.

That, indeed, is the philosophy at which A. N. Whitehead arrived in his 'theory of organic mechanism', which he regarded as applying not only to 'living organisms' but to smaller organisms such as molecules, atoms and electrons. He maintained that the whole concept of materialism applies only to the abstract entities which science isolates from the phenomena that it studies. 'The concrete enduring entities are organisms, so that the plan of the *whole* influences the very characters of the various subordinate organisms which enter into it. . . . Thus an electron within the living body is different from an electron outside it, by reason of the plan of the body. The electron blindly runs either within or without the body; but it runs within the body in accordance with its characters within the body; that is to say, in accordance with the general plan of the body, and this plan includes the mental state.'

Whitehead regarded this principle of modification as being general throughout nature and not as representing a property peculiar to living bodies: 'molecules may blindly run in accordance with the general laws, but the molecules differ in their intrinsic characters according to the general organic plan of the situation in which they find themselves. . . . This doctrine involves the abandonment of the traditional scientific materialism, and the substitution of an alternative doctrine of organism.'

All this, of course, is wholly acceptable to the biologist; it is mostly a part of his everyday thinking. Perhaps one may be using words in a different sense, but it seems to me that the character of an electron as it is detached from an organic substrate by a specific dehydrogenase and shepherded along the cytochrome chain to activate molecular oxygen and cause this to unite with the liberated hydrogen ion, is different from the character of an electron of the same organic substrate in a bottle. This electron, if it could think, might well imagine that it enjoyed freedom of will; but *we* know that it is subject to the living environment. That living environment is a system of active enzymes. These enzyme proteins owe their existence to a system of ribosomes and associated nucleic acids, which in turn derive from the self-reproducing nucleic acid chain which is the gene system. It was on these grounds that I ventured elsewhere to define 'Life' as 'a *structure* which controls the chemical processes in its aqueous environment' — that is, in the *milieu intérieur* of the cell.

The philosophy of Kant, which I suppose most of us tend subconsciously to accept (because it provides the line of least resistance for the mind, and we are inherently lazy when it comes to thinking) teaches that what we deal with in science and in everyday life are 'phenomena' and that behind these is the ultimate reality, the 'noumena' or 'things-in-themselves' which are beyond our comprehension — and that if we did know about them they would explain everything. Whitehead among the philosophers of our day condemns this attitude as being 'the great refusal of rationality to assert its rights . . . we have to search whether nature does not *in its very being show itself as self-explanatory.'*

That is an encouraging thought to come from a philosopher. It is the assumption on which science works — albeit scientists do not claim to see the end of the tunnel. If in the end it should prove to be so, science and philosophy would be reconciled at last. Karl Pearson, in the first edition of *The Grammar of Science* (1892), asserts that 'to draw a distinction between the scientific and philosophical fields is obscurantism'. Personally I think that that assertion was premature. Science is certainly not immune to obscurantism — but that is a distemper to which philosophy is infinitely more susceptible.

Science, however, is founded on faith and lives by faith. Without a deeply rooted instinctive belief in the existence of laws which reign throughout nature, the incredible labours of scientists would be without hope. We must just soldier on in that faith to whatever end it may ultimately lead.

INDEX

DATE DUE

SEP 1 7 1982			